PIPE FITTINGS

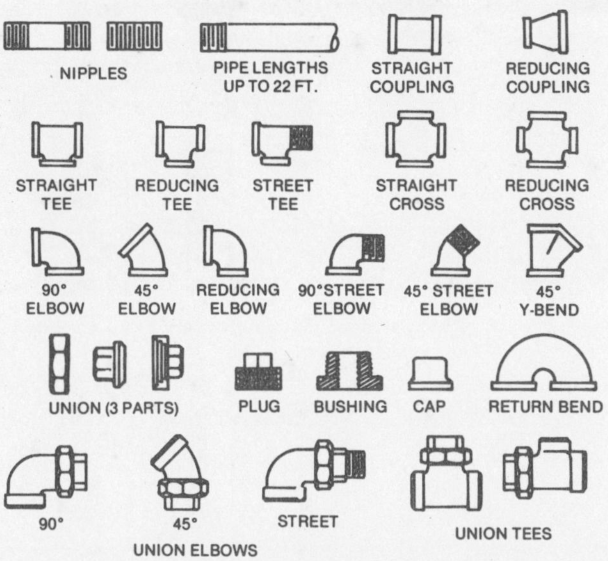

Here are the common steel pipe fittings. Nipples are simply short lengths of pipe threaded on both ends. Reducing fittings join two different sizes of pipe.

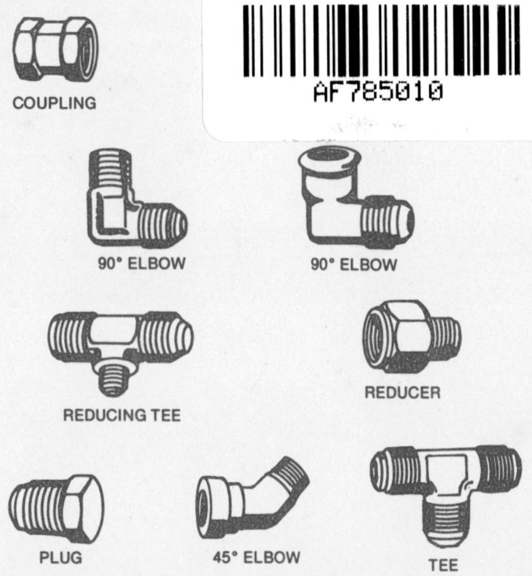

Compression fittings of the flared-tube type are the easiest for the novice to handle when working with copper tubing.

STANDARD STEEL PIPE (All Dimensions in Inches)					
Nominal Size	Outside Diameter	Inside Diameter	Nominal Size	Outside Diameter	Inside Diameter
1/8	0.405	0.269	1	1.315	1.049
1/4	0.540	0.364	1 1/4	1.660	1.380
3/8	0.675	0.493	1 1/2	1.900	1.610
1/2	0.840	0.622	2	2.375	2.067
3/4	1.050	0.824	2 1/2	2.875	2.469

SQUARE MEASURE

144 sq in = 1 sq ft
9 sq ft = 1 sq yd
272.25 sq ft = 1 sq rod
160 sq rods = 1 acre

VOLUME MEASURE

1728 cu in = 1 cu ft
27 cu ft = 1 cu yd

MEASURES OF CAPACITY

1 cup = 8 fl oz
2 cups = 1 pint
2 pints = 1 quart
4 quarts = 1 gallon
2 gallons = 1 peck
4 pecks = 1 bushel

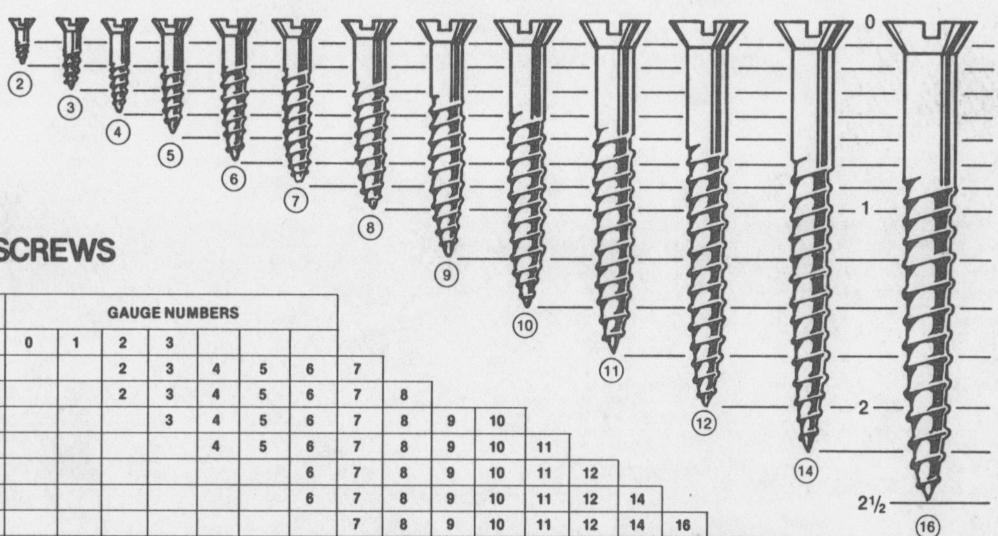

WOOD SCREWS

LENGTH	GAUGE NUMBERS																
1/4 INCH	0	1	2	3													
3/8 INCH			2	3	4	5	6	7									
1/2 INCH			2	3	4	5	6	7	8								
5/8 INCH				3	4	5	6	7	8	9	10						
3/4 INCH					4	5	6	7	8	9	10	11					
7/8 INCH							6	7	8	9	10	11	12				
1 INCH							6	7	8	9	10	11	12	14			
1 1/4 INCH								7	8	9	10	11	12	14	16		
1 1/2 INCH							6	7	8	9	10	11	12	14	16	18	
1 3/4 INCH									8	9	10	11	12	14	16	18	20
2 INCH									8	9	10	11	12	14	16	18	20
2 1/4 INCH										9	10	11	12	14	16	18	20
2 1/2 INCH													12	14	16	18	20
2 3/4 INCH														14	16	18	20
3 INCH															16	18	20
3 1/2 INCH																18	20	24
4 INCH																18	20	24

WHEN YOU BUY SCREWS, SPECIFY (1) LENGTH, (2) GAUGE NUMBER, (3) TYPE OF HEAD—FLAT, ROUND, OR OVAL, (4) MATERIAL—STEEL, BRASS, BRONZE, ETC., (5) FINISH—BRIGHT, STEEL BLUED, CADMIUM, NICKEL, OR CHROMIUM PLATED.

In this volume . . .

A FINE CRAFTSMAN'S WORK speaks for itself—in the design, in the joinery, most of all in the finish. And the secret of a topnotch finish, of course, is preparing the surface. To give your own work a professional touch, read "Choose the right abrasive" on page 20.

BUILD THIS HANDSOME pine bench, a reproduction of one in Lincoln's law office. See page 90.

SAVE MONEY! Troubleshoot your airconditioner yourself. See charts, take-apart diagrams on page 50.

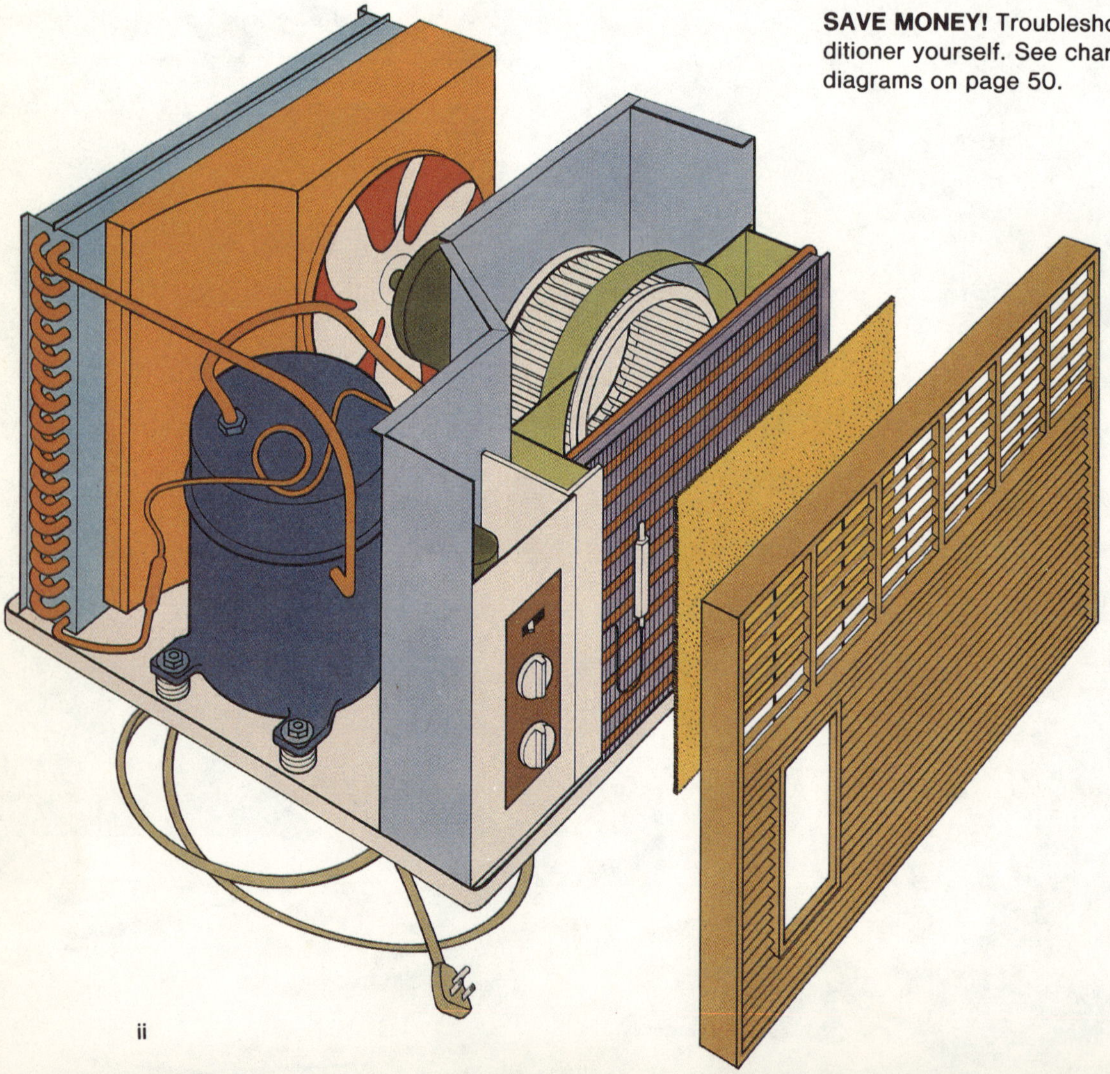

MODERN GLUES hold everything together, from airplanes to shoes. But no single glue will hold everything. Some glues are quick-setting, others slow; some shrink in joints, some fill gaps. For a complete rundown, see "Stick with the right glue" on page 35.

IF YOU TRUST the lives of your family to a smoke alarm, make sure it's a good one. See buying tips on page 66.

IF YOU ARE a wilderness camper, don't miss the article on page 151 describing the latest gear for backpackers.

YOUR GAME MAY BE TOPS but occasionally you'll need to restring your racket. With a simple home-made jig you can do it yourself. See the complete instructions in Vol. 18 on page 2851.

Look what you'll find in other volumes!

YOU'LL FIND three handsome mobile cooking centers in Vol. 12 on page 1865. And these versatile rollabouts can be used indoors or out. The article includes complete plans and step-by-step photos.

BENCHES ARE IMPORTANT to any deck or patio. Here we show benches and steps that can be used for lounging. You'll find plans for two other simple-to-build but beautiful benches in Vol. 2, page 264.

HERE'S ONE MODERN VERSION of the old-fashioned gazebo, a back-yard entertainment center. You'll find still another version, with built-in barbecue, in Vol. 9 on page 1346.

EVERYONE WANTS TO BE a woodcarver, and Vol. 4 offers everything you need to know to give it a try. The article includes dimensions and detailed instructions for carving a snack dish, a trinket box, a mirror embellished with two partridges, and a cat. See page 604.

ONE OF THE SUREST WAYS to succeed when you're remodeling or redecorating is to cover one or more walls with wood. And the easiest way to cover a wall with wood is to use plywood paneling. Prefinished paneling gives each of the rooms shown here a feeling of warmth, yet each has its own individuality. You'll learn the various ways to apply paneling, how to treat windows and doors, how to make cutouts for electrical outlets, and all the other tricks of the trade, in the article, ''How to work with plywood paneling'' in Vol. 13 on page 2056.

THERE'S AN ART to applying the right finish to a piece of furniture—or refinishing an old piece. The choice of finishes is so broad it can be confusing. If you know the advantages and disadvantages of each, the selection is easy. You'll find an authority's evaluation in Vol. 8 on page 1208.

THIS BEAUTIFUL CADDY will add grace to any buffet table. It holds silverware and napkins for all your guests in elegant style. Make it in just a few hours from the plans in Vol. 10, page 1594.

Popular Mechanics

do-it-yourself encyclopedia

in 20 volumes

a complete how-to guide for the homeowner, the hobbyist—
and anyone who enjoys working with mind and hands!

All about:

home maintenance
home-improvement projects
wall paneling
burglary and fire protection
furniture projects
finishing and refinishing furniture
outdoor living
home remodeling
solutions to home problems
challenging woodworking projects
hobbies and handicrafts
model making
weekend projects
workshop shortcuts and techniques
hand-tool skills
power-tool know-how
shop-made tools
car repairs
car maintenance
appliance repair
boating
hunting
fishing
camping
photography projects
radio, TV and electronics know-how
clever hints and tips
projects just for fun

volume 1

ISBN 0-87851-066-4
Library of Congress Catalog Number 77 84920

MANUFACTURED IN THE UNITED STATES OF AMERICA

foreword

For over 80 years *Popular Mechanics* has been the world's most authoritative source for how-to-do-it information.

That know-how now has been refined and published between the covers of these 20 volumes. Here you'll find more than 900 challenging articles on a wide variety of important subjects, from home maintenance to car repair and craft projects. These articles are enhanced by:

- ☐ More than 10,000 photos and drawings that show you exactly what to do and how to do it.
- ☐ More than 1,000 clever hints for solving home and shop problems.
- ☐ Countless tips to stimulate your enjoyment of handicrafts, sports and hobbies.
- ☐ An Index of more than 6000 entries, thoroughly cross-referenced, that will enable you to find desired information quickly and easily.
- ☐ "See also" listings, displayed with each major article, telling you where you can find related information that may be of special interest to you.
- ☐ Pure enjoyment. Countless hours of fun and satisfaction for anyone who enjoys working—and playing—creatively.
- ☐ A Table of Contents, in this volume, showing every major article in all 20 volumes. Turn the page and look at it now. It will give you an idea of the scope of your encyclopedia. In addition, for your convenience, you'll find an individual Table of Contents in each volume.

Our aim, in preparing this *Popular Mechanics Do-It-Yourself Encyclopedia,* has been to make it the most accurate and informative how-to encyclopedia ever published.

THE EDITORS

contents

The right glue, p. 35.

Tabletop hockey, p. 58.

Colonial chair, p. 102.

"Sunken" tub, p. 214.

Platform beds, p. 252.

Butcher block, p. 468.

VOLUME 3

VOLUME 4

Boating pictures, p. 356.

Butler's table, p. 472.

Boating pictures, p. 356.

It's a travelpod, p. 526.

Recorder repairs, p. 598.

Shelf clock, p. 750.

VOLUME 5

VOLUME 6

VOLUME 7

Beauty for a deck, p. 920.

Home offices, p. 935.

Colonial dry sink, p. 1050.

Classic oak table, p. 987.

Family room ideas, p. 1174.

VOLUME 8

VOLUME 9

How to frame pictures, p. 1264.

Portable grill, p. 1370.

Gun cabinet, p. 1378.

Swivel hi-fi center, p. 1444.

Foldaway hobby center, p. 1454.

Hutch table, p. 1516.

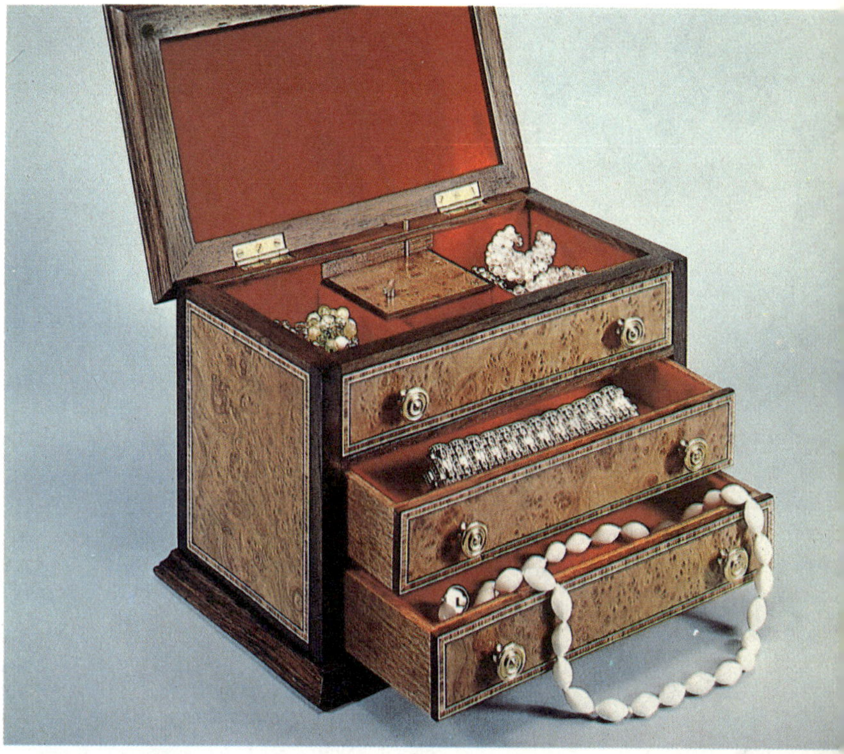

Jewelry box, p. 1562.

Patio appliance center, p. 1622

Candlestand lamp, p. 1664.

The art of marquetry, p. 1772.

Outdoor tables, p. 2013.

Nesting party tables, p. 2070.

VOLUME 12

VOLUME 13

Foyer set, p. 2162.

Plexiglas projects, p. 2205.

Putting green, p. 2356.

Circus train, p. 2348.

Remodeling, p. 2421.

Electric serving cart, p. 2570.

Scuba diving, p. 2692.

Homemade snowplow, p. 2724.

Strawberry barrel, p. 2816.

Rustic stool, p. 2793.

Hand tools, p. 2899.

VOLUME 19

VOLUME 20

Underwater photography, p. 2980.

Weekend projects, p. 3062.

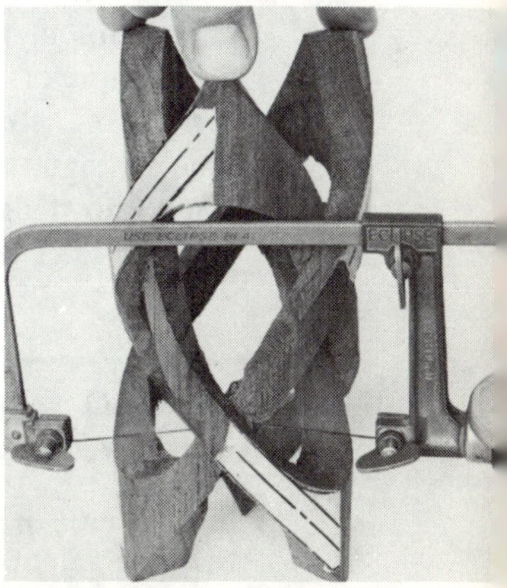

Wood sculpture, p. 3118.

Choose the right abrasive

With today's abrasives you can handle virtually any job—remove big chunks of stock rapidly or rub down the smallest uneven spots to a glossy finish. But you must know how to choose your materials and use them properly

THERE'S NOTHING like a belt sander to peel off the old finish in a hurry. Choose an open-coat belt for this kind of work, though, or you'll soon find the belt gummed and clogged with the old finish.

"ONE THING I've noticed about do-it-yourselfers. They work too hard. I tell 'em to choose the right paper, then let the paper do the work." That's Edwin Johnson, interior restoration expert, talking. Like any woodworker, he finds sandpaper a basic tool in his workshop.

But you must *choose the proper paper.* And that may be more difficult than it sounds. A manufacturer may call a particular sandpaper grit "Tough industrial abrasive—medium." Not much help. That term "medium" is hardly exact.

If you can find a veteran hardware-store operator with long personal experience, you've found a goldmine of information. He'll be able to prescribe precisely the paper you need. But how do you distinguish the man who speaks from personal knowledge from the man who parrots all-purpose sales talk?

Also, you'll find that ordinary words, in the abrasives field, are much less precise than you might expect. To begin with, sandpaper rarely has any real sand. And the backing isn't always paper. (Manufacturers prefer, in fact, to call their product "coated abrasives" in today's market.)

The abrasive grit is what does the cutting, and the great bulk of the jobs are done by four different kinds. They are flint, garnet, aluminum oxide, and silicon carbide. The first two are natural minerals; the last two are synthetic.

two natural minerals

Flint is the only one that's similar to real sand. Actually, it's made of white quartz crystals on a tan kraft-paper backing. Flint papers are the least expensive; the backing is seldom very strong and the grit comes off most easily. But flint is probably the right choice for those who have only rare use for coated abrasives—those who tend to use a sheet for a bit, then throw it away.

Almandite, an iron-aluminum mineral, is the one generally used for *garnet* grit in the United States. The bulk of U.S. almandite comes from a large deposit on Gore Mountain in the New York Adirondacks. It's reddish in color, sometimes orange, and does a better job than flint because its

SEE ALSO

Belt sanders . . . Circular saws, portable . . . Discs, wood . . . Finishes, wood . . . Furniture, care of . . . Joinery . . . Moldings . . . Pad sanders . . . Sanders, belt . . . Sanders, disc . . . Sanding . . . Scrapers . . . Shapers . . . Wood finishes

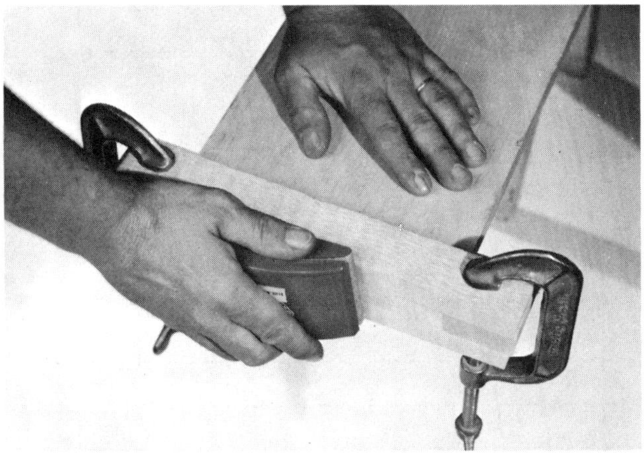

END-GRAIN sanding benefits from scraps clamped to the work as shown. This helps to keep the ends square and prevents your rounding off the edges.

AN UNPADDED sanding block usually saves time and work on rougher surfaces. It cuts high spots down faster, sands out hollows, and leaves true surface.

A CONTROLLED TOUCH makes all the difference in sanding. Even metal can get a mirror finish despite coarse paper, with a light touch and enough time.

A "SHOESHINE" approach works well on turnings or round corners. The method helps to maintain a constant radius while it leaves a smooth surface on the work.

grains are very sharp. Heat-treating increases the mineral's natural hardness and toughness, but garnet still dulls too fast for metal working.

new synthetic grits

The "tough industrial abrasive" that manufacturers like to refer to is usually *aluminum oxide.* It's off-white to gray-brown in color, often with specks of black. Crude bauxite ore is purified, and titanium oxide is added for extra toughness, in making this grit. Crushing rolls are controlled to get the sharpest fragments. Makers then grade these for size and add them to the appropriate backing.

Aluminum oxide grit is chunkier than *silicon carbide,* but the silicon carbide crystals are the sharpest and hardest of the synthetic abrasives. Silicon carbide paper is iridescent black, often tinged with green. The crystals are generally considered less tough than aluminum oxide, although some tests do dispute that view. In any case, the silicon carbide cuts under light pressure faster than any other abrasive material.

There are a couple of other coated abrasives whose names you've probably heard: emery and crocus cloth.

Emery is a natural combination of corundum and iron oxide; its grains are blocky and cut slowly. They tend to polish the material being worked on.

Crocus is powdered iron oxide—rust. It's very soft and bright red. The value of crocus is in polishing operations where you want to remove only the very minimum of stock.

Technical Grades		Simplified Grades		Other Grades	
Aluminum Oxide Silicon Carbide Garnet & Flint					
Mesh	Symbol	Flint	Emery	Flint Finishing	Emery Polishing
600					4/0
					3/0
500					2/0
400	10/0				0
360					
320	9/0			7/0	½
280	8/0			6/0	
240	7/0			5/0	1G
220	6/0			4/0	2
		Extra Fine			
180	5/0			3/0	3
			Fine		
150	4/0			2/0	
120	3/0	Fine			
			Medium		
100	2/0				
80	0	Medium	Coarse		
60	½				
			Extra Coarse		
50	1				
		Coarse			
40	1½				
36	2				
		Extra Coarse			
30	2½				
24	3				
20	3½				
16	4				
12	4½				

THE SAME terms may indicate a variety of grit sizes, depending on the abrasive material used. This chart decodes the common terms. The mesh number is the most precise. It tells the number of threads per inch for a screen that will pass a particular size grit material.

Whatever the grit material, the grain size is critically important. That's what controls the depth of the scratches that remove material from the workpiece. And that is the reason you shift in stages to finer and finer grits, leaving smaller and smaller scratches and, therefore a smoother and smoother surface. But identifying grit size from the variety of terms used can be confusing.

how rough is 'medium'?

In selling to the general public, the coated abrasives industry tends to rely on the terms *fine, medium,* and *coarse* instead of being specific. (Carborundum also uses the terms *extra fine* and *super fine.*) Even those manufacturers who use numerical designations sometimes stick with such old symbols as ½ or *6/0* or *1G*—meaningless until you've learned their particular code.

The various grade systems don't match. Take 180-mesh grit. Depending on the system being used, it might be called *3* or *3/0* or *5/0* or *extra fine.* All can indicate the same grit size.

But mesh numbers classify all grits by the openings per inch in fine silk screens used to sort them. The 22 screens range from 12 openings per inch to 600. The table on page 22 translates various grading terms into the mesh-number system. It's the only system that includes everything.

Some manufacturers still show mesh grades only on products for industrial customers. Still, mesh numbers are taking over, if slowly. Learn to use them. Know what number 80 or 120 or 180 paper does for you. Then you can rely on numbers instead of advertising adjectives. If you can't find specific data on the package, it may be on the back of the paper itself.

Industry people who resist citing mesh numbers explain that slightly different grit sizes can give almost identical results: 80-grit paper with the continuous stroke of a disc sander or 90-grit paper with hand sanding or 100-grit paper with the short strokes of a vibrating sander all can produce about the same finish. Thus the different numbers might be confusing, they say.

choose a protective package

The package has other importance when you're shopping for sandpaper. Many of us discard a coated abrasive after only a bit of its productive life. If you choose the paper carefully, you should also pick one of the packages that serve to protect the supply for re-use. A stiff cardboard envelope with a hole from which to hang it is one handy form. But be sure you store it in a dry place, warns Edwin Johnson. Humidity ruins sandpaper.

The *backing* is nearly as important as the grit. The backing has to hold together if your paper is to have any staying power. Generally, today's papers do a good job. But strong backing is especially important for machine sanding, whether you're using a disc on a portable drill, an orbital sander or a belt sander.

available in four weights

The paper comes in four weights: A, C, D, and E. Few specialists feel A has much value, although it's likely to be the backing for bargain flint. Discs cut from A-weight paper are likely to give up without much fight, and the clamps of a vibrating sander may well tear it. C- and D-weights do a better job and E is as heavy as paper backing comes—more than three times as heavy as A-weight. E is commonly used on commercial floor-sanding machines.

Cloth backing is also available, in two weights. J-weight is the more flexible while X is stronger and more durable.

"Fibre" backing, actually a hardened rag-stock paper, has more body than any other backing. It's sometimes combined with either cloth or ordinary paper. Those combinations are usually for industrial use, however.

Even with good backing and the right range of grits, certain jobs can give you trouble. Loading, in which the stock being removed (swarf, it's called) fills the spaces between grit particles, is frustrating. When the spaces between grains load up, the sharp edges can't reach down and cut as they should.

an answer to loading

A standard approach has been to use open-coat paper, in which 30 to 50 per cent of the backing's area is exposed, carrying no grit.

Special anti-loading treatments are a recent development. A particular chemical, usually zinc stearate (from soap family), covers grit and all. In use, the edges cut through it instantly, but the rest of the coating gives the swarf no grip.

From 3M, such paper is called Fre-Cut. From Carborundum, it's Dri-Lube; from Norton, No-Fil; from Clipper Abrasives, Anti-Klog; and from Midwest Abrasive Company, Lubricut.

You can doctor your own sandpaper similarly. Just rub a bar of soap across the grit. But think ahead. The soapy compound has to be removed before you paint or otherwise finish the surface. Unless you plan further sanding anyway, you might well stay clear of the soap.

What Carborundum calls Sand Screen is a still newer response to loading. This material is open-mesh plastic screening coated with aluminum oxide or silicon carbide grit. Such products from 3M are called Wetordry Fabricut; from Norton, Screen-Bak; and from Armour, Abrasive Screen Cloth.

Carborundum people are enthusiastic: "It's great for something like sanding that gummy anti-fouling paint from a boat hull. When this stuff starts to load up, all you do is slosh it around in a bucket of water. Then go back to sanding."

buy paper in bulk

If you have lots of sanding to do, buy the paper in bulk. Paint stores often sell a dozen sheets for the price of 10. For a big job, buy what the industry calls a "sleeve"—50 or 100 sheets, depending on the grade. Don't forget the need for careful storage, however.

How about steel wool for woodworking? Johnson finds it messy and prefers sandpaper. Others agree, though at least one experienced hardware man sees an exception: "Use 0-0-0 steel wool after each coat of polyurethane and the finish will be like glass," he says.

Steel wool comes in seven grades. From fine to coarse, they are 0-0-0-0, 0-0-0, 0-0, 0, 1, 2, and 3. Steel wool is almost identical regardless of brand. You may as well shop for price.

With abrasives as with the rest of your shop equipment, pick the right materials and use them right. You'll end each job with a smooth finish!

Save yourself from drowning!

Startling discoveries by experts indicate about a third of the country's 'drowning' victims didn't drown, and that many such victims, declared dead, are not. Here's what to do if you fall overboard.

By RICHARD F. DEMPEWOLFF

NEAR JACKSON, MI, an 18-year-old college student driving alone "lost it," went sideways off the road and plunged through the ice of a deep pond. The rolling car eliminated any hope that air might be trapped in the passenger compartment. The youth struggled, took on water and lost consciousness.

Luckily a following driver spotted the accident and alerted the authorities. It was 38 minutes later, however, before rescuers pulled the victim from the water. There was no apparent pulse; no signs of life. He was declared "dead at the scene."

While the body was being loaded into the ambulance, however, the "dead" man gasped. Startled rescuers immediately began revival efforts. At the University of Michigan Hospital in Ann Arbor, Dr. Martin J. Nemiroff and a team of colleagues worked over the boy for two hours. After 13 more hours of respiratory support, the student "woke up." He instantly recognized his mother, who was at his bedside.

Attendant doctors, who had expected brain damage in anyone deprived of oxygen for more than four minutes, were even more surprised shortly thereafter when the lad picked up his college career and completed it with A grades.

The apparently unusual case, it turns out, isn't so unusual at all. Today, after several years of scientific investigation prompted and encouraged

SEE ALSO
**Boat camping . . . Boating, safety . . .
Boating, white-water . . . Canoes . . . Ice fishing . . .
Inner-tube water sports . . . Life preservers . . .
Outboard motors . . . Sailboats . . . Sports, water**

HUNTERS and fishermen falling overboard from boats are prime hypothermia victims. As shown here, waders will float a fisherman who lies still.

HELP position extends survival time.

MARKED AREAS lose body heat.

DON'T gun it while standing aft.

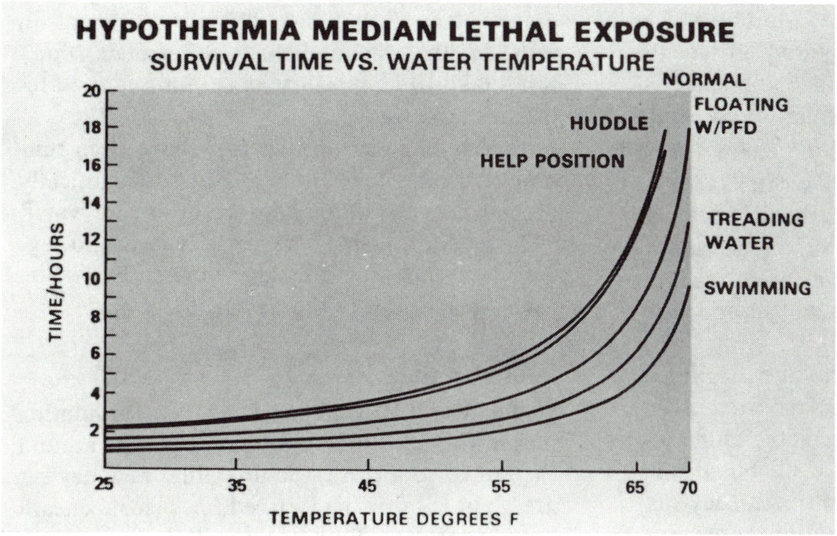

CHART shows survival time lost in cold water by swimming or other exertion.

FOAM BELT pad protects thorax from cold and keeps the head high.

IMPROPERLY WORN life vests lift out of water and lose buoyancy value.

THIS HUNTING jacket PFD insulates body, and floats. Hood warms head.

SKI BELTS are not approved as PFDs. They provide too little buoyancy.

by the U.S. Coast Guard and the Michigan Sea Grant Program, investigators know that sudden contact of the head and face with "cold" water (anything below 70° F. is classified as "cold" by the Coast Guard) may touch off a primitive response in humans known as the "mammalian diving reflex."

The frigid water triggers complex physiological responses that shut down the blood circulation to most parts of the body except heart, lungs and brain. Though the blood contains only a limited amount of oxygen, it can be enough, investigators have learned, to sustain life and prevent damage to brain tissue for considerable periods of time, once the body's internal temperature has dropped. A cooled-down brain needs less oxygen than one at normal temperature.

This phenomenon has long been known to researchers. It permits deep-diving mammals like whales, porpoises and seals to remain active at frigid depths for long periods.

In humans, unhappily, the phenomenon is not quite that convenient—despite the unique life-extending time it may provide in rare cases.

"Hypothermia," the medical term for dropping the body's internal temperature below its normal 98.6 ° F., can produce a number of disastrous results. While it may take 10 to 15 minutes before the "core" temperature starts to drop, surface tissues cool quickly. A victim may experience labored breathing and stiffness of limbs and hands.

As core temperature drops to 95 ° there will be violent shivering; at 90 ° to 95 °, mental facilities cloud; at 86 ° to 90 ° there's muscular rigidity and loss of consciousness. Below 86 ° come diminished respiration and possible heart failure. Below 80 °, respiration becomes almost undetectable and death is imminent.

Investigators now believe that something like a third of all the boating drownings reported in one recent year, according to best available estimates, probably were not drownings at all but deaths due to hypothermia. Even more tragic, they suspect that in some 20 to 30 percent of those cases, the victim probably was not dead when found even though there was no discernible pulse, no apparent breathing, eyes were dilated, color was bluish and rigidity had set in—all usual signs of death in familiar warm-water drownings.

threat to hunters

For the past few years, Lt. Cmdr. David S. Smith, state liaison officer for the U.S. Coast Guard's Second District headquarters in St. Louis has been traveling the country spreading a new gospel about these discoveries and what people can and should do about them. He points out that the primary cause of death in autumn hunting accidents is not gunshot wounds, but "drowning," and that many of those so-called drownings are death from hypothermia.

"Some victims don't even have water in their lungs," he reveals. "We lose all kinds of them every year. They make a blind out of a 14-foot boat, stand up to shoot, lose their balance and go over the side. Water in many lakes seldom gets above 60 °, even in summer. During spring and fall floods it may get down to 40 °. Worse, those guys usually are hypothermic to start with from sitting there on a cold morning waiting for the ducks. On top of it, they've been drinking to keep warm. The birds come over, the nimrods stand up, stiff and wobbly, fire, and over they go. The cold water hits them and that's it."

Another favorite gaffe, Smith points out, is to reach over with one hand, while standing, goose the outboard throttle, and get pitched over the transom when the boat surges ahead.

How do you protect yourself in cold water? For boatmen, the Coast Guard emphasizes "personal flotation devices" (now the preferred term for lifejacket). "And you don't just carry them along," says Dave Smith. "You *wear* them." In tests, Smith has found that even experts sometimes take 10 minutes trying to climb into a lifejacket in the water.

The commander and his crew have been running tests on a new family of PFDs, scientifically designed for flotation and warmth in cold water. "The medical people," he says, "have found several body areas extremely vulnerable to the cold—head, sides of thorax and the groin."

insulation vital

One new PFD is an insulated, hooded hunting jacket with built-in flotation. A strap goes around the crotch so it can't ride up. Other new devices are foam plastic pads laced in place beneath outer garments. Both types will keep a man's head well above water; the hooded jacket protects it from weather.

Though not as insulative, approved life vests are even a help in an emergency. "Unfortunately," Smith observes, "most people don't know how to put them on properly. In tests, even Coast Guard personnel didn't know kids' from adults' sizes, and one Academy instructor tried to put on an approved vest inside out."

Actually, ordinary woolen clothing will provide flotation if the person in the water doesn't panic and force the air from the fibers, Smith says. And despite what you may have heard, a fisherman's chest waders will pop his feet up and float him if he doesn't thrash.

cold water dos and don'ts

DO:

1. Wear a float coat, a PFD or several layers of clothing when you're hunting or fishing in a boat. When the water temperature is 50 ° F., a clothed person can survive an average of three hours in a PFD.

2. Try to keep lungs filled with air to maintain buoyancy.

3. Use minimum movement to prevent the escape of trapped air in your clothing. An average person who is treading water or swimming in a PFD will lose body heat about 35 percent faster than he would when holding still.

4. Take advantage of floating objects, such as boats, paddles and so forth for added buoyancy.

5. Maintain HELP (Heat Escape Lessening Posture—see diagram on page 25) until help arrives. If two or more people are in the water, huddle.

DO NOT:

1. Panic. Most victims are conscious when they enter the water; most drownings happen only 10 feet away from safety; action taken in the first 10 seconds can mean survival or death.

2. Struggle. You'll squeeze out air trapped in your clothing. Ingesting cold water may constrict the breathing passages and induce "dry drowning."

3. Swim for land that's over a mile away.

4. Remove clothing.

5. Use so-called "drownproofing" techniques in water that's colder than 72° F.

What about drownproofing?

The principles of a procedure known as drownproofing undoubtedly have saved many lives in shallow, sun-warmed lakes and pools where water temperature climbs above 72° F. in summertime. The technique involves floating almost motionlessly for long periods, relying on the natural buoyancy of the body and its tendency to hang in a semi-vertical position in water, head just breaking the surface. Potential drowning victims tend to thrash around in futile efforts to "climb on top" of the water, but the drownproofing concept teaches them to stay alive through maximum conservation of energy.

Instruction in the technique usually begins at poolside, practicing the correct position—head forward, arms down, legs together. With a friend to help at the pool's shallow end (left), the student kneels on the bottom and tilts head back to bring nose and mouth above surface to inhale fresh air, then tilts head forward to exhale. Final step (center) finds student hanging suspended (arms and legs positioned as in the right photo) in deep water by herself—nose and mouth above the surface where they can take air as needed—without need for exertion. At that point, the student has been "drownproofed."

In water below 72° F., however, forget drownproofing, says the U.S. Coast Guard—unless you're caught with only bathing attire and no flotation gear. In cold water, the greatest body heat loss is from the head and neck. Since drownproofing requires immersion of those areas, the onset of hypothermia, followed by death, can be brought about with distressing swiftness.

If you are unfortunate enough to go overboard without attire containing some insulative or buoyant potential, then drownproofing, treading water or swimming may be your only chance.

How to plan a room addition

Take your time in planning. Do the job right by sketching several different concepts, contacting the correct authorities, and locating the materials before you start to build. With this kind of planning you'll build an addition you won't want to change later

By MIKE McCLINTOCK

■ HOW MANY TIMES have you wished you could alter the layout of your house? Whether it's relocating a door or closet, widening a hall or raising a roof, most houses have an area that should and could have been planned better. If you're thinking about an addition, now's the time to consider all your options and work all the bugs out of the plan.

The first step is to find out any limits you must work within. Your assessors' office may have a tax map for your area that shows the size of your property and location of your house. Get a few copies so you know what you're working with. Next, ask your local building department about limitations on yard spaces around your house. Most codes specify how close you can build to your property line. When you get these figures, lay them out on your tax map using the map scale.

Now you have some boundaries. As you think about your addition—how big and where it will be—pencil it in on the map adjoining the house. Even though you may be planning your dream room, remember that you may be giving up something like a shade tree or natural runoff for ground water. Make sure you locate the septic tank and underground piping such as a gas line. I've heard horror stories about porches with spe-

SEE ALSO
**Attic dormers . . . Ceilings . . . Contractors . . .
Family rooms . . . House additions . . .
Insulation . . . Moldings . . . Remodeling . . .
Sheathing . . . Siding**

cial cuts, fittings and hinges to get at the septic tank that was forgotten when the porch was built. Balance your wildest dreams with a practical solution and pick the best site available.

make the first plan

Start working on a larger scale. Get a pad of ¼-inch graph paper and lay out the dimensions of your house, one square for one foot. Include interior room sizes and mark door openings. Put a thin piece of tracing paper over this and sketch out a rough plan for the overall size of your addition. Do one sketch of the biggest and best, one of the smallest, and as many variations as you can think of in between. Even if you decide that you don't like the overall idea in a drawing, keep it. You may find it contains a good idea that you'll wind up incorporating in the final plan.

the easy way to move furniture

Take some colored construction paper and measure out, to scale, the approximate sizes of furniture you expect to use in a room. Pick out a few sketches you like best and try different furniture arrangements on them. This is likely to cut down on the number of designs because you'll find some layouts are a natural for the furniture you have in mind—and some just won't work at all. Now go back to the graph paper and put in more details. Locate windows, closets and doors exactly, and the thickness of all interior walls (figure 4 to 5 inches to scale). If your sketch starts to look messy, retrace it on a clean sheet of paper.

you'll have to compromise

Here come the first big decisions. The easiest way to compromise is to multiply the total floor area of your addition by a per-square-foot cost estimate. This figure can be obtained by talking to new homeowners and builders in your area. If you contemplate using expensive materials like plaster, tile, parquet floors and hardwood cabinets, you'd better add $5 to $10 to the figure. This system makes it somewhat easier to eliminate your more elaborate designs. Your addition should be just what you want, but it should also be practical and it has to be affordable or you'll have no addition at all.

make the second plan

Here are some new rules. They'll save construction time and material costs. If you're figuring the width of a room at 17 feet, try 16. This way, two sheets of 4 x 8 plywood and 16-foot joists will fit. You'll be saving a bundle on materials by eliminating waste. Get a copy of local building codes or contact your building inspector. You may find that by making your room 6 inches narrower you can use 2 x 8 joists instead of 2 x 10s. Before you put all this into a final plan, find out about materials. See what's available at local lumberyards. Get some catalogs (with prices) and look at flooring, tile, windows and doors. You may find a good-looking siding like Texture 1-11 that comes in 4-foot widths. It eliminates the need for plywood sheathing (in most areas) and will cut costs considerably. This may buy you back that extra few feet of space you want in the room.

a time for final decisions

Hopefully you've picked your location and you should have a sketch that's very close to the final plan. Considering materials, costs, availability and your needs, make the last adjustments and draw the final sketch neatly. Before proceeding with a contractor or starting the job if you're doing it yourself, make an appointment with the building inspector. His job is to be sure you live in a safe, secure house, so take his advice.

don't rush it

Take your time with planning. Give yourself an opportunity to make mistakes now, on paper. Moving a wall later on is expensive. Since you're going to live in the addition, you're really better equipped than anyone else to plan its layout. Even if you expect to see an architect for a design, you'll have something specific to show him that reflects your needs.

How will it look? If may be difficult to visualize the elevation from a floor plan. Drawing a simple elevation of each exposed side will help. Work from dimensions on your plan to get the length of each wall. It's important that the addition looks like part of the house; not like a box stuck against it. So make the heights of all doors, windowsills and fascias the same as they are in the house. Sticking with the same siding and paint color helps, and definitely use the same color shingles.

For your drawings, get dimensions from your existing house and transfer them, to scale, to your elevations. Orient the drawings by marking each one north, south, east or west elevation. If you are really ambitious, use the plan dimensions to build a scale model.

Take your time. Make a good plan now, and you won't want to change anything after it's built.

Add a greenhouse—an elegant addition

By MIKE McCLINTOCK

THE SUN is shining, snow is on the ground, icicles are hanging from the roof, and the roses are blooming. This combination seems impossible, but there's one place it can happen—in a greenhouse, a beautiful addition to your home.

That's the conclusion I came to after several attempts at designing a freestanding unit and wondering where to locate it and how to heat it. The strong lean-to design of the final greenhouse is so clean and simple that it will look good with any style home. You'll get the most use out of it in the winter when it captures enough of the sun's energy to keep your garden growing through the

YOU'LL HAVE a bumper crop of flowers blooming all year inside this beautiful greenhouse. The classic design will boost your house value.

SEE ALSO

**Benches, potting . . . Cold frames . . . Decks . . .
Dry sinks . . . Gardening . . . House additions . . .
House plants . . . Planters . . .
Strawberry barrels . . . Terrariums . . .
Transplanting . . . Vegetable gardening**

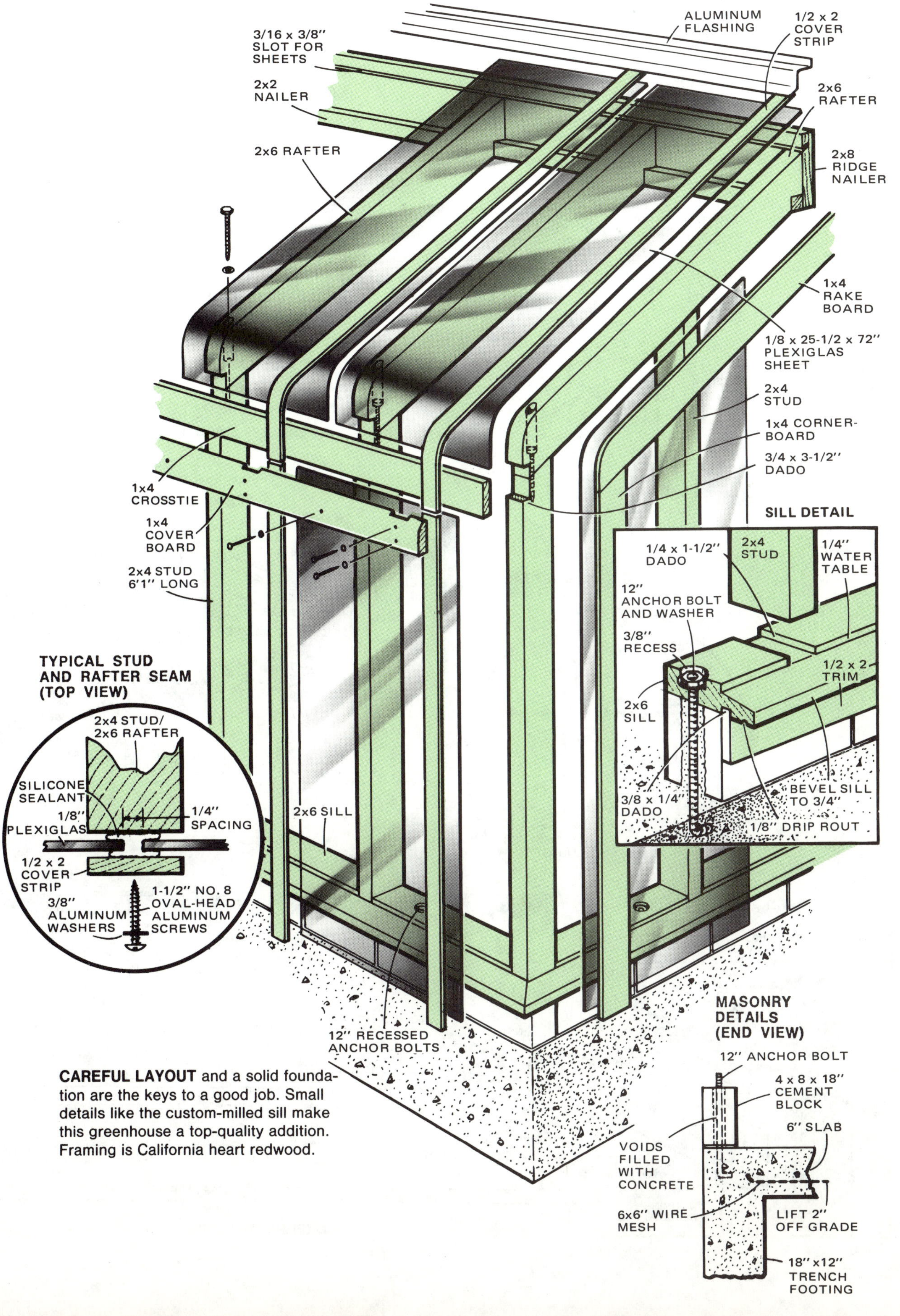

CAREFUL LAYOUT and a solid foundation are the keys to a good job. Small details like the custom-milled sill make this greenhouse a top-quality addition. Framing is California heart redwood.

RAFTER DETAILS

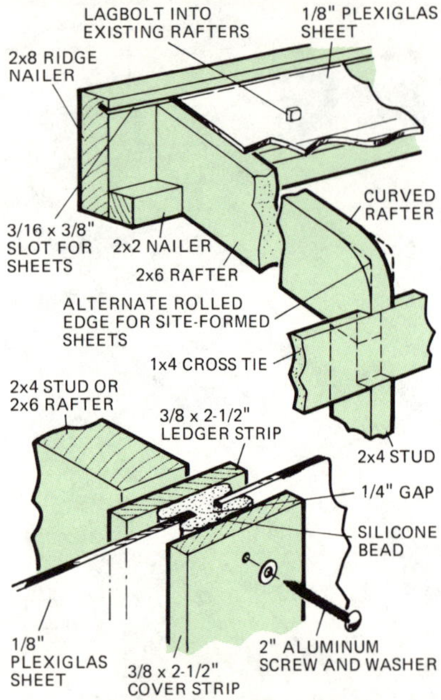

HURRICANE DETAIL (EXPLODED VIEW)

sleet and the snow. I'm looking forward to sitting "outside" in the greenhouse on a bright, 35° F. Sunday morning, and reading the papers in 75° F. comfort.

Making the greenhouse a part of your home gives you a lot of advantages. You'll need less material, and the adjacent house wall will protect the plants from winter winds. You'll be able to enter without going outside. You won't have to install lengthy electric or gas lines. But a great increase in heating efficiency is the best reason to go with a lean-to design. When there's no sun, you can let house heat spill into the greenhouse and take the load off its heater. When the sun is out, you can reverse this process and let that sweet hot-house air spill into the room and save on your fuel bill. It's the simplest form of solar heating.

The structural design is simple, solid and flexible. Each bay is modular so you can add as many

ALTERNATE FOOTING

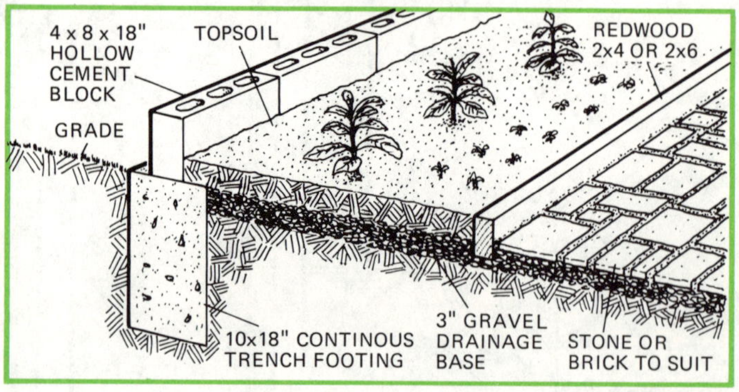

CORNER DETAILS

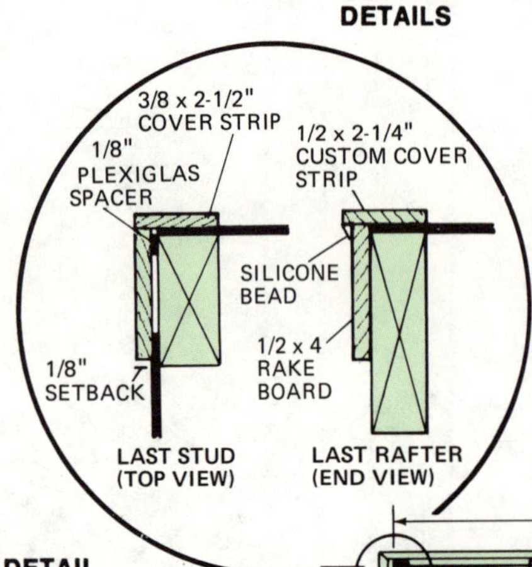

COVER BOARD DETAIL

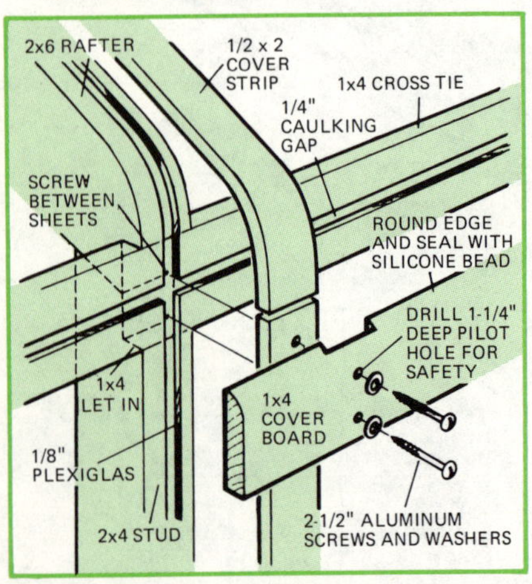

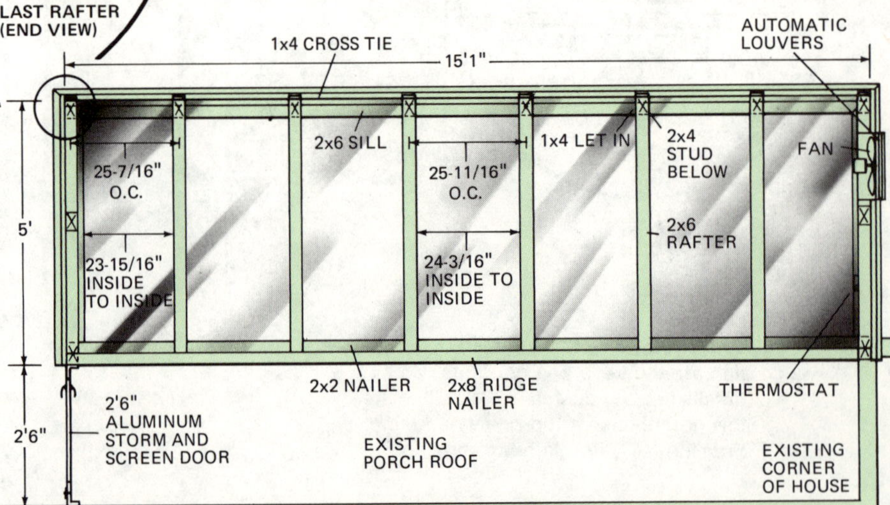

OVERHEAD VIEW

LAYOUT LINES should be checked for accuracy before you build the 2 x 6 forms (1). Run a flat 2 x 4 across the edges of the forms to level the slab. You can finish with a rough or smooth troweling, depending on the floor surface you want (2). Set up the block while the concrete is still wet, checking the level carefully (3). All studs should be plumbed and braced (4). Inset shows how to set up the rafters for bolting to the studs. Accuracy and strength here are most important.

as you want to get just the right length. The height of the eaves is figured for a 6-ft. sheet of Plexiglas. This gives you comfortable headroom with the added height of the 8-in. cement block and sill. The run of the rafter also conforms to a 6-ft. sheet. We got extra space by attaching the ridge to an existing overhang. The design will also work against the flat wall of a house where you extend rafters and use 8-ft. sheets, another stock length.

Here's a rundown on the materials. The footings are concrete. We put down a full slab (a center drain is nice but unessential). You can also use a simpler and less costly perimeter footing (see alternate detail). The cement-block edging was laid while the concrete was still wet to get the best possible bond. This detail raises the wood sill off the ground and gives you more headroom. Many greenhouse designs call for a 3-ft. masonry wall; our design eliminates this expensive, time-consuming job and increases the growing area by letting in more light.

All timber is construction grade, heart redwood. It is milled from the center of the tree, contains virtually no sap, can be left untreated and still withstand high moisture. This is crucial since all sealers contain a mildecide agent with vapors that are harmful to plants months after application.

We chose ⅛-in. Plexiglas from Rohm and Haas (even though it's softer than glass and more expensive than fiberglass) because it transmits light well, can be cut or trimmed easily (a sharp plywood blade will do it) and has an elegant appearance. The biggest consideration was our two young boys who like to play baseball in the yard. Materials including an 8-ft. bench, heater, fan and thermostat, cost about $700 when we built it.

This is a large undertaking, but it's an addition with unusually high payoffs: good looks, a major jump in equity in your home, extra solar heat and, if you're an enterprising gardener, high-vitamin, unprocessed and nearly free vegetables.

Plexiglas comes slightly oversized, so we widened the framing centers and cut sheets down the middle. Be sure you comply with your local building codes. To maintain 60° F. on a cold day, your heater should produce 5000 B.T.U. for every 10 square feet of greenhouse.

One last note: Curving the Plexiglas to a wide arc is tricky with heat tape. Your supplier can bend the sheets to your design or you can use our alternate method for a single, tight bend at the eaves.

REMOVING A RIVET by drilling out the peened-over end can be a problem, because the rivet will revolve with the drill bit. What works for me is backing the rivet with a fine, flat file—being careful, of course, not to drill into it.—*B. F. Borsody, Palmetto, FL.*

AFTER A FEW thousand miles, two-piece wheel covers with plastic centers can develop annoying noises at low speeds. Eliminate them permanently with a bead of silicone rubber sealant around each center on the inside, coating the spring clips at all pressure points.—*Parry C. Yob, Fair Oaks, CA.*

A SPRING LAMP-SHADE clip and the base from a discarded iron, bolted together, make a rest for a hot soldering iron. The threaded part of the clip was just the right size for the hole in the base plate.—*Ken Patterson, Regina, Sask.*

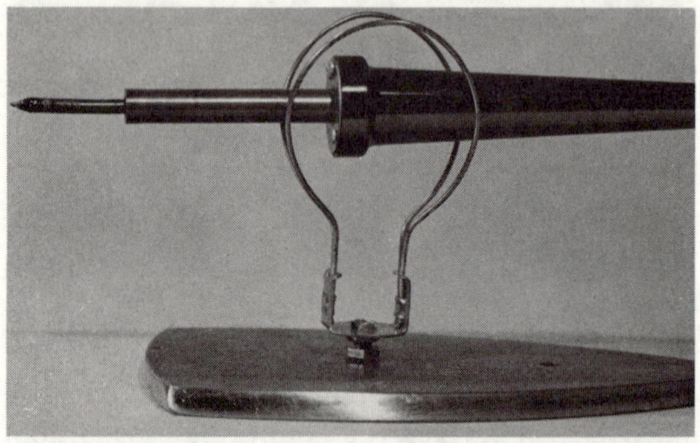

EVEN THE SMALLEST needle or pin is too big to clear the tiny port of an aerosol valve, and ordinary wire is too limp. But a bristle snipped from a common wire brush is the right size (about .015 in. dia.) and stiff enough.—*W. G. Tilsher, Rosemead, CA.*

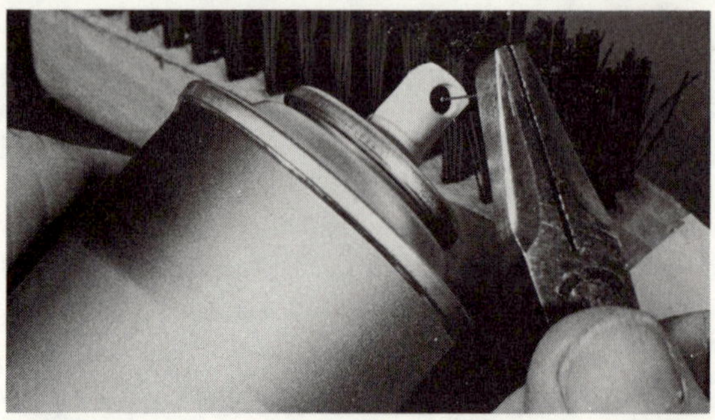

A LIGHTED HOUSE number is easily made by fastening metal numerals on a piece of translucent white plastic, which is hung from cup hooks. The numbers on the white background are lit from behind by the porch light at night.—*T. J. Gray, Springfield, MO.*

Stick with the right glue

The wild and wonderful array of today's adhesives—including some old timers still unsurpassed—can handle just about any job you have. But you'll need to know the field if you want the special combination of characteristics your project requires

CHOOSING THE right glue—and handling it right—will hold your work together. That may seem an obvious statement, but modern adhesives will keep nearly anything together—from buildings to airplanes.

Bear in mind, however, that no one glue will do everything. You have to know which is best for what.

Actually there are only about a dozen basic types of glue. The question of which one to select will depend on the specific characteristics of the glue and the nature of the job. Many glues are quick-setting, while others are not. Offhand, a quick-setting adhesive would seem to be ideal and so it is—for small assemblies. But what happens when a quick-setting glue is used on a large, complex assembly?

Trouble. It may be difficult to get all the necessary surfaces joined together before the glue on some joints begins to dry. It may well start to dry before you can apply clamping pressure, or even before all the surfaces are ready.

Warmth—whether of the air, the glue, or the material to be bonded—makes such problems more likely. Whether an adhesive depends on a chemical reaction or simply on the evaporation of its medium, almost any adhesive sets faster at higher temperatures. That's why some craftsmen put the glue container in a larger container and surround it with ice.

SEE ALSO

Clamps . . . Dovetail joints . . . Drawers . . . Finishes, wood . . . Joinery . . . Legs, furniture . . . Moldings . . . Sanding . . . Veneering . . . Wood bending . . . Wood finishes . . . Woods

tight fit—or loose

The fit of a joint can also influence your choice of glue. Most glues work best when surfaces match well. For joints that don't mate perfectly, a glue with good gap-filling properties is the obvious choice. Sometimes joints *must* be loose-fitting so the work can be assembled. Projects with dowel or mortise-and-tenon joints that angle toward or away from each other often re-

CHOOSE THE GLUE FOR THE JOB

KIND	USES	GAP FILLING	STRENGTH	WATER RESISTANCE
Hide (animal)	Structural bonding of wood: indoor furniture, cabinets, veneer. Available as liquid.	Good	High	Poor
Casein	Structural bonding of wood for most applications; particularly good for oily woods such as teak, lemon, yew. Can be used at any temperature above freezing. Mix powder, water.	Good	High	Fair
White (polyvinyl resin)	All-around household and shop glue for furniture making and repair, model and hobby work, paper and leather. Ready to use.	Poor	Medium	Poor
Aliphatic resin	Structural bonding of wood for furniture assembly, casework: edge and face gluing. Ready to use.	Good	High	Poor
Plastic resin	Structural bonding of woodwork where considerable moisture resistance is desired. Mix with water.	Poor	High	Good
Waterproof resorcinol resin	Structural bonding of wood exposed to soaking: furniture, framework, boat building and repairs. Two components.	Good	High	Excellent
Contact cement	Nonstructural bonding of wood, paper, fabrics, glass, cork, felt, linoleum. Laminating veneers and plastic compositions (Formica, Micarta and so forth) to countertops and vertical surfaces. Ready to use.	Poor	Medium	Very good
Epoxy resin	Structural bonding of rigid materials: wood, metal concrete, brick, tile, glass, china, some plastics and any application requiring high strength or extreme outdoor exposure. Two components.	Good	High	Excellent
Hot melt (glue gun)	Bonding wood, metal, leather, fabrics, plastics. Household repairs, hobby and craftwork. Ready to use.	Good	High	Excellent
Mastic adhesive	Installing plywood and hardboard paneling, gypsum wallboard to wood, plaster, concrete. Bonds ceiling and wall tiles, floor tiles. Ready to use.	Very good	Medium	Excellent
Silicone seal	Bonding glass, metal, pottery, porcelain: aquarium construction, weatherstripping, caulking. Ready to use.	Good	Medium	Excellent
Super glues*	Bonding glass, metal, wood, rubber and numerous other nonporous materials. Ready to use. *A wide variety is available. Check labels for specific applications.	Poor	High	Excellent

quire joints that are loose. The glue must fill the gaps.

How about moisture resistance? Can you get by with a water-resistant glue or must you have one that's water*proof*? It depends on the outdoor project you're working on, how much it will be exposed to the elements.

A chair put together with water-resistant glue will serve nicely on a covered porch, but the same chair would require waterproof glue if used out on the lawn or open patio.

Still another factor to consider in glue selection is its resistance to heat. Thermoplastic glues like the popular white polyvinyls become soft at temperatures above about 150° F. Such glue would be a poor choice for a project such as a

GLUES THAT require mixing must be measured carefully; a postal scale can help. Mark measuring cups and spoons so you don't accidentally contaminate one component with the other.

END GRAIN soaks up glue fast, so it should get two coats. Give it a thin coat first, add glue to the mating surface, then recoat the end grain before joining pieces.

NEWLY GLUED surfaces are slippery. Start a few nails through a butt joint before applying any glue. Projecting points will grab the mating piece as the two join, preventing skidding.

TEMPORARY CLEATS help ensure that you space shelves accurately. After you lay a bead of glue, spread it with a brush to be sure you have glue distributed evenly along the joint.

ON ANY JOINT, a larger gluing surface means stronger construction. Lap joints, dadoes, and tongue-and-groove joints are among those that offer extra gluing-surface area.

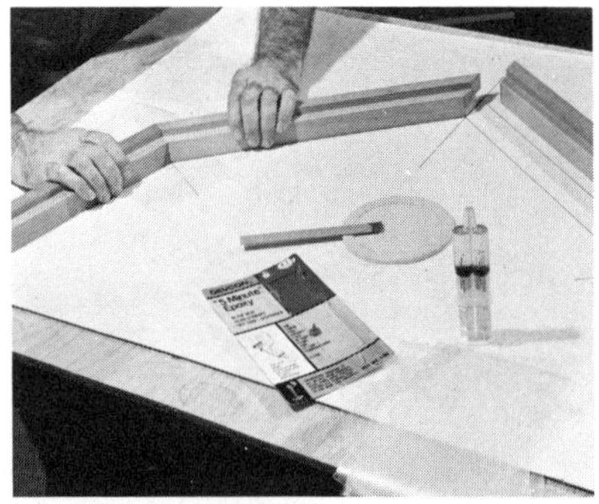

SOME IRREGULAR assemblies are nearly impossible to clamp. Select a fast-setting glue such as 5-minute epoxy so your hands—with a steady grip—can substitute for clamps.

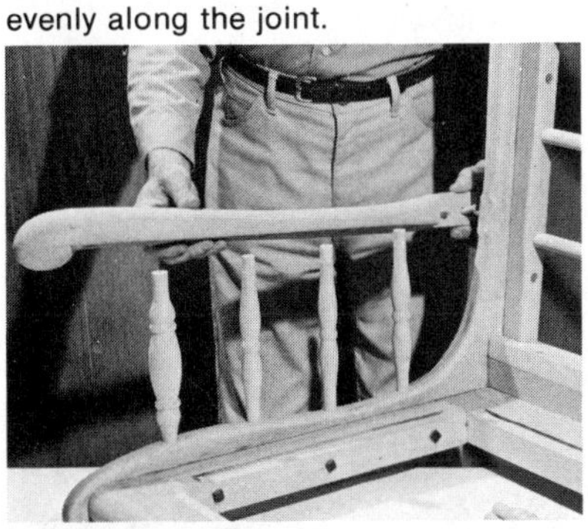

PARTS YOU will have to nurse into place can't have tight-fitting joints or fast-setting glue. Make the joints a bit loose and use a gap-filling, slower-setting glue.

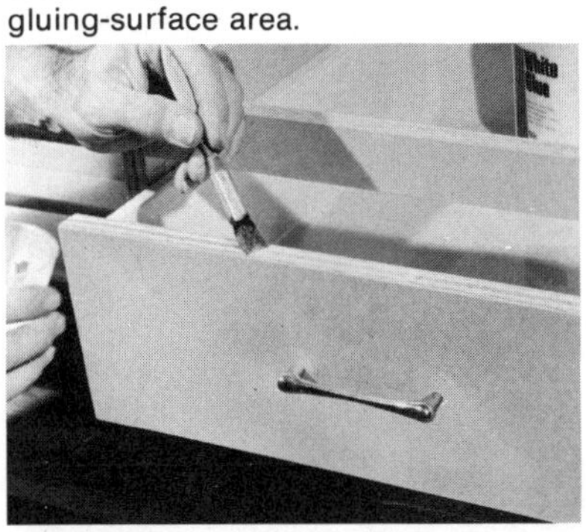

WHITE GLUE cut half-and-half with water is excellent for sealing edges of plywood that will be painted. It prevents the grain on the edges of the plies from showing through.

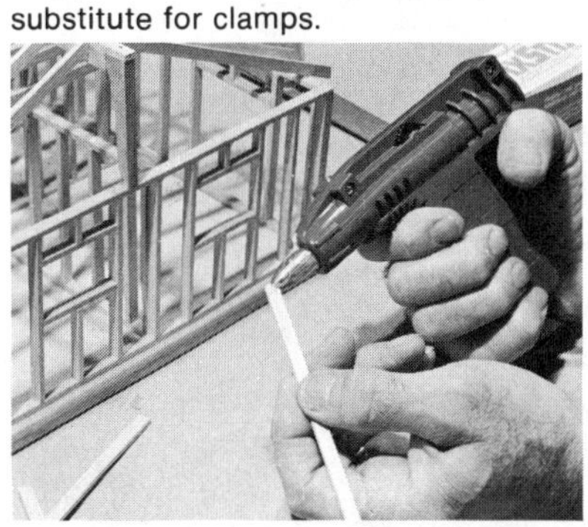

HOT GLUE from an electric glue gun provides quick stick for a variety of craft jobs and do-it-yourself projects. You'll find it handy in gluing together parts of models.

radiator enclosure or something that will be placed near a furnace.

follow directions

These are examples of the considerations you should keep in mind while you decide which glue to use. The projects you work on will indicate others. Be sure to check the manufacturer's instructions thoroughly and follow them to the letter. He wants his glue to perform in a way that satisfies you, and his instructions are written with that in mind.

Several of the more powerful adhesives require mixing by the user. Accurate measurements are important. When a powder is to be mixed with a liquid (sometimes water) and pro-

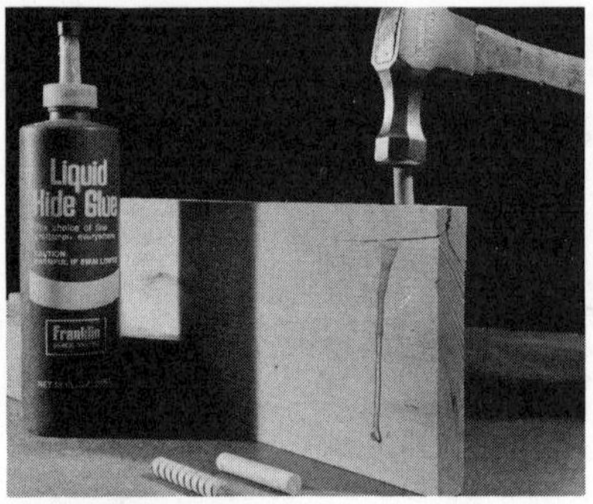

HAMMER TEST shows how glue trapped at the bottom of a hole can split the work under clamping pressure. Always plane a flat on a dowel for such jobs, giving excess glue an escape route.

PAPER SHEETS keep contact-cemented surfaces apart as you position them. As the sheet comes out, the exposed, glue-laden surfaces grab each other firmly. There's no reconsidering!

SUPERGLUES can bond wood trim, even to slick plastic laminates, without nails or clamps. But check the label; some don't work well on particular kinds of surfaces.

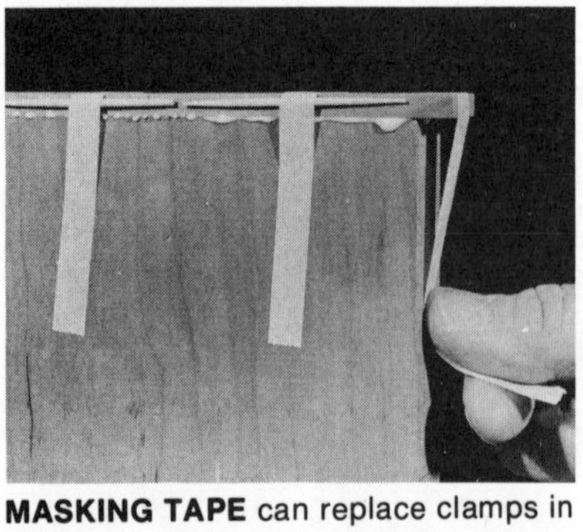

MASKING TAPE can replace clamps in gluing edge strips. Toothpicks at the strip's edge take clear of glue squeezing out. Slightly larger pieces of scrap will give more clearance.

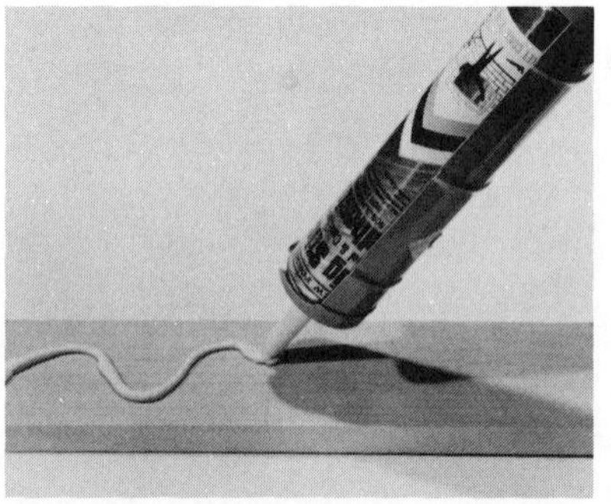

MASTIC ADHESIVE works great when you're installing furring strips on a concrete wall. If the original wall is uneven, however, big blobs from a can will do a better job.

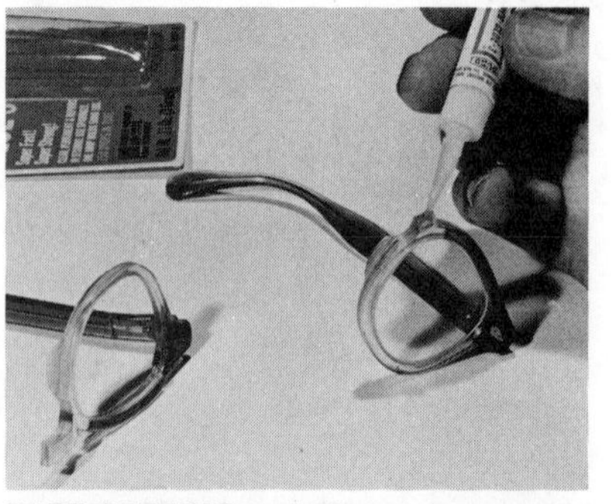

FAST SETTING and strong, some new superglues can even repair eyeglass frames. But some don't work on particular kinds of plastic; check the label in advance.

BULK MASTIC adhesives are more economical on large jobs like putting up sheets of paneling. A serrated tool lets you spread it evenly, yet assures you're using enough.

SPRAY ADHESIVE is a great way to stick fabric to wood. Coat both surfaces and let them set a moment or so before joining them. It gives you new decorating possibilities.

A TOURNIQUET or sometimes a simple strap will help when other clamps don't offer much. For furniture, a glue that swells wood fibres locks parts together securely.

portions are by volume, you'll be wise to "fluff up" the powder first to get an accurate reading on the volume. When proportions are by weight, a postal scale is handy.

Be careful not to contaminate your stock of one element with traces of another. Old craftsmen often use a pair of teaspoons that have been retired from active table service. They paint the handles with contrasting colors to avoid interchanging them by accident.

kinds of glue

• **Polyvinyl (white) resin glue** is a good all-around household and workshop glue for furniture repairs. It sets fast at room temperature, dries clear leaving an invisible glue line, and can be used for paper, leather and cork as well as wood. It's quite strong, but softens under heat and is not waterproof. White glue also doesn't handle sanding well; wipe off what squeezes out—promptly.

• **Liquid hide (animal) glue** is an old-time favorite in the furniture industry. It's made from bones, hooves and hides of animals, makes a tough, lasting bond, has excellent gap-filling properties and is very slow-setting. This makes it ideal for large assemblies.

A disadvantage is that it is not waterproof. Hide glues lost some popularity for a while with the coming of the synthetics, but are now making a comeback. The availability of hide glue as a liquid has helped broaden its acceptability. Originally it was available only as sheets or flakes. You had to soak it until it dissolved and keep it hot until it was applied and quickly clamped. Some users also found the aroma unappealing.

• **Casein glue** is made from mild curd, hydrated lime and sodium hydroxide. It is available in powder form and is mixed with water for use. It can be used at any temperature above freezing, has good strength and is fairly water resistant. It is very abrasive to tools and will stain some woods such as redwood. It is especially effective on oily woods such as teak and lemon. It is good as a gap-filling glue.

• **Plastic-resin glue** is a dry powder made with urea resin. The catalyst or hardener is incorporated in the powder. It is mixed with water to a creamy consistency for use. Highly water-resistant and stain-free, it sets very hard to produce a bond stronger than most species of wood. It's a good choice for salad bowls, serving trays and other articles subjected to moisture. Joints must be well fitted, however, because this glue is a poor gap-filler.

• **Aliphatic resin glue,** a relative newcomer among the synthetic resin glues, is a creamy, light tan liquid and comes ready to use. It is somewhat similar to polyvinyl white glue but has decided advantages. It is strong, highly resistant to heat and takes sanding very well. It's a good gap-filler, actually holding better in a thick glue line than in a thin one. But it isn't waterproof.

• **Resorcinol water-proof glue** is a two-component adhesive. When the wine-colored resorcinol resin is combined with the dry-powder catalyst, it cures at room temperature. It is 100-percent water-proof; it will withstand extreme cold as well as boiling water, acids, alkalies and solvents; and it is excellent for building or repairing boats, outdoor furniture and toys. It is quite expensive, leaves a dark glue line, is slow-setting and fills gaps rather well. But it cannot be used below 70° F.

• **Contact cement,** a neoprene-based, ready-to-use liquid, is an excellent adhesive for bonding plastic laminates to plywood. Also recommended for joining combinations of wood, cloth, cork, leather, ceramics and thin metal. It is applied to both surfaces and allowed to dry for about 30 minutes before assembly. The parts bond immediately upon contact and require no clamping. The regular type is highly flammable and must be used with good ventilation and no open flame. A nonflammable, latex-base type is also available for use where a fire hazard exists.

• **Hot-melt glue-gun glue** is a remarkably handy household and shop adhesive. Special adhesive cartridges in stick form are inserted into the chamber of the electrically heated gun and provide the quickest and easiest method of bonding two surfaces. You simply press to squeeze out a bead of hot melted adhesive that sets in 60 seconds.

The glue sticks to almost anything except a few stubborn plastics. It is, completely waterproof and works well as a gap-filler in loose joints. A caulking cartridge is also available for use in bathrooms, outside the house and on boats, autos, concrete, vinyl pool liners and inflatable toys.

• **Multi-resin hot-melt glues** don't depend on a glue gun; they're often sold in foil trays. You melt the glue on a hot plate or similar device. Such brands as "Hot Grip" bond to plastics that defeat other adhesives.

• **Epoxy resin adhesive** is a two-component resin and catalyst material that produces a very strong waterproof bond. Equal amounts of resin and hardener are mixed together for use. Many epoxies are available with curing times ranging from five minutes to more than one hour. All have excellent gap-filling properties. Most will work even on wet lumber—especially advantageous on outdoor construction where thoroughly dry lumber is rare. Another plus: Odd-shaped fabrications practically impossible to clamp are easily put together with fast-setting epoxy. Ordinary hand pressure for a few minutes does the trick.

Measuring equal amounts of the two components is made easier by new packaging methods. The two are marketed in what functions like a double-barrelled tube. A single key at the rear squeezes both tubes equally so equal amounts are automatically extruded.

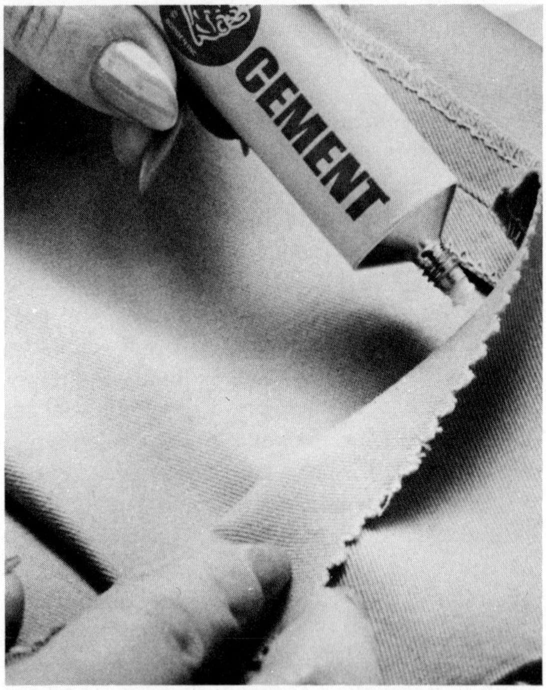

FABRIC CEMENT such as Elmer's is water-based, but is said to be laundry and dry-cleaning safe. Besides helping seamstresses, it works on leather, canvas, fur and other fabrics for craft and hobby projects.

WINDSHIELD SEALER forms a clear, tough, flexible film that holds glass to synthetic rubber, stainless steel, aluminum and wood. The fast-drying material is water-based, but still is water-resistant.

Now there's even a water-phase epoxy combination. It serves as either a coating or an adhesive. Before it sets, you can use water to wash it from brushes and tools, but after it sets, it's completely waterproof. Complete setting takes about 8 hours.

• **Superglues** are modern adhesives with amazing holding power, particularly suitable for bonding non-porous materials such as metals, glass, ceramics, porcelain, rubber and most plastics. Among them are the cyanoacrylates, urethanes and silicones. Most live up to the claims made for them provided they are used precisely according to the manufacturer's instructions. *Caution:* These superglues stick to anything including human skin. Take care to avoid getting any on your hands during use.

• **Mastic adhesives** are heavy-bodied pastes that are extremely tacky and fast-bonding. They are available in cartridge tubes for easy application with a caulking gun when you're installing wall panels, stair treads, metal thresholds, ceramic tiles, parquet flooring and other building materials. Specialized varieties are designed for masonry work such as brick and block laying, patching and repairing. Some are available in more economical five-gallon cans.

From Borden, "Elmer's Panel Fast" is a light colored mastic for adhering wall panels to studs or furring strips. After a bead of mastic ⅛ to ¼ inch wide is laid along the stud, it's best to delay hanging the panel for up to 15 minutes. Good bonds develop in 48 to 72 hours, but it takes 28 days for the mastic to reach full strength. It can even be applied to wet lumber.

Solvents are potentially a problem with many adhesives. Standard contact cement includes naptha or toluol, for example. Toluene, acetone, and xylene are among other popular solvents. Such solvents give off flammable vapors at temperatures as low as 40°F. (4°C.) or even 15°F. (—18°C.) in the case of acetone. The National Safety Council says the vapors' main hazard sometimes comes from their "profound narcotic effect." However, the vapor can also build up until it's explosive.

As this report is written, the Consumer Product Safety Commission is considering what steps it should take in regard to solvents. And industry sources are saying that solvent adhesives are on the way out.

In any case, you're well advised to pick water-base glues when you can. Solvents are less likely to be a problem and clean-up will be easier.

Build an A-frame swing set

This play center for the kids includes a swing, slide and more

By CHARLES R. HENTZ

USING AN A-FRAME for strength, this swing set is very stable and can be built for about $300. If you can find some materials at the junkyard it will cost less.

Choose a 16 x 18-ft. site for the swing set. It should be fairly level and clear of shrubs and other obstacles. In addition, the sliding board will extend about 12 ft. from one side. Level four block footings before starting on the A-frame.

To construct the frame, assemble the two A-shaped sides on the ground. Use temporary gussets at the vertex and bolts at other intersections.

Raise, position and plumb each preassembled side with the aid of a helper. Use 1 x 2 furring as temporary braces until you can nail on the floor joists, ridge board and plywood floor. Temporary braces extending from the front (pole side) and rear (slide side) to ground stakes should remain until the roof sheathing is in place. Frame the swing set as shown in the plans.

Note that swing-support headers are pinned to header joists. Bore ⅜-in.-dia. holes in these joists and insert ⅜-in.-dia. steel rod. Bore mating holes in the support header and slip it over the pins. Heavy-duty 5-in. corner braces can also be used in place of pins.

The foot of the slide must be securely anchored to a concrete base, since this will prevent the A-frame from swaying. Prepare a form and locate anchor bolts for securing the slide to the base plate. After the concrete has been poured and allowed to set, the slide rails can be attached. Notice that the rails are built in three sections. Use ⅜-in.-dia. x 3-in. carriage bolts to join them together and counterbore so threaded ends of bolts don't snag children.

Secure the top end of the rails to the 2 x 4 loft joists. Use a mending plate and No. 10 rh screws or bolts. Fasten the rails to the slide base plate after it has been secured to the anchor bolts in the concrete.

Next, build the bottom end of the slide. The underside of the lower rail boards are curved at one end. Use the lid of a 20-gal. trash can to mark the arc before cutting.

Now attach the galvanized sheet metal to the underside of the slide rails. Use ¼-in.-dia. x 1½-in. lagscrews with washers. The metal edges should be recessed about ¾ in. from the rails' outer edges. Leave enough extra metal at top and bottom so it can be wrapped under the cross members and then fastened securely with more lagscrews.

SEE ALSO
Playgrounds . . . Porch swings . . . Swings

On the opposite side of the A-frame install the fireman's pole. Sink it at least 1 ft. into the ground or into a concrete footing. Attach the top to the ridgeboard with metal strapping. Other accessories, as shown in the plans, can be added at your discretion. Use ⅜-in. nylon rope or chain to hang the various ladders, swings and trapezes.

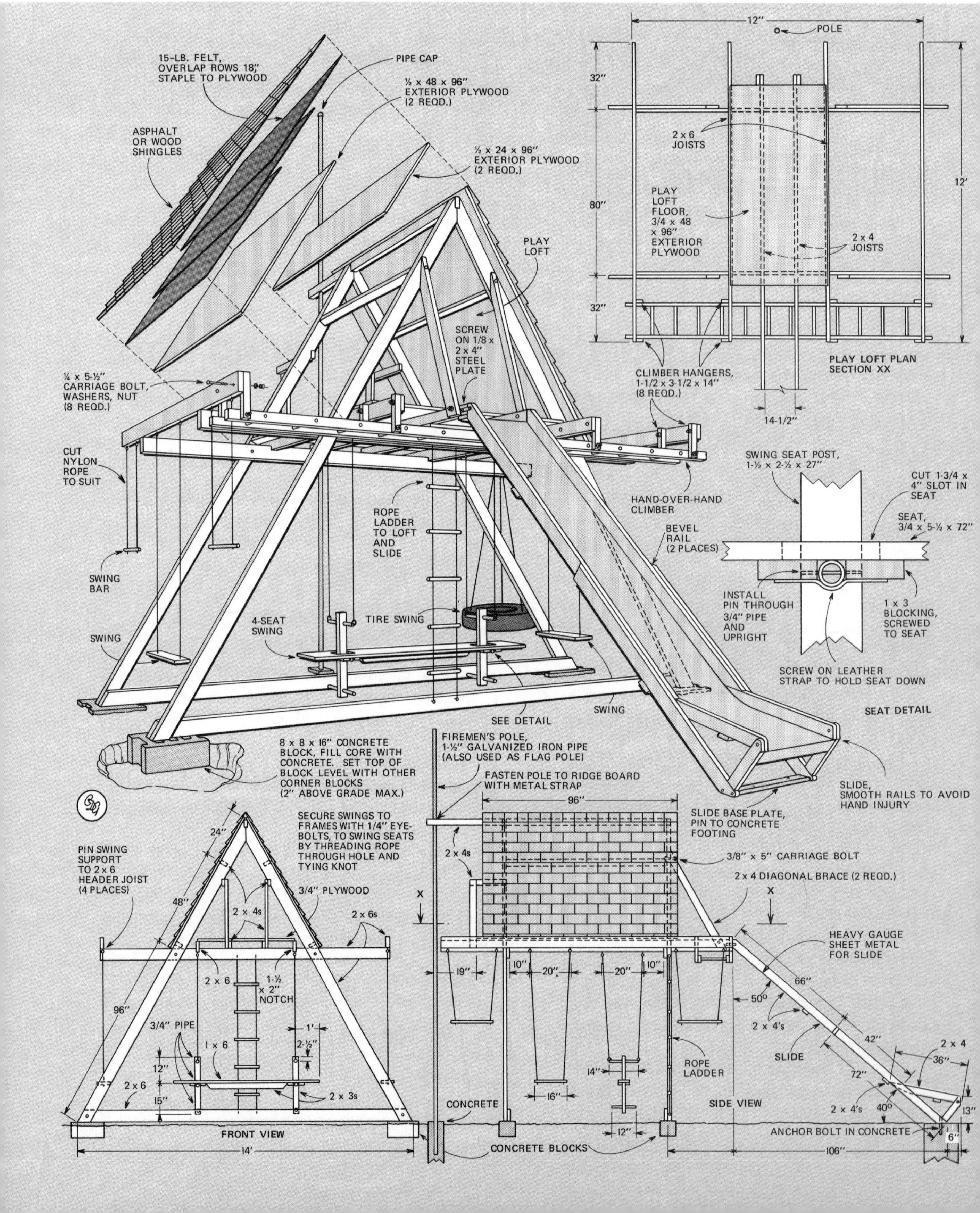

IF YOU LIVE in a climate where the warmth of summer often goes over the edge to plain uncomfortable, you need relief with airconditioning.

There are three options: Install central air, snap in a window unit or build a healthy-sized room unit into the wall.

The first choice is expensive, time-consuming and a luxury considering the costs of electricity.

A window unit will give you some relief but knocks out the use of one window and often doesn't fit very tightly or attractively.

A NEAT INSTALLATION doesn't intrude on the decor of the room. This airconditioner is a GE unit rated at 6000-BTU-per-hour. The size of the unit you need is determined by the area you want to cool, climate, and house construction.

Build in a room airconditioner

many advantages

Room airconditioners built into the wall have many advantages: Since installation is not limited to a window, you can pick a central location allowing maximum airflow. Airconditioner brackets can be easily positioned on the outside wall. You can get a tight, draft-free seal around the unit housing by filling the seams with scraps of insulation and sealing with beads of flexible caulking. You can trim and paint inside and out to match your house.

where to locate

Try to position the unit where you'll get the most mileage from the cool air. That means facing the length, not width, of a rectangular room and avoiding obstructions like large bookcases and other furniture that can block the airflow.

Also try to locate close to a grounded circuit, and if possible avoid areas where cables in the wall will have to be moved.

how big a unit?

ASHRAE (the American Society of Heating, Refrigeration and Airconditioning Engineers) recommends that you contact a reputable installer in your area to figure out how big a unit you'll need for the area you want to cool.

START BY laying out the opening for your unit on the inside wall. Cut 1½ in. inside a stud to allow for a 2 x 4 frame. Thus you should only have to cut away one stud. Drill through a corner of the opening to mark the layout on the wall outside.

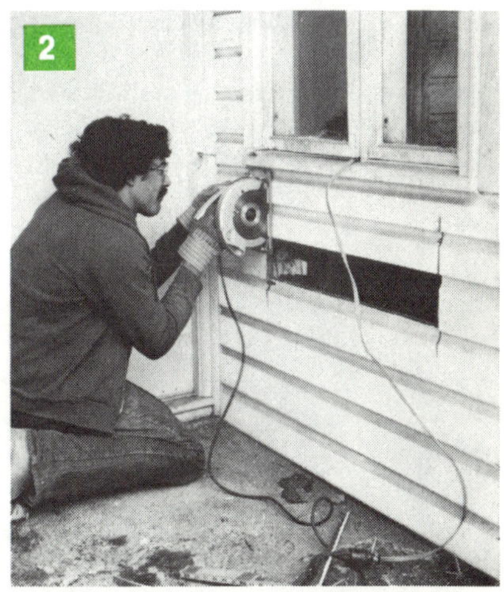

CHECK FOR NAILS before cutting the opening. With a circular saw, start with a plunge cut along the layout lines and finish corner cuts with a handsaw. Peel away siding, tarpaper and sheathing and remove the insulation underneath to reveal the studs.

SEE ALSO

Airconditioners, auto . . . Energy, saving . . . Family rooms . . . Heat pumps . . . Home improvement

continued

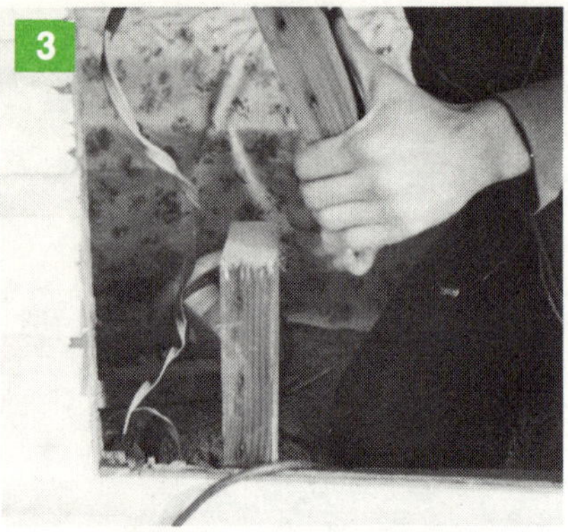

SAVE SOME insulation for filling in around the airconditioner housing. To remove stud in the opening, cut it 1½ in. above and below the opening (again to allow for the 2 x 4 frame) and slice it in half to make removal easier.

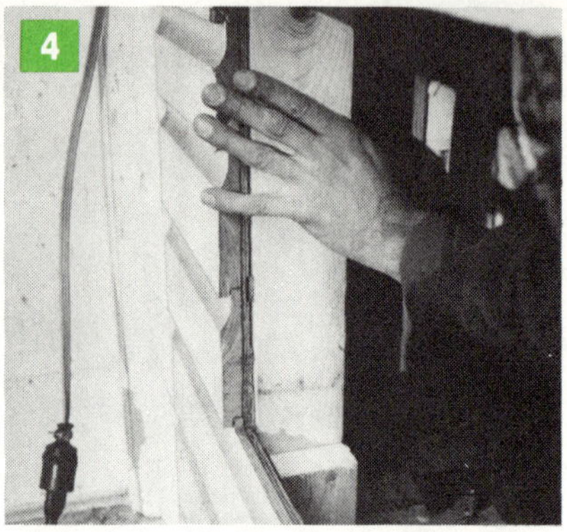

CHECK THE UNIT and opening dimensions and leave 1/16-in. clearance on each side for fitting. Tack a 2 x 4 header between the side studs and support it at each end with a short stud down to the floor sill. Toenail with 8d common nails.

A 2 X 4 SILL is toenailed to the side studs to support the unit. Add a short 2 x 4 at each end and (on some units) two in between. Drive 10d nails down through the sill and header into the center studs. Make sure that all nailheads are flush.

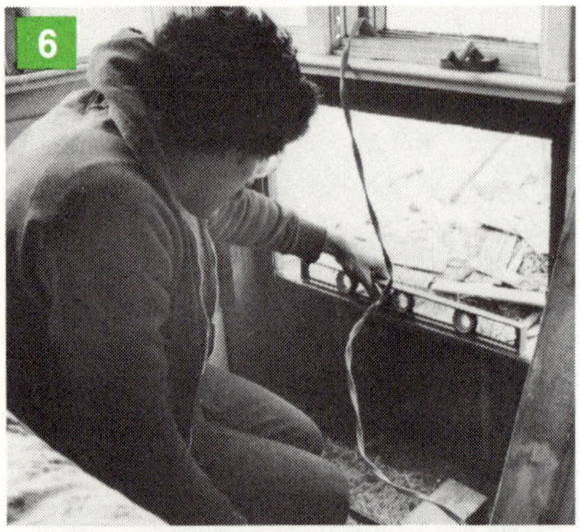

AS YOU FRAME opening, check dimensions and be sure the sill of the frame is level. At this point, screw the air-conditioner support bracket to the exterior wall. Recut insulation and staple in place.

CUT DRAFTS by adding 15-lb. felt or polyethylene vapor barrier inside; then replace the wallboard. You should be able to reuse the original piece. Nail it on and apply tape and compound to visible joints.

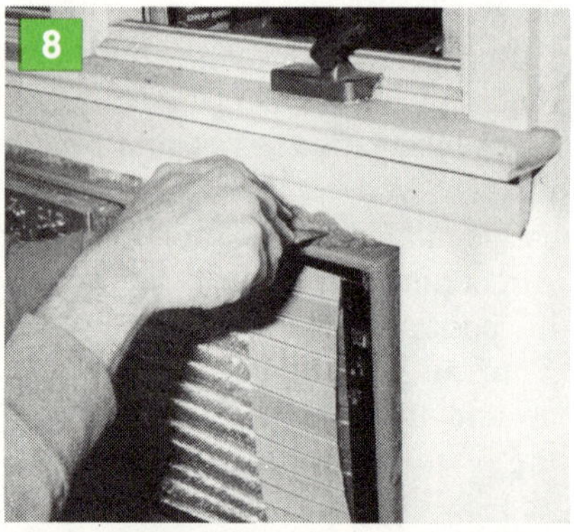

STRIP SOME fiberglass from the insulation and force it into seams between the housing and the frame with a putty knife. Leave an even margin around the housing to the interior wall. Caulk and cover with trim to suit.

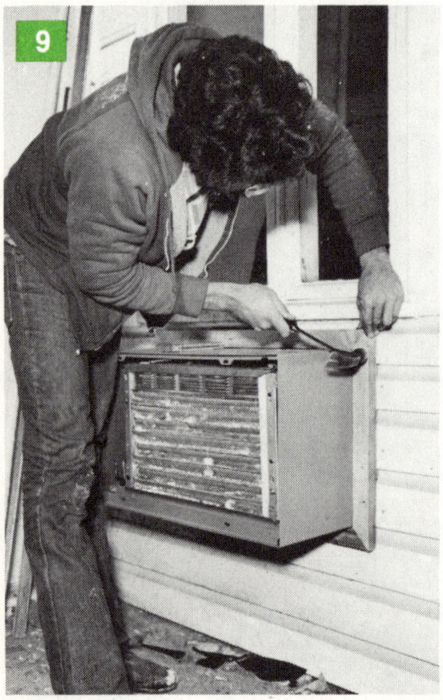

ONCE UNIT is in place, seal the seams with butyl caulking. Any neat trim can be nailed around the housing. The GE unit shown has an aluminum grille that's screwed onto the casing. For appearance, the unit can be painted to match your house.

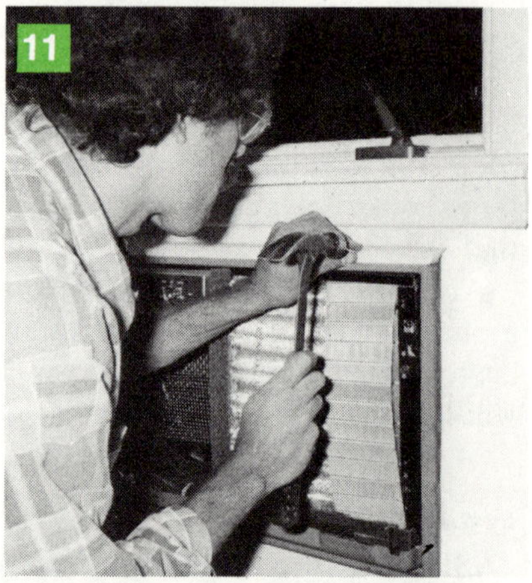

WE USED quarter-round molding on the interior. Miter the corners and set finishing nails. Putty the holes, sand, prime and paint. A grille with adjustable vent panels clips inside the housing. Controls are clustered behind a tinted fold-down panel.

Peeling under windows

Although I seem to have no such trouble elsewhere, the outside paint persists in peeling under several windows. I've done these areas over several times, but the paint still peels. What's the cause and remedy?—Harry Osbourne, Springfield, Mass.

If you remove the trim pieces (aprons) under the stools (sometimes mistakenly called window sills), you will likely see a narrow crack or opening. Moisture from inside the room is forced through this opening by vapor pressure into the space between the inside and outside walls. From here it gets under the paint film and eventually lifts it. Brush the dust from the opening and fill it with spackling compound, forming a fillet with your finger. When the compound is dry, prime it with aluminum paint, then apply a coat of oil-base paint or enamel. This usually cures the trouble.

Loose at the edges

Vinyl tiles in my kitchen have loosened and turned up at the edges. Can I restick 'em or must I replace?—Robert Marion, Chicago.

You might try running an iron, set on low heat, over the edges. If there is no accumulation of dust or wax under the edges, this can work. Be careful not to overheat and damage the tiles.

If the iron doesn't do the trick, you'll have to lift the edges, clean out dust and debris with a wire brush and work vinyl adhesive underneath. Wipe up any excess adhesive and weight the treated joints until the adhesive has set. This is the sure cure, but the job won't be quite as neat as it was originally—some of the turned-up edges many show in oblique light.

Splintered tread

One of my basement-stair treads is splintered at the edge. I don't know how it happened; the splinter just suddenly appeared. It's about two-thirds the length of the tread with one end still holding. Can it be repaired some way or should I replace the tread?—R. M. Desmond, Austin, Tex.

Before replacing the tread I'd try a repair. If the splinter is still intact, it should fit back in place with little if any offset. Mix a small amount of waterproof glue; then pry the splinter up very carefully, just enough to work in the glue between the meeting surfaces. Cover as much of each surface as possible without breaking the splinter off entirely. Force it back into place and hold it there with strips of adhesive tape. Wipe away any excess glue. When the glue dries, sand the area smooth and repaint in matching color.

Cove correction

A short section of the cove base in my bathroom has loosened and won't stick back in place. I've tried twice; the cement hardens but won't hold. This section is about 18 in. long and at the side of the toilet bowl. What to do now?—H. Cole, Redwood City, Calif.

It seems as if you didn't do a very thorough job of cleaning behind the cove. Usually the top end of the cove will loosen first, admitting dust and other debris. Unless this dirt is removed first, the cement just won't stick.

Do an all-out job of cleaning both the cove (scrape the old cement off the back, too) and the surface, then spread cove base adhesive (of a type appropriate for your cove material) as uniformly as possible with a notched trowel. Replace the cove and apply pressure if possible or use well set 4d finishing nails where required.

Extra insulation in attic

I need more insulation in my attic to keep out both heat and cold. At present there are 3-in. batts between 2x6 joists. Should I add more batts or use a pour-type insulation?—Ross Ihler, Cincinnati.

It might be permissible to use batts over batts but I think I would prefer the pour-type, especially if you are now experiencing no problems with moisture in the attic.

The pour-type insulation is somewhat easier to handle in cramped quarters, is quite as effective, and may be a bit cheaper in the end. The fill should be at least flush with tops of joists, or perhaps a little over.

Regluing oval picture frame

I have an antique oval picture frame measuring 20x25 in. Apparently it's made of four curved pieces joined with a peculiar dovetail-like joint. One piece is loose and needs regluing. How do I clamp the frame until the glue dries?—Mrs. R. Peabody, Bangor, Me.

Such frames are usually joined before machine-shaping with a modified "box" dovetail or box joint. Clean the open joint of all old hardened glue, taking care not to alter its shape.

Clamping of the frame probably will be a little tricky but can be done with a band clamp, or "web" clamp available from Albert Constantine & Son, 2050 Eastchester Rd., Bronx, N.Y. 10461. Or a rubber gluing clamp (a heavy rubber band) can be obtained from Brookstone Co., Dept. C-12, Brookstone Building, Peterborough, N.H. 03458.

How to keep cool for less money

■ TO STAY COMFORTABLE this summer and save money, too, you will want to use cooling equipment with capabilities that match the load your home imposes. You will want to use new or existing equipment as efficiently as possible, and you will want to make sure that conditions in and around the house are helping your cooling equipment do its job, not fighting it. This page and the three that follow will show you how to get the most comfort for the least money.

The Square Feet Method of determining cooling-load capacity, explained below, was developed by the Assn. of Home Appliance Manufacturers, which also issues a more detailed load estimate form, and publishes test results, including efficiency ratios, for room aircon-

ESTIMATING COOLING LOAD

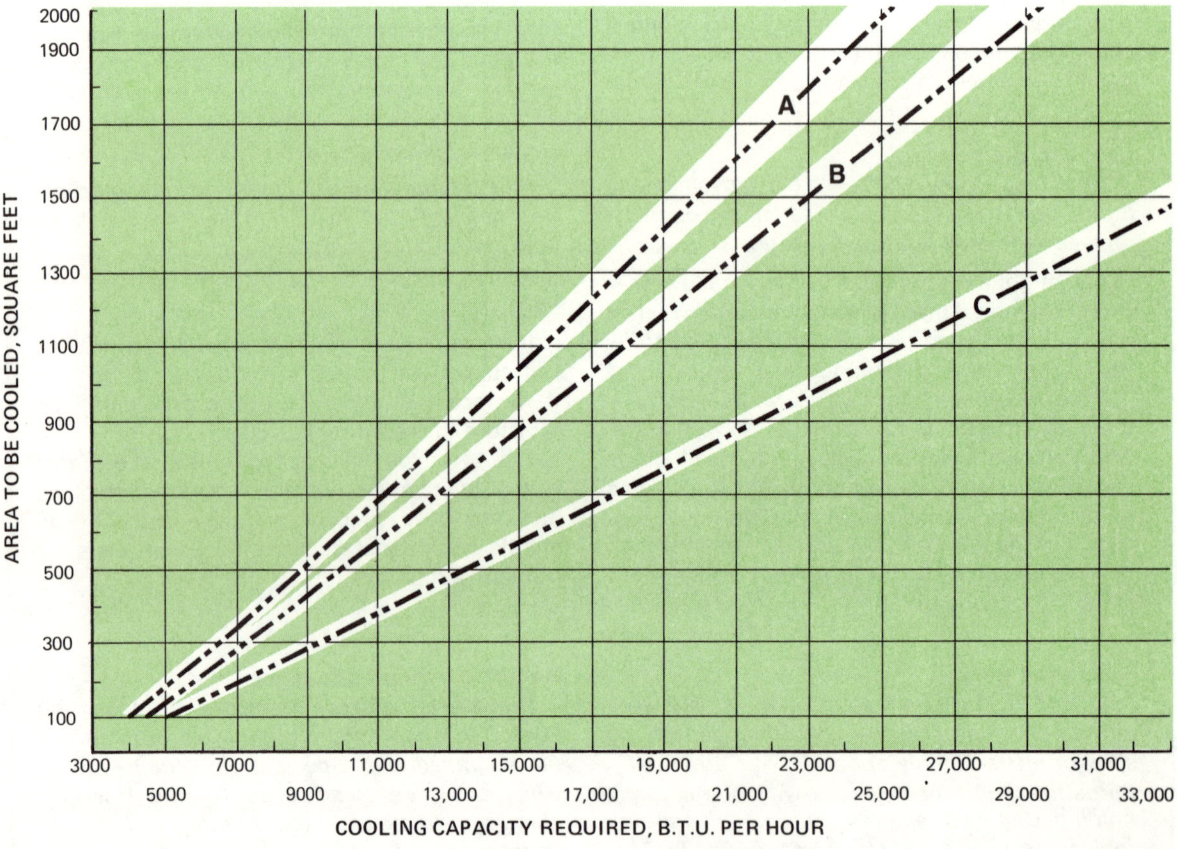

For most efficient cooling, a room airconditioner must be sized to suit its load. Too small, and it won't do the job; too large, and it will fail to control humidity, and its compressor will run intermittently—while you will have paid more for the unneeded capacity. AHAM's method of determining cooling load uses the graph above. To begin with, determine the area to be cooled (in square feet) and locate this figure on the left side of the graph. Then move across to the intersection of band A, B or C, depending on the condition of the space above—band A, occupied space above; band B, attic above insulated floor; band C, attic above uninsulated floor. From the intersection, move within the appropriate band to the left for more northerly exposure or to the right for more westerly exposure. From this point, read down to the bottom of the graph and note the number. This is a preliminary figure for the cooling load. Now subtract 30 B.T.U. per hour for each linear foot of wall separating the area to be cooled from other cooled rooms. If more than two people occupy the area, add 600 B.T.U. per hour for each additional person; if only one person occupies the area, subtract 600 B.T.U. per hour. Add 4000 B.T.U. per hour if the area should contain a kitchen.

SEE ALSO

Attic dormers . . . Attic ventilators . . . Energy, saving . . . Heat pumps . . . Winterizing, homes

ditioners sold in this country. Write AHAM, 20 North Wacker Dr., Chicago, Ill. 60606 for literature.

Insulation makes a dramatic difference in the cost of both cooling and heating. A 6-in. layer of insulation installed between attic-floor joists will pay for itself in a few years. Wall insulation also makes a sizable difference, but insulating walls of an existing house usually requires an expert.

If you do not like to come home to a warm house, consider using a timer control (with enough rated capacity for your airconditioner) instead of running airconditioning all day with no one at home.

A thermostat setting of 78° F. will give reasonable comfort and save money. On the hottest days, do not try to keep the indoor temperature more than 15° lower than outdoors.

COMPLETING THE ESTIMATE

Now locate your geographic area on the map at the right and multiply your previous B.T.U.-per-hour figure by the appropriate factor for your location. The resulting number is the cooling capacity you require; if, however, the room airconditioner is intended primarily for night use, reduce this amount by 30 percent.

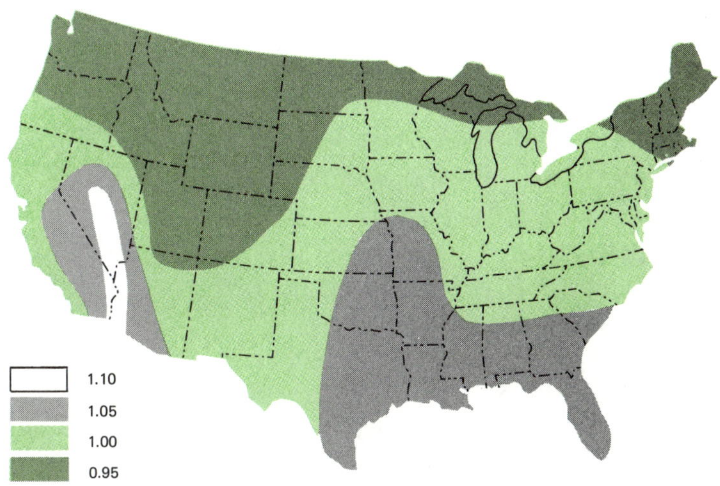

BUY EFFICIENCY YOU CAN USE

A room airconditioner's energy efficiency ratio (EER) is found by dividing its electrical input in watts into its cooling capacity in B.T.U. per hour. EERs between 5 and 7 are common for smaller units, but high-efficiency models with EERs of 11 and higher are also available, and cost more initially. From the price of electricity in your area, and knowledge of your family's habits of cooling use, you can estimate how long a high-efficiency unit will take to repay its higher initial investment.

INSTALL AND OPERATE EFFICIENTLY

Where possible, install a room airconditioner on the north side of the house or shade it to keep direct sun off the case. Insulate central airconditioning ducts, especially where passing through hot attic spaces; seal leaks with tape or caulking compound. With either type of airconditioning, check and clean (or replace) filters regularly, keep condenser surfaces clean and follow manufacturer's instructions on lubrication. With central airconditioning, locate the thermostat on an inside wall, in a spot with good circulation, out of sunlight and away from pipes and appliances. Operate with all occupied rooms at the same temperature.

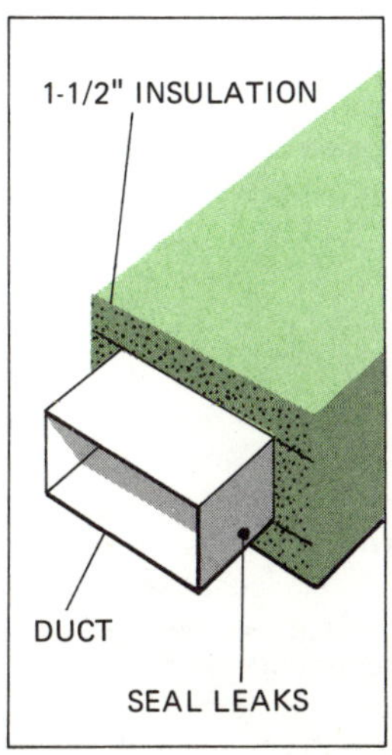

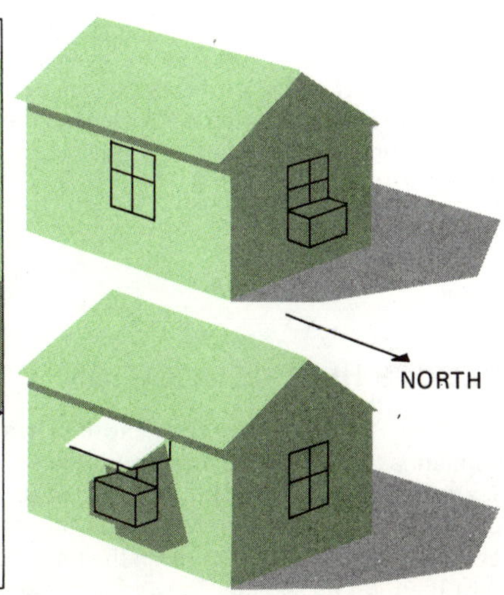

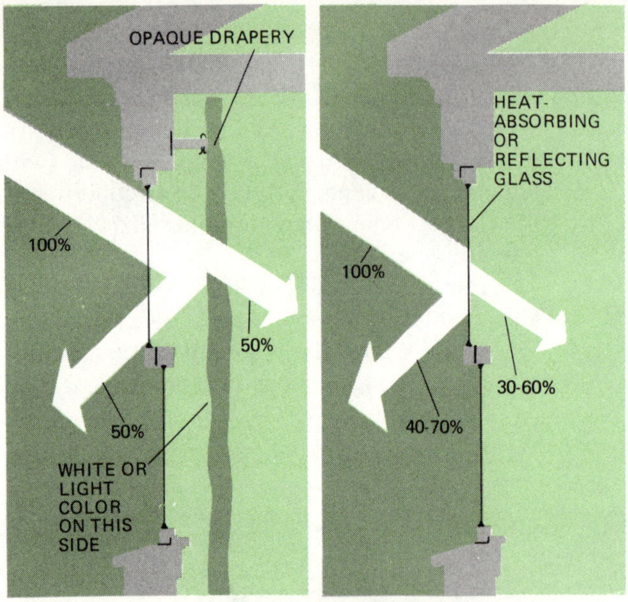

KEEP THE SUN OFF AND OUT

Sunlight admitted to the space being cooled turns into heat, and most window glazing provides a greenhouse effect by keeping that heat from escaping as infrared radiation, so the more light kept out the better. Draperies or blinds, if opaque and light-colored on the outward-facing side, can reduce heat gain (through windows) up to 50 percent. Keep them drawn during daylight hours. For new construction or reglazing of large areas, consider heat-absorbing and reflecting glasses; these can cut solar heat gain from 40 to 70 percent. Awnings, overhangs and screens can reduce solar heat gain by 80 percent, but must not trap hot air near the window. Shade trees do the same job, but take time to grow. Though no factor in solar heat gain, double glazing insulates and reduces heat gain by conduction from outdoor air. So do storm windows—leave them all year on windows not needed for ventilation.

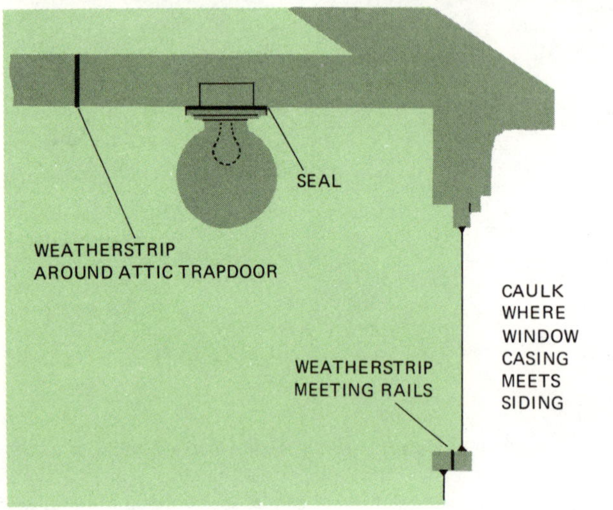

REDUCE INFILTRATION

Infiltration of hot, humid outdoor air cannot be completely avoided, and a certain amount of fresh air is necessary. But building construction is far from airtight, and you can increase indoor comfort by reducing infiltration with weatherstripping and caulking, and by stopping air leaks between cooled spaces and uncooled spaces like the attic. Close your fireplace damper, and if air registers are not part of a central airconditioning system, they should be closed also.

REDUCE HEAT GENERATION

Cooking, lighting, showers, clothes washing and electric appliances all add to the load your cooling system must handle. Try to reduce use of lights and larger appliances as much as practical. Shower and do laundry during cooler times of day or evening, and use exhaust fans in the bathroom and kitchen—but turn them off as soon as showering or cooking is completed.

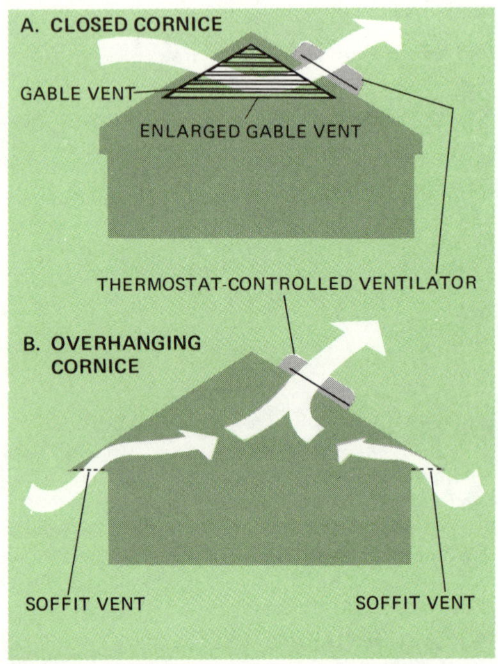

IMPROVE ATTIC VENTILATION

A hot attic radiates heat downward, and an inadequately ventilated attic can easily reach a temperature of 150° F. While insulation between attic-floor joists cuts radiation, cooling the attic by improving its ventilation will also increase comfort in living areas. A powered ventilator (louver) governed by a thermostat is mounted as high on the roof as possible, and used with gable or soffit vents of adequate size. General practice calls for net free area (effective area) of such vents to equal 1/300 of the attic floor space.

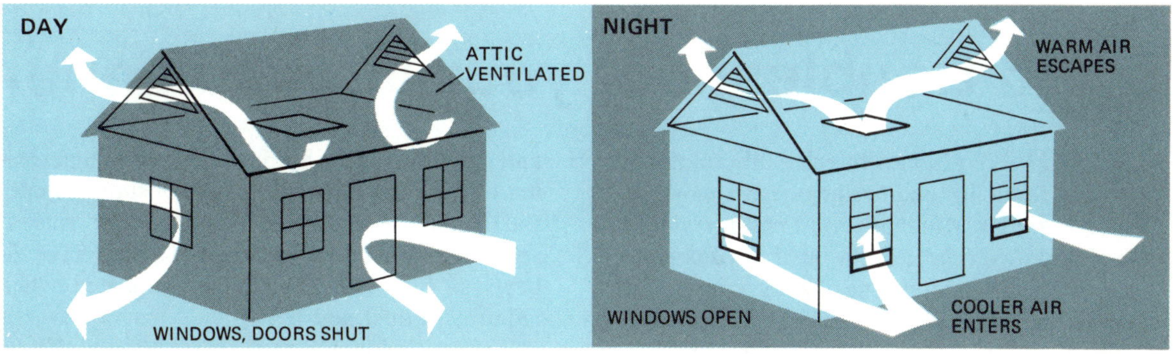

COMFORT WITHOUT AIRCONDITIONING

Houses without airconditioning can still be livable if closed up tightly when outdoor air becomes warmer than indoor. Circulation to the attic should be prevented. At night, cooler air can be allowed to enter via windows. Warmer air rises through entrance to the attic and escapes out vents in the gables.

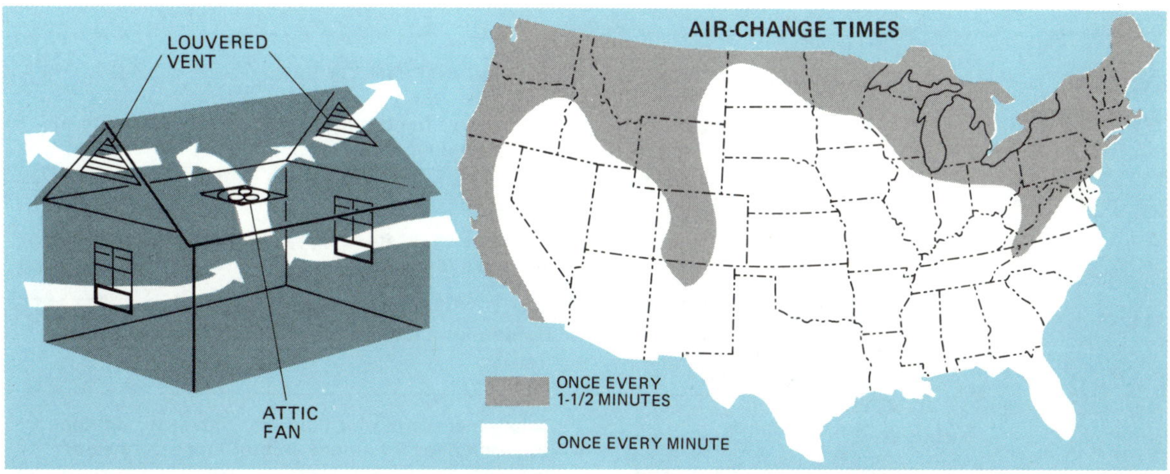

COOLING WITH AN ATTIC OR WINDOW FAN

Still air seems warmer than it is, and moving air helps cool you by speeding evaporation of moisture from the skin. Whenever the outdoor temperature is lower than the indoor temperature, as at night, attic and window fans can provide fairly effective cooling. These fans are rated in cubic feet per minute (c.f.m.). To determine the size you need (as a minimum), calculate the volume of the area to be cooled. This figure is the size you need if your locality is within the unshaded portion of the map; if your locality is within the shaded portion, divide the volume by 1.5 to determine needed capacity in c.f.m. For daytime ventilation, draw air from the shaded side.

COOLING BY MEANS OF EVAPORATION

In sections of the country with naturally dry climate, cooling by evaporation is commonly used, and may cost less than airconditioning. Water is sprayed on absorbent material through which air is drawn by a fan. This air, which has been cooled by the evaporation of water, is then returned to the living area, where the air is changed every 1½ to 3 minutes.

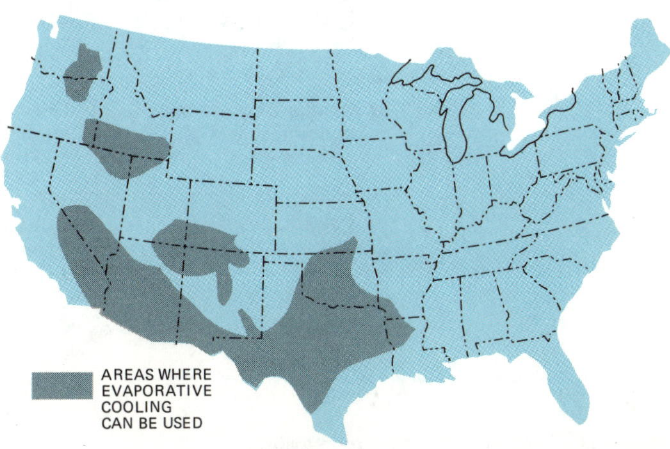

How to troubleshoot your airconditioner

IF YOU FIND after a winter's "hibernation" that your room airconditioner doesn't work as well as it did last summer, don't call a serviceman right away. There are a number of checks you can make to determine what's wrong and pinpoint the part or parts that need replacing. You'll be surprised at what you can save by being your own appliance repairman.

It may be that the air filter is simply dirty. A dirty filter restricts airflow over the cooling coil and cuts efficiency. Some models have a permanent-type germicidal filter made of spongy material that can be washed in soap and water, rinsed, squeezed dry and reinstalled. Others have fiberglass filters that should be replaced when laden with dust and lint.

The unit's inner compartment should also be cleaned. Although there are two types of chassis—one that slides out like a drawer and one that has to be totally removed from the

Noisy operation

POSSIBLE CAUSES	ACTION TO TAKE
1 Tubing vibration.	Reshape or bend tubing so there is no rubbing of tubing against metal.
2 Fan blade loose on shaft or bent.	Check to make sure that blade does not spin freely on motor shaft. Bend or straighten fan blades until the noise is minimal.
3 Fan motor loose on mounts.	Tighten fan motor mounts. Check motor alignment.
4 Loose parts.	Check installation for tightness, cover for tightness, and look over the entire unit for loose screws or washers.

Unit drips water

POSSIBLE CAUSES	ACTION TO TAKE
1 Cabinet not properly leveled.	Adjust unit so that it has a slight downward pitch toward outside end (Maximum pitch ¼ in.)
2 Condensate drain holes plugged.	Check and clean holes of any blockage.
3 Slinger-ring fan on condenser out of adjustment.	Check slinger-ring clearance from base pan. It should be 1/16 in. Too much clearance reduces water pickup.
4 Extreme humidity.	Sweating formations are normal under these conditions. Try to improve all seals and minimize window or door openings.

SEE ALSO
Airconditioners, auto . . . Energy, saving . . . Heat pumps

window—both are cleaned the same way: Use a vacuum cleaner to blow dirt and lint off the condenser and evaporator. Then clean the compressor, fan motor and blades and tubing with a quickly evaporating solvent such as trichloroethylene, sold in hardware and paint stores.

When reinstalling a window unit, especially the chassis-type that does not slide out, be sure it is properly tilted for condensate flow and drain of water (usually ⅛ to ¼ in. low on the outside). Finally, make sure the unit is plugged in.

During the hottest days of summer, it's good practice to operate the airconditioner on MAXIMUM or HIGH COOL. At this setting, air is cooled, filtered, dehumidified and circulated at the highest rate. On average summer days and at night, switch the unit to LOW COOL to reduce current draw and prevent possible icing up of the evaporator on cool nights.

Unit will not run

POSSIBLE CAUSES	ACTION TO TAKE
1 Blown fuse or open circuit breaker.	Check voltage at wall receptacle with test lamp. If lamp doesn't light, replace fuse or reset circuit breaker. Make certain airconditioner is off.
2 Broken or loose wiring connection.	Check service cord at wall outlet and cord connections on control switch.
3 Defective thermostat.	Unplug unit. Turn thermostat to Cool position. Check for continuity (uninterrupted connection) across thermostat's terminals with a continuity tester, available at hardware stores. If no continuity exists, replace the thermostat.
4 Defective start capacitor.	Unplug unit. Remove start capacitor (the smaller of two capacitors located behind control panel). Replace with new capacitor of the same rating.

Fan runs, compressor does not

POSSIBLE CAUSES	ACTION TO TAKE
1 Defective thermostat.	Turn thermostat to High Cool, place jumper wire across thermostat terminals. If compressor comes on, replace thermostat.
2 Defective run capacitor.	Unplug unit. Remove run capacitor (the larger of two capacitors behind control panel) and replace it with new one of the same rating.
3 Overload switch open or defective.	Remove overload switch (may be attached to outside of compressor). Place continuity tester across overload terminals. There should be a reading if overload is at room temperature (70° F.). If no reading, replace overload.
4 Loose or broken wiring connections.	Check all wiring and terminals. Clean all rust and replace defective wiring and terminals.
5 Mechanical "stall" or defective compressor.	Temporarily hook up compressor directly to power line to see if it will run (try this only on 117-volt models, not on 220-volt types). Do this for just a few seconds. If compressor fails to start, a new compressor may be needed.

REFRIGERANT CYCLE IN AIRCONDITIONER

Refrigerant cycle at the right is in all window airconditioners. All have same components and pattern of flow. The amount of refrigerant used in system is only difference.

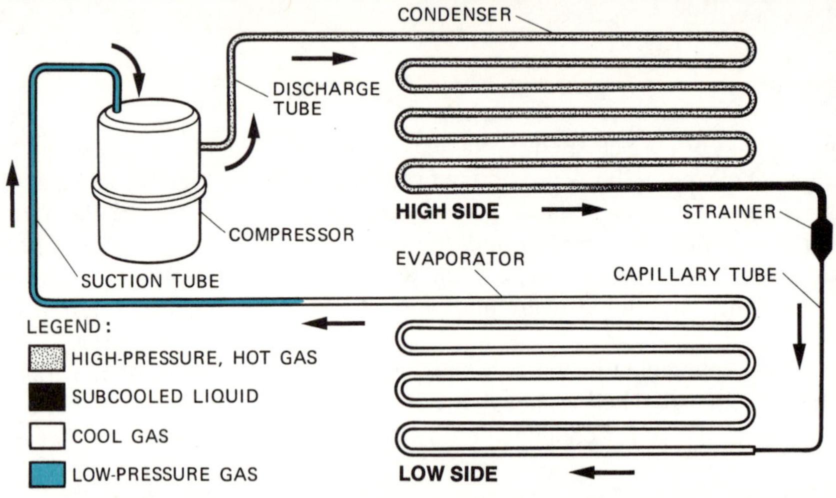

Compressor runs, but fan does not

POSSIBLE CAUSES	ACTION TO TAKE
1 Defective fan switch.	Unplug unit. Place continuity test lamp across High, Medium and Low terminals on switch (refer to the manufacturer's schematic). If no reading is indicated at any or all terminals, replace switch.
2 Defective fan capacitor.	Unplug unit. Replace fan capacitor (usually common with run capacitor) with one of exactly the same rating.
3 Defective fan motor winding.	Unplug unit. Check each winding (High, Medium and Low) of fan motor with continuity test lamp. Refer to wiring diagram for proper connections or bridge tester across switch terminals and ground on motor housing. If no reading is indicated in any winding, replace fan motor.
4 Blower wheel binding.	Try to spin blower wheel. Failure of wheel to spin freely is a result of improper clearance. Adjust blower wheel on motor shaft or blower shroud surrounding the fan assembly.

Unit blows fuse or trips circuit breaker

POSSIBLE CAUSES	ACTION TO TAKE
1 Unit restarted too soon after running.	Allow three to five minutes for the system to balance (pressures to equalize) before turning the unit on again.
2 Circuit overloaded.	Place the airconditioner on a line by itself and check for proper fusing.
3 Stuck or defective compressor.	See the section "Fan runs, compressor does not," page 51.
4 Defective run capacitor.	Unplug the unit. Then replace the defective part with a new run capacitor which has exactly the same capacity rating.
5 Wiring shorted or grounded to frame.	Check all electrical connections to the compressor and behind the control panel. Connections should be tight and should not touch any metal parts of the airconditioner.

Unit short cycling

POSSIBLE CAUSES	ACTION TO TAKE
1 Thermostat short cycling.	Evaporator is either blocked or dirty and must be cleaned. Make sure that only the thermostat sensing bulb is touching the evaporator and is clamped tightly to it.
2 Defective condenser.	Check the fan operation. If the fan should become hot and stop, replace the motor. Check the blades for clearance.
3 Condenser dirty.	Blow out the condenser (using the blower of your vacuum cleaner) until light can be seen through the fins.
4 Defective overload.	If the compressor isn't overheated, and the overload is at room temperature, and no continuity is read across the overload terminals, replace the overload switch.
5 Unit restarted too soon after running.	Allow from three to five minutes for the system to restore its pressure balance; then try restarting the unit again.

INTERNAL VIEW OF TYPICAL A/C COMPRESSOR

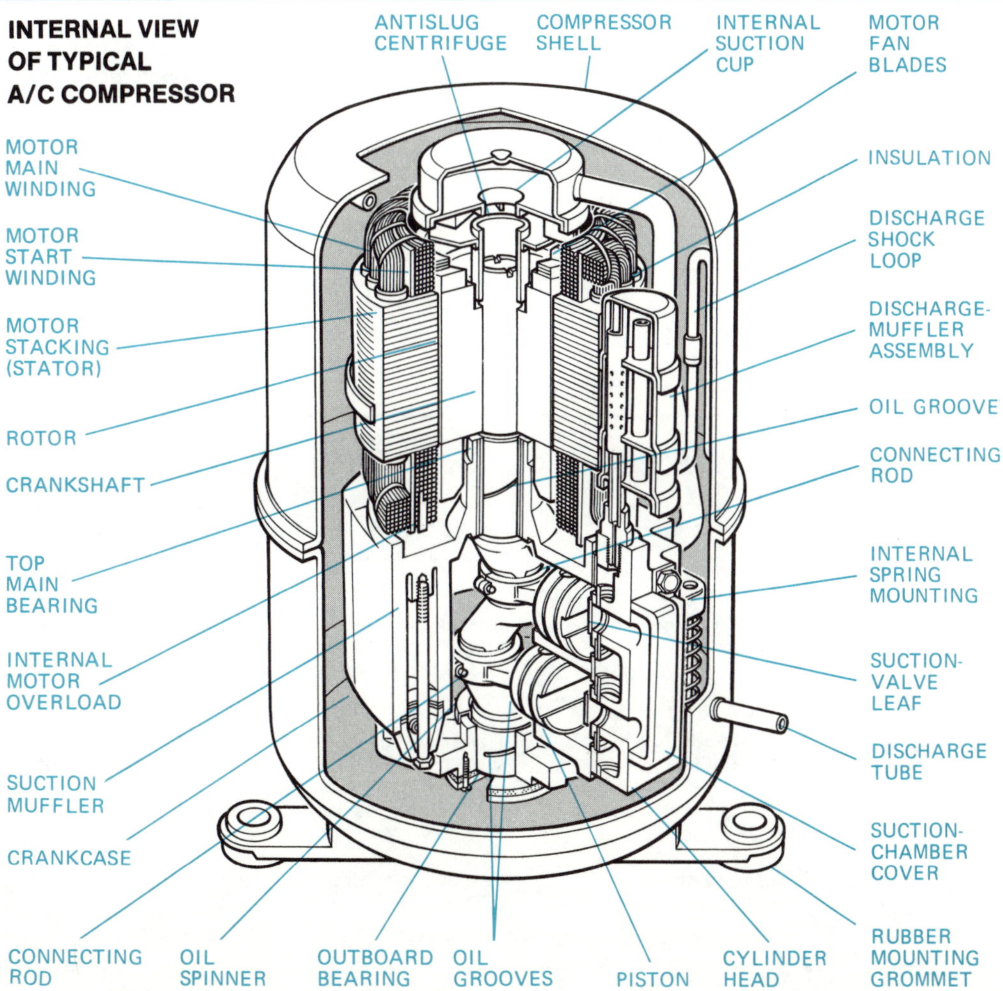

Unit not cooling

Heat survey: Multiply volume of room in cu. ft. by 10 if another room or an insulated attic is above, by 18 if not. Multiply result by factor for exposure of the longest wall (north 16, east 17, south 18, west 19) and divide by 60 to get B.T.U. rating.

POSSIBLE CAUSES	ACTION TO TAKE
1 Thermostat set warm.	Turn thermostat to a higher setting.
2 Filter dirty.	Check filter for dirt accumulation. Light should be able to pass through it. Replace or wash filters according to brand.
3 Condenser dirty or restricting airflow.	Blow out condenser with vacuum cleaner and clean fins of all dirt buildup.
4 Compressor won't run.	See section "Fan runs, compressor does not," page 51.
5 Leaking seals.	Check all seals around window. Make sure windows are shut and that curtains or furniture don't block unit.
6 Undersized unit.	Make heat survey of room for correct B.T.U. size of unit. Check according to accompanying directions.
7 Refrigerant leak.	Check amperage (current draw) of unit while it runs (you can do this if you have an ammeter handy). Compare current reading to manufacturer's nameplate amperage rating to see if motor is drawing current properly. If current draw is below rated amperage and everything else checks okay, this may indicate a refrigerant leak. Test for leaks by rubbing soapy solution over outside of tubing and around joints. Watch for bubbles that show up leaks. If leaks are found, call serviceman to repair and recharge unit.

PROPER EXTENSION-CORD WIRE SIZES AND LENGTHS

(For use with 117-volt airconditioning units)

LENGTH OF CORD (in feet)	AMPERES REQUIRED (see nameplate on units) 6	8	10	12	14	16	18	20
	AWG Wire Size							
to 25	18	18	16	14	14	12	12	12
26-50	16	16	14	14	12	12	12	10
51-75	14	14	12	12	10	10	10	8
76-100	14	12	12	12	10	10	8	8

Evaporator frosts over

POSSIBLE CAUSES	ACTION TO TAKE
1 Restricted airflow over evaporator.	Check for dirty filter, blocked air passages, lint buildup on the blower wheel or blocked fins on the evaporator. Clean all items.
2 Outside temperature too low.	If temperature outside drops below 70° F., either turn unit off or set thermostat at Low Cool and fan at Low Speed.
3 Thermostat too high or defective.	Lower setting of thermostat. If problem still exists, turn thermostat off and check for continuity between the terminals. If a reading exists, thermostat is defective and must be replaced.
4 Refrigerant leak or undercharge.	See section "Unit not cooling" above).
5 Low fan speed.	Check fan for higher speed, binding at housing, loose blade on shaft or defective motor. Correct or replace motor.

TYPICAL OUTLET RECEPTACLES

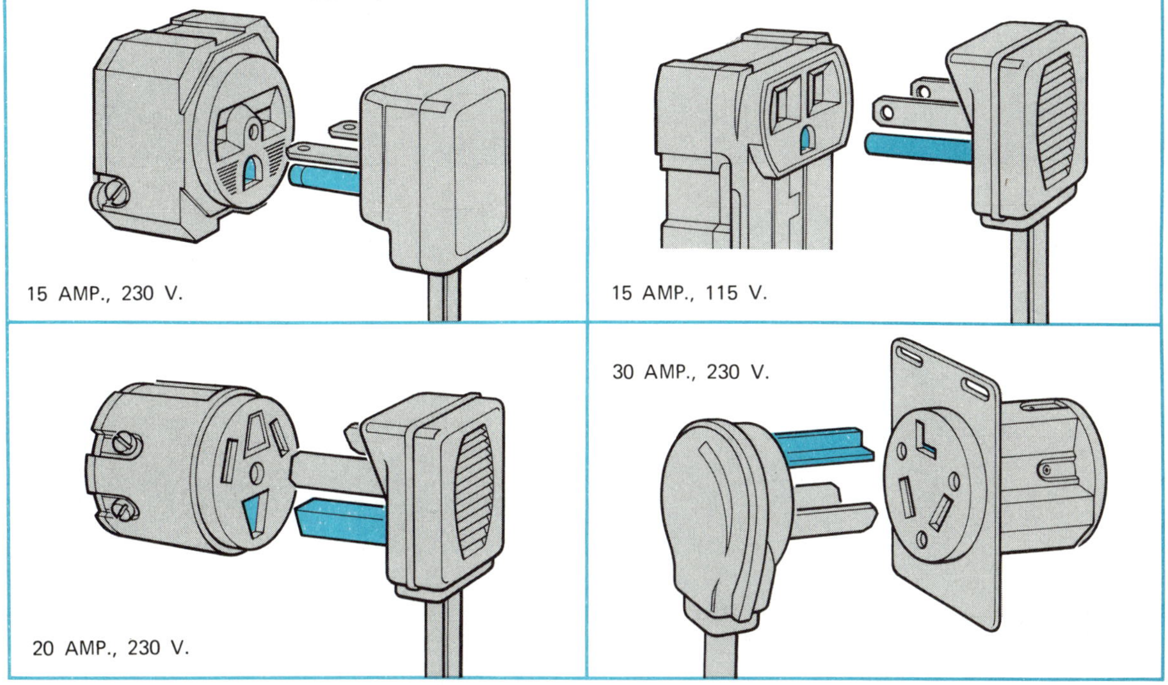

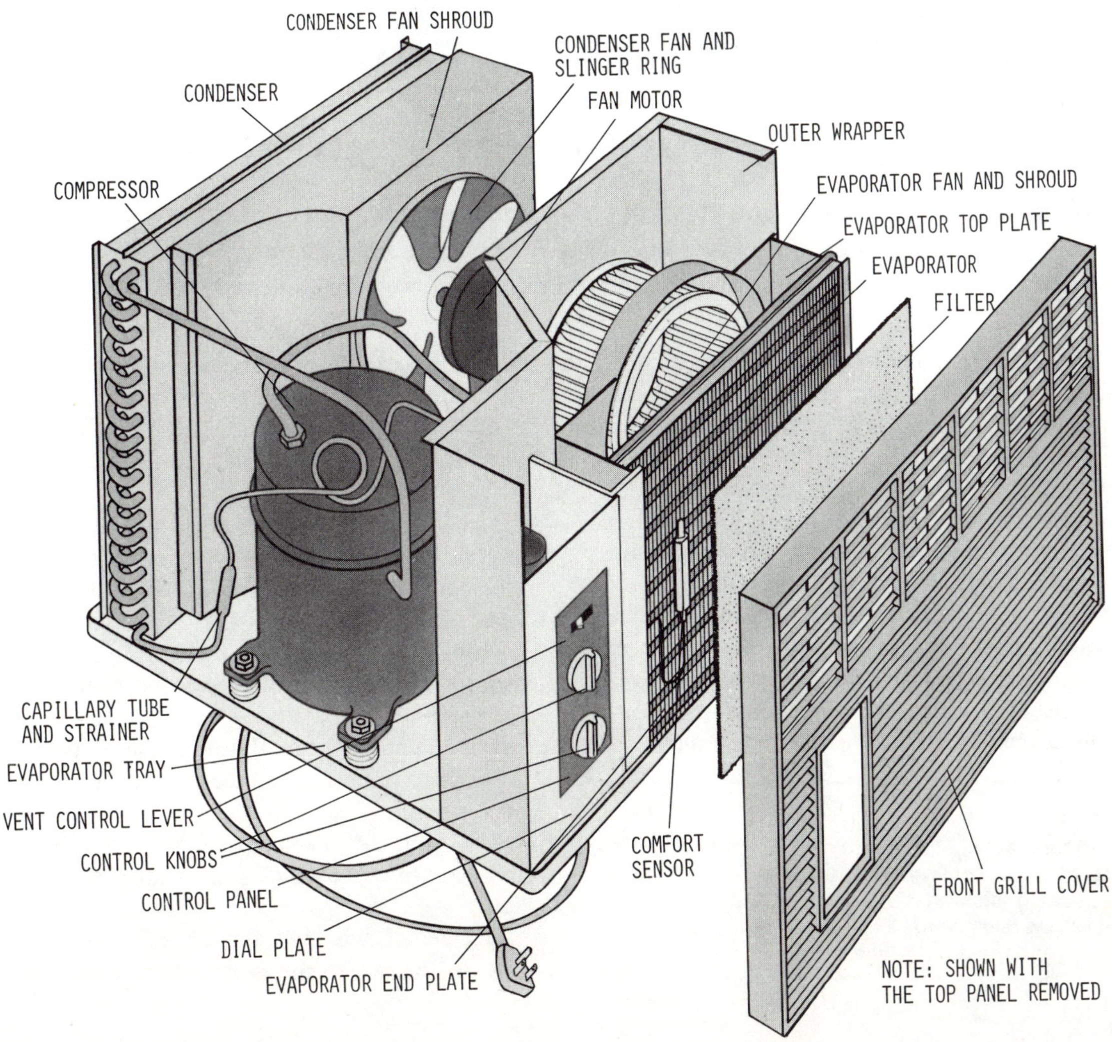

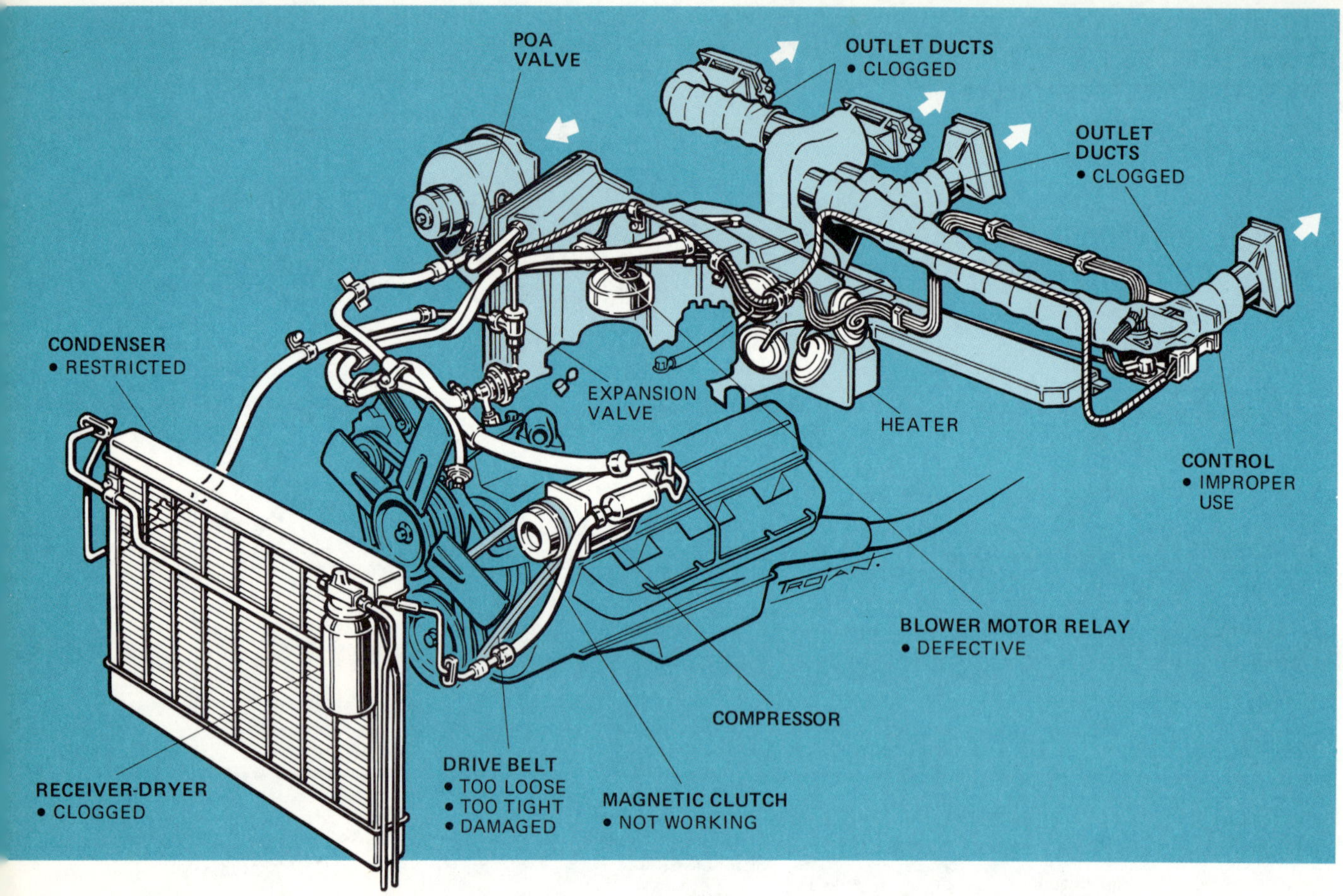

Quick checks on your car's airconditioner

Why isn't the airconditioner keeping your car cool? Many owners don't know how to maintain their system for proper operation. Here are some hints for keeping your air conditioner running at maximum efficiency and making minor repairs yourself

■ A MAJOR PROBLEM for many auto owners is insufficient cooling from their airconditioners. The typical complaint goes something like this: "It worked fine for the past few years. Now it won't cool." Although special equipment is needed if the refrigeration system does require service, the refrigeration system may *not* require that service. And if it doesn't, your chances of correcting the trouble yourself are good.

Of course, if you can prevent problems from developing, you can save yourself some hefty repair bills. To avoid difficulties with your airconditioner, keep the following points in mind:

SEE ALSO

**Alternators, auto . . . Autos, ramps . . .
Belts, auto . . . Cooling systems, auto . . .
Electronic ignition, auto . . . Engines, auto . . .
Exhaust systems, auto . . . Gaskets, auto . . .
Ramps, auto repair . . . Tune-up, auto**

1. An airconditioner should be operated at its maximum setting for at least five minutes once every week all year long. This allows the compressor to pump oil, which lubricates the compressor seal.

2. The cooling system of a car equipped with airconditioning should be provided with ethylene glycol antifreeze all year long. Protection to at least −15°F. will keep the heater core from freezing in summer and provide sufficient inhibitors to protect the cooling system itself against corrosion.

Manufacturers generally agree that if a car has an airconditioner, antifreeze should be changed once a year.

3. If your car's been parked in the hot sun and you want to cool it quickly, here's the best way to do it:

- Open all windows and drive the car.
- At the same time, set the temperature con-

trol lever to the coolest setting or "off" and set the airconditioner control at maximum cooling.

■ Set the blower fan switch on the highest setting that you have available.

■ After a few minutes, when the car has cooled, close the windows and reset the airconditioner controls for individual comfort.

troubleshooting your car's system

If you still experience difficulties after following the operational tips given above, there are some simple repairs you can attempt yourself before turning the car over to an airconditioner repair shop. Proceed as follows:

1. Are you manipulating controls properly? Consult the car owner's operation and maintenance manual.

2. Replace fuses. Check the fuse or fuses protecting the unit. Normally, there is a fuse located in your car's main fuse panel, which is generally beneath the dashboard on the bulkhead or, in some foreign cars, under the hood in the engine compartment. Replace this fuse and see if it solves the problem.

If performance doesn't perk up, look for another fuse. If the car has one, it is often located in a fuse holder in the engine compartment, somewhere near the compressor. The best way to find this fuse, if there is one, is to consult a wiring schematic which outlines the airconditioner circuit.

When you locate the fuse, replace it.

3. Inspect the drive belt which operates the compressor. If the belt is loose, glazed or damaged, it will affect compressor action, which will reduce the flow of refrigerant. The result is insufficient cooling.

You can get a good idea of the way the drive belt is working by starting the car's engine with the airconditioner turned on. Watch the belt. If it's slipping, the pulley won't rotate or will hesitate. Tighten the belt if it's loose, or get a new one if it's damaged. Also check the pulley to make sure it's in good shape.

Although less common, very serious problems may occur in some models if the drive belt is much too tight. Consult your dealer if you suspect this is a problem.

4. Start the engine and switch the airconditioner control for maximum cooling. Look closely at the magnetic clutch, which you will find on the front of the compressor. Its purpose is to connect and disconnect the drive pulley from the compressor, allowing more or less pumping of refrigerant.

With the airconditioner set for maximum cooling, the magnetic clutch should be rotating. If it is difficult for you to see "rotation," have someone in the car turn off the airconditioner and then turn it back to the maximum cooling setting. If the clutch is not working, then the compressor will have to be disassembled.

By the way, if the pulley is making noise when the compressor is *not* operating, but doesn't make any noise when the compressor is working, the pulley-bearing assembly is defective and should be replaced as soon as possible.

5. The condenser core may be restricted with debris, such as leaves and dead bugs. This will reduce cooling.

Using a soft-bristle brush with a long handle, brush debris from the condenser. You can use compressed air to clean the condenser, but this must be done carefully in order to avoid damaging the fins. Don't point any heavy blasts directly at the condenser. Shoot several short bursts at an angle.

6. Make sure the receiver-dryer, also called the receiver-dehydrator, is unclogged. The receiver-dryer is a container that holds liquid refrigerant. The unit also removes traces of moisture that may have been left in the system after it has been purged and evacuated. If the receiver-dryer is clogged, the flow of refrigerant will be restricted and cooling will be reduced.

Operate the airconditioner at maximum cooling for five minutes; then run your hand over the receiver-dryer. If the outlet end feels cold, the receiver-dryer should be replaced, which will require discharging and evacuation of the system.

7. Is the system short of refrigerant? Wipe off the sight glass of the receiver-dryer and observe if slow-moving bubbles, signs of vapor, are visible. A shortage of refrigerant might be indicated. However, keep in mind that continuous bubbles may appear in the sight glass in a perfect system if the ambient temperature is below 70° F.

If bubbles are apparent and you want a better indication of refrigerant charge, place a piece of cardboard or an old bedspread over half of the condenser. If the sight glass now clears, the charge is adequate.

8. Warm air leaking into the inside of the car will reduce the cooling effect of a properly functioning system. All holes and crevices should be sealed with body sealer, commonly called dum-dum, which is available at automotive supply outlets. Look for leaks in the firewall and on the underside of the vehicle.

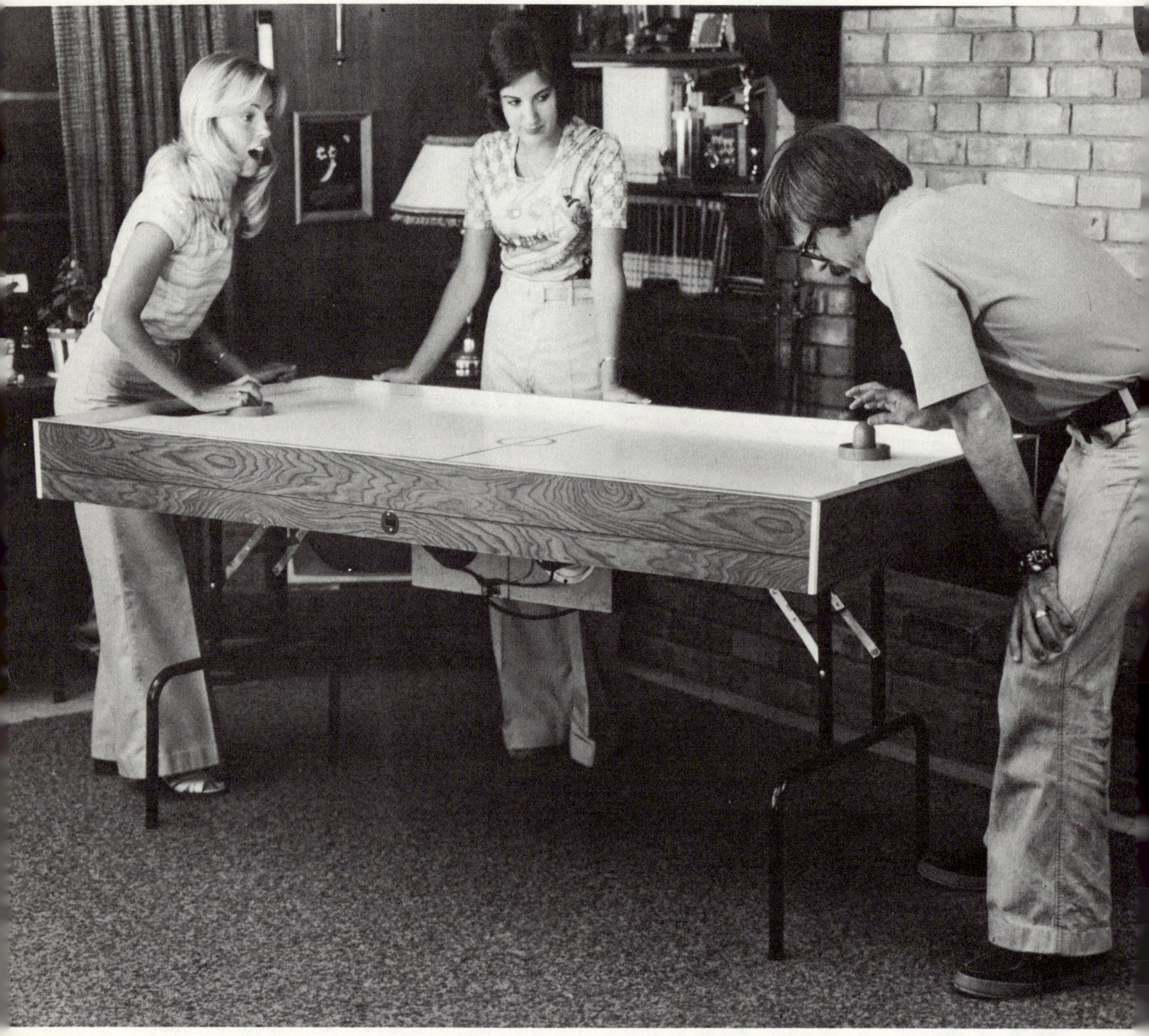

Build a tabletop hockey game

This family game requires lightning reflexes. The hockey puck travels at amazing speed on a cushion of air

By GEORGE M. KALER

YOU'LL SOON FIND you have to be as quick as a fox to play hockey with an air-cushion puck. The floating puck travels at lightning speed on a cushion of air created by a fan and some 2360 tiny air jets in the playing surface.

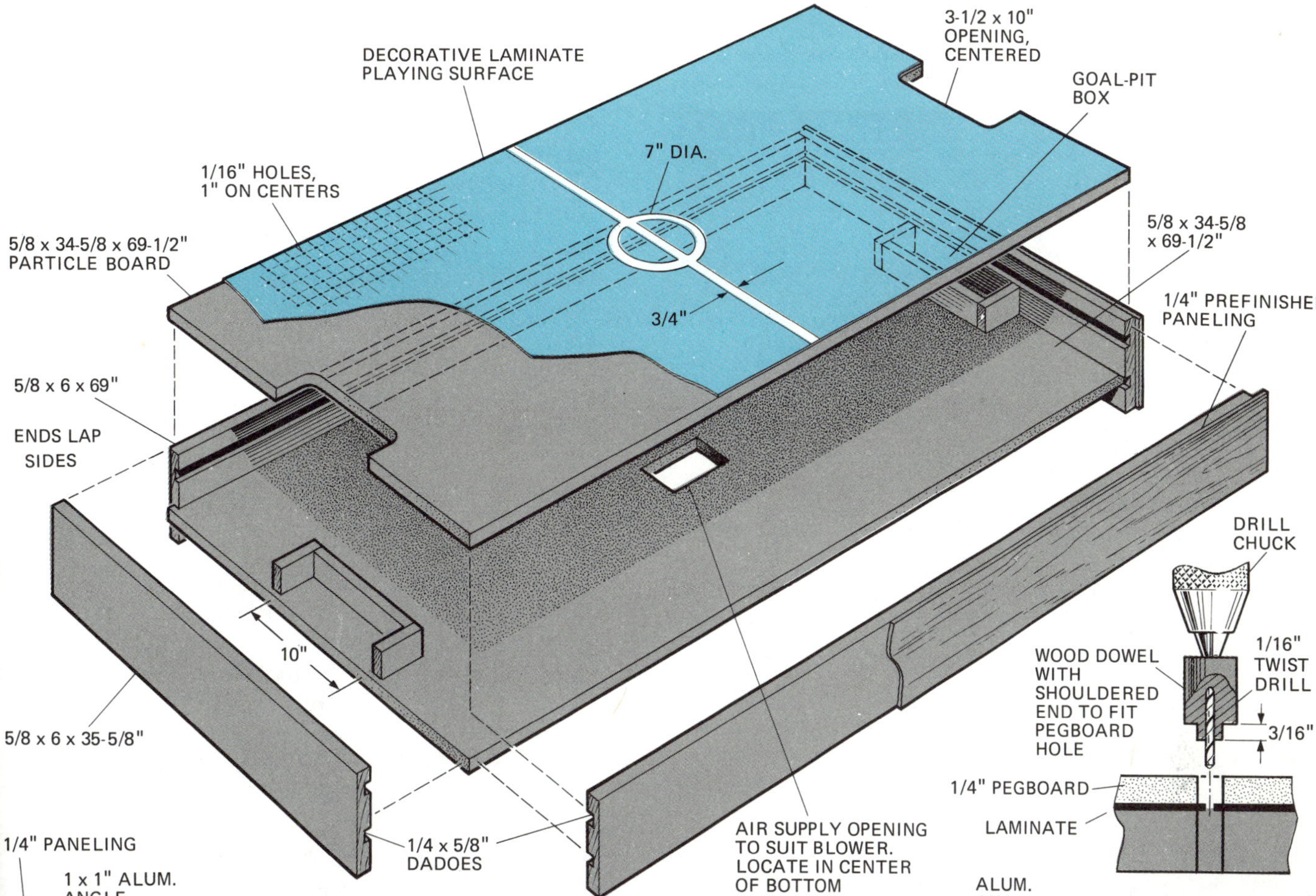

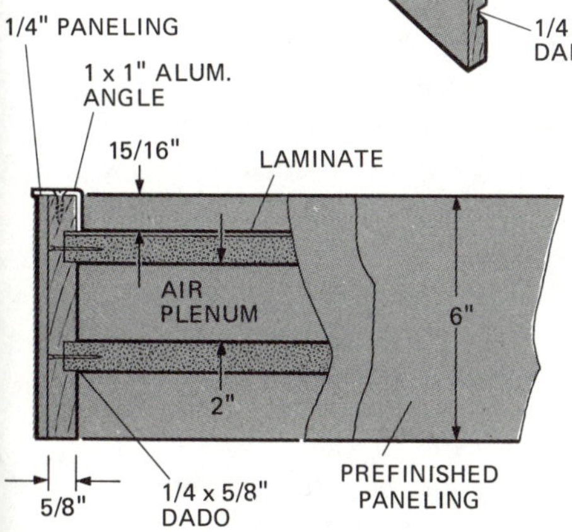

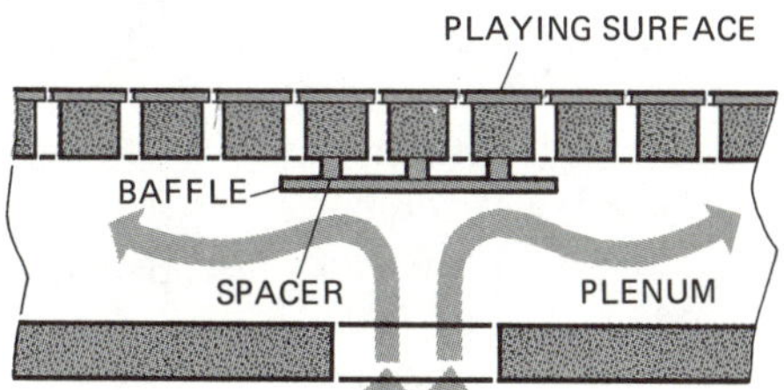

DETAIL A

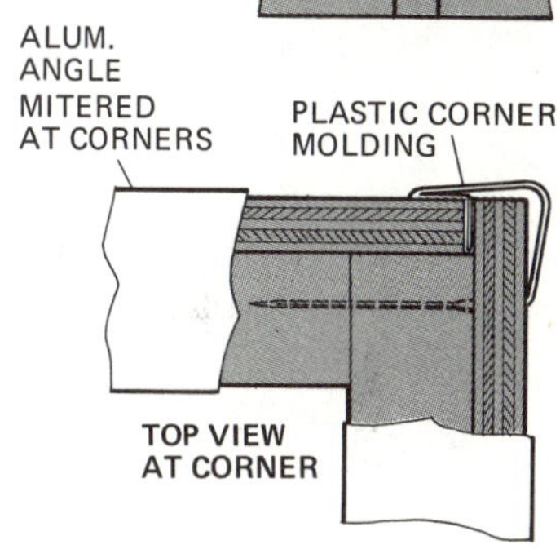

TOP VIEW AT CORNER

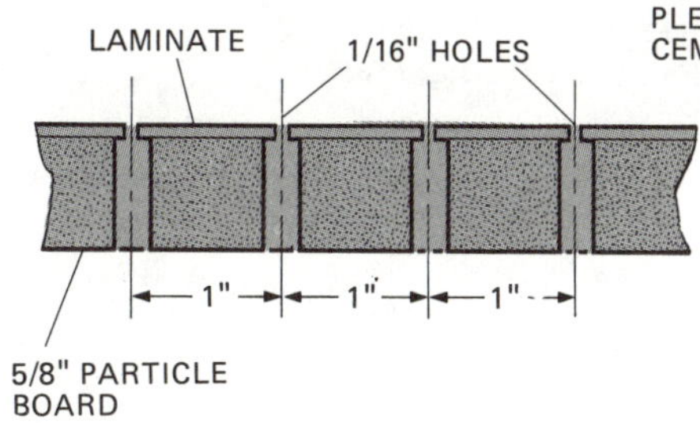

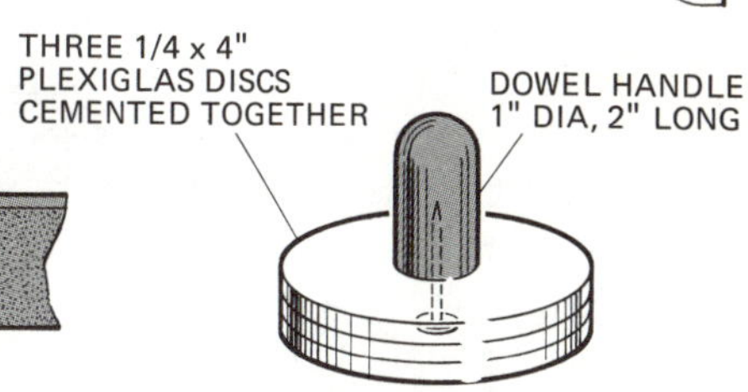

GOALIE MALLET (2 REQD.)

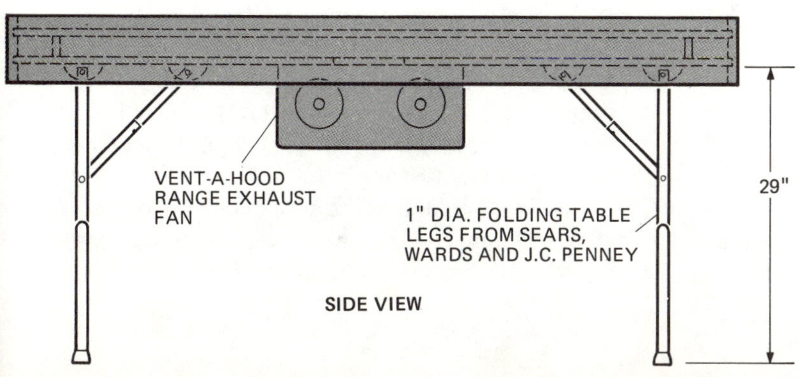

SIDE VIEW

PUCK

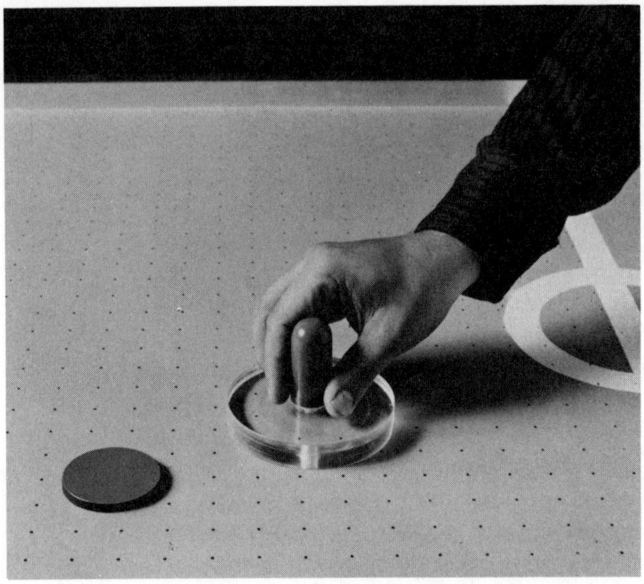

GOALIE MALLETS AND A PUCK can be bought or made at home. Each mallet consists of three ½-in.-thick plastic discs that are cut with a fly cutter in a drill press and cemented together. A dowel held with a screw provides a handle.

Please take note that the name Air Hockey is owned by the Brunswick Corp., which also holds three basic patents on the game. The game may be made for personal use but not for sale.

The playing surface is made first. It consists of a ⅝-in.-thick particleboard base honeycombed with ¼-in. holes on 1-in. centers and a plastic laminate facing with an equal number of 1/16-in. holes. The particleboard is drilled first, then the laminate is cemented to it and the 1/16-in. holes drilled. The spacing and drilling of the 4720 holes is not the endless job it may seem, thanks to ¼-in. pegboard which is used as a drilling guide for both sets of holes.

Cut the particleboard, laminate and pegboard the same overall size (34⅝ x 69½ in.) and see that holes in the pegboard are centered equally along the edges. Clamp the pegboard to the top of the particleboard, edges aligned, and with a ¼-in. bit in your electric drill go from hole to hole in the pegboard.

Now cement the laminate to the particleboard with contact cement. Apply a coat to each surface, wait about 15 minutes until the cement is tacky to the touch, then bond the two together. Remember that once the coated surfaces touch, you can't shift them, so position the laminate carefully.

To drill the 1/16-in. holes using the pegboard you'll need to make a shouldered stop from a short piece of ½-in. dowel to center the bit in the ¼-in. holes. The shouldered end can be formed with the dowel chucked in your electric drill. First run a 1/16-in. bit through the center of the dowel, letting the drill protrude about ⅛ in. Then with bit and dowel still chucked in the drill, turn down the end of the dowel with a chisel so it's ¼ in. in diameter and 3/16 in. long. The tighter the dowel on the bit, the better it will resist loosening in use. Clamp the pegboard to the top of the laminate, even with the edges, and drill the 1/16-in. holes. It will take about two hours to zip through the 2360 holes.

plenum under playing surface

A bottom in the boxlike assembly forms a 2-in. air plenum under the playing surface. Make it the same size as the top and cut an opening in the center as shown to suit the blower used. I selected a used Vent-a-hood range exhaust fan with two 1/25-hp, 1550-rpm motors, each driving a 3½ x 4½-in. squirrel-cage blower. The blowers put out a total of 290 C.F.M., which enters through a 4⅜ x 7¼-inch opening. You'll notice in detail A that an air baffle, slightly larger than the blower opening, is made and attached to the underside of the playing surface directly over the inlet. Make the two goal boxes to measure 3¼ x 10 in. inside and glue them to the underside of the playing surface, along with the baffle, then glue the boxes to the bottom, making sure the two panels are aligned.

Dadoes in the 6-in.-wide particleboard sides make the plenum airtight. Use glue and nails and let the ends lap the sides at the corners. It is important that the plenum be airtight. You can paint the sides or cover them with wood-grain Con-Tact paper. The original was faced with prefinished paneling. Here you can lap and butt the ends at the corners and hide them with outside corner molding, or just miter and glue the ends without molding. One-inch aluminum angle fitted around the top and inside provides a metal bumper for the puck. It's mitered at the corners and attached along the top with ovalhead screws in countersunk holes.

Each player has a goalie mallet made by cementing three ¼-in.-thick Plexiglas discs together and attaching a dowel handle. The puck is simply a 2½-in. disc cut with a circle cutter from the same material. (Mallets and puck may be purchased from Sears.)

Folding tubular legs are attached to the bottom of the plenum to clear the blower unit. You can buy them from several mail-order firms.

ORDINARILY, WHEN YOU spray-paint small parts, the final step of the job is prying them loose from the work surface after they have dried. But, if you lay them on a platform made from hardware cloth, the problem is eliminated. The wire screen should be bent or supported to keep it 1 in. above the paper spread below to catch the overspray.—*Walter E. Burton*

IT'S A WASTE to throw away an old permanent magnet; it can be used in the shop for holding various things. The photo at the left shows how two magnets—one a horseshoe type, the other a unit from a cabinet catch—were used to steady a rod being soldered to a metal strip. The magnets are clamped to a V-block that rests on the vise anvil.—*Walter E. Burton*

DISCARDED PHOTOGRAPHIC FILM can be used as practical erasing shields or stencils simply by cutting appropriate openings in it. Round openings can be formed with punches, other shapes with a pointed knife. The erasing shield on the right is being used to correct a drawing; on the left is a punched-hole stencil and a sample of the work done with it.—*Walter E. Burton*

SINCE A FRAMING SQUARE occasionally goes out-of-square, it should be checked periodically with a second square. If not true, it can be corrected by placing the square on an anvil and peening it with a punch. To close the legs, strike the back of the corner as shown; to spread them, punch the inside edge. Check for square after each blow.—*Lloyd L. Long*

HOW'S THIS FOR realism? The Andrews Aeromaster biplane even sports a smoke generator.

Air thrills on a small scale

Radio control brings all the thrills of real flight. You can soar, race, or even fly helicopters

■ THE F4U-4 CORSAIR, gleaming with Marine markings, taxis to the end of the runway, pauses while the pilot goes through his preflight check, then turns into the wind. There is a roar as he pours on full throttle and the gull-winged fighter begins to roll, picks up speed, and gracefully lifts off. The gear retracts, the flaps come up, and the pilot pulls the plane into the tight climbing left turn of a carrier join-up.

The chief difference between this flight and one that might take place on any Navy Air Station is that the pilot isn't sitting in the cockpit. He's standing at the flight line, radio-control box in hand, manipulating miniature controls that fly the plane through every maneuver its full-sized prototype can do.

His eyes pinned to the fighter, now at 200 feet and flying away from the field, the pilot turns the craft back toward the flight line and begins a series of precise aerobatics—a loop, followed by an Immelmann and a couple of snap rolls. By now it has flown past the field, so the pilot does a split-S and brings it back parallel to the runway. Dropping flaps and wheels, he makes a neat 180 into the wind and touches down on the centerline. After rolling out, the plane taxis to the flight line and stops at the pilot's feet. He cuts switches and the flight is over.

This F4U is a ⅛ scale model, magnificently detailed. Built from a kit and enhanced with over 600 hours of work, the plane is an excellent example of the craftsmanship and flying ability of a

SEE ALSO

**Bottle craft . . . Cannon models . . .
Carving, wood . . . Hobby centers . . .
Metal casting . . . Modelmaking . . . Ship models . . .
Shops, modelmaking . . . Telescopes . . .
Tin-can crafts**

very experienced radio-control enthusiast.

A beginner in this exciting sport doesn't attempt to build scale-model planes of this caliber nor to fly complex maneuvers, but from the beginning, he can enjoy all the thrills of piloting his own plane—and can look forward to the time when his work matches that of this F4U pilot.

Sooner or later, every would-be pilot gets the urge to try his hand at the excitement of radio-controlled flying. The question is, what is the best way to start?

Old hands at this kind of flying have seen hundreds of successes and failures. They've seen money wasted, and they've seen discouraged beginners walk away from their equipment. But they also have seen raw beginners develop into prize-winning builders and flyers. They know what it takes to get into flying.

The first step, they say, is to visit a local flying field and talk to the pilots. The second step is to join a club. Club members are a storehouse of vital information, and most clubs welcome neophyte members. You can learn how to buy and build a plane, how to select the right radio equipment and engine, and how to get the plane ready for that first flight.

Most clubs have certain members designated as instructors; by the time your first plane is ready to fly, the instructor is ready to take you through all of the steps. He'll check the flight

F4U4 CORSAIR fighter in 1/8 scale is a beautiful gull-wing plane built in 600 hours of work from a kit that cost $79.

CHEROKEE ARCHER and Cessna Cardinal 177 (below) come ready to fly—ideal for pilots who aren't modelers. In flight the Cessna is a stable trainer.

"BUDDY BOX" dual control setup is the best way to learn to fly. The ribbon flag shows the frequency being used.

conditions and the condition of your plane and its radio equipment. He'll show you how to break the engine in, and range-check the radio.

Then he, not you, will take the plane off and fly it around on a check flight. He may make several flights, adjusting the rigging and trim. Then your flight instruction will begin, and the parallel between this kind of flying and the real thing will become apparent. Your instructor will handle the controls most of the time, turning them over to you for short periods. You'll gradually get the feel of flying, and the touch of the controls. As you master one bit, he'll move you on to the next. You'll go through level flight, turns, landings, take-offs—the whole curriculum.

Then will come that great event, your first solo flight. The whole club will turn out to watch and if you bring it off without spinning in or cart wheeling on your landing, you'll be the hero of the day.

Those of us who have gone through both real and scale-model flights agree that the scale solo flight is just as exciting as that first solo in a full-sized aircraft. The feeling of accomplishment as you walk from the flight line is exactly the same—and you can hardly wait for the next opportunity.

Radio-control flying requires an investment. Training-plane kits run $40 to $60, with scale-model kits upwards of $100. Engines are about $50, and a 4-channel radio runs from $180 to $250. In addition, you'll need accessories totaling around $80. But those who are in it feel they get more than their money's worth in fun and accomplishment.

Model flying offers a variety of categories, including precision aerobatics (called pattern flying), scale-model flying, pylon racing, helicopter flying, soaring, and the biggest category of all, sport flying. The plane you fly fits into one of these categories. An aerobatic plane, for example, would have a retractable landing gear, flaps, spoilers, dive brakes, and even variable-pitch propellers. A sport plane would be any model from a trainer up that you enjoy flying on a Sunday afternoon.

Soaring—flying sleek gliders—has gained a lot of popularity recently. The gliders are launched by a kind of big sling shot, then controlled by radio as they seek the lifting air in thermals. If you know what you are doing you can achieve flights up to several hours.

Helicopter flying is probably the most demanding. Operating the controls on one of these, they say, requires three hands and two heads. If you can chew gum and fly a helicopter at the same time, you are really coordinated!

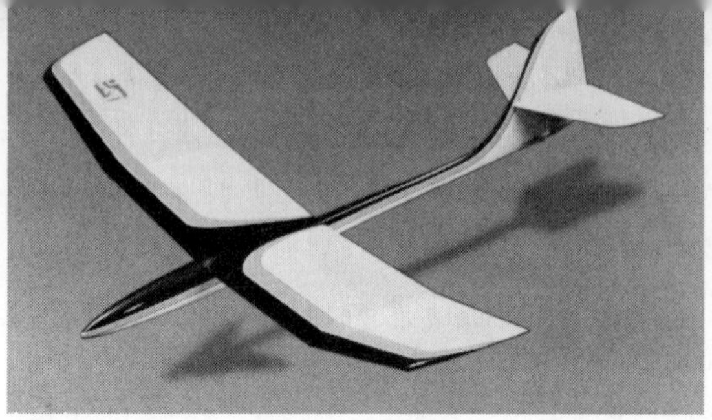

SAILPLANES are increasingly popular. This Airtronics Sagitta has a 98-in. wingspan.

The best advice is: Don't try RC flying alone. First, join one of the hundreds of clubs. Second, even if you don't join a club, always have someone with you when you fly. Third, believe that you need help and instruction in getting started—it will insure that your investment in equipment won't be wasted by early discouragement.

Finally, old hands recommend that you join the Academy of Model Aeronautics, AMA for short. This organization issues licenses to its members, sanctions contests, and provides insurance coverage in case your baby injures someone's property. It also publishes *Model Aviation,* a magazine to keep you up-to-date on the sport. Through the AMA, you belong to the FAI (Federation Aeronautique Internationale), the world organization that governs sports aviation. The address of AMA is 815 Fifteenth St., N.W., Washington, DC 20005.

Once you have soloed and become one of the local hot pilots, what's next? Well, you can show off at the local fly-for-fun contests, then expand all the way up to the annual AMA Nationals—the big league of RC flying. Or construction may be your bag, and it could lead you to displaying your handiwork in shows, including the prestigious event held in Toledo each year. An award here for the plane you built is like an Oscar to an actor.

F8F-2 BEARCAT has a 60-in. wingspan.

Loose marble top

I've bought a nightstand with a marble top about 15 in. square. It is not attached. What adhesive or glue should I use to fasten it in place?—Roy Wilkins, Rochester, N.Y.

Although it may have been done, I've never seen a marble top of any size attached with adhesive. Usually it is held in place with some form of cleating that's made a part of the original construction and finished to match the wood. One marble top I've seen had shallow holes drilled near the four corners on the bottom face. Short locating dowels were fitted loosely in these holes to hold the top in place. I saw a small top recently that had a single cleat, or stop, cemented to the underside, but I suspect that this may not have been done originally.

As for your particular case, you might well find that a tape having adhesive on both sides will do an adequate job in holding the top in place.

Flooded asphalt-tile floor

The tiled floor (asphalt tile) in part of my basement was flooded recently. Water remained on the floor about three days and drained away slowly. Will the tile loosen?—Ruben Asp, Racine, Wis.

I don't know. But if tiles have not loosened at joints or corners by now, they are not likely to do so in the future, especially if they were properly installed originally. I wouldn't lose any sleep over this situation.

Crack patch

My patio floor is of natural stone laid in a concrete bed. Only 10x12 ft., it's cracked diagonally all the way across, right through the stones. The crack is a hairline part of the way and not more than ¼ in. at the widest. Do I fill it as is, chisel it wider or what?—C.E., N.J.

By "laid in a concrete bed," I assume you mean the stones were originally bedded in concrete over a gravel fill, and that the openings between the stones were concrete-mortared flush with the surface. Settling of whatever the builder used as fill has undoubtedly caused the crack. There's a possibility that the crack may open farther, but I'd try filling it "as is." Several types of concrete crack fillers are available, some of which come in a cartridge for use in a caulking gun. The main problem is to clean the crack thoroughly, removing all dirt and loose debris. Usually you can do this with a strong stream of water from a hose while using a small screwdriver or other pointed tool to loosen any embedded dirt. Thoroughness of the cleaning will determine the success of the repair patch.

A thin mix of concrete patcher will probably run deeper into the fine crack than most other patchers. Fill the crack a little over flush and then brush off lightly. Cover it with wet sacks or cloths and keep them damp for at least 36 hours.

Lumpy lawn

Why is my lawn so rough and bumpy under trees? I have a wide curb shaded by large trees and under these the lawn surface is so rough it is difficult to hang onto my power-mower handle. Is there any way it can be made smoother?—I.H., Ill

If you look closely during a heavy rain you will see water falling in streams from the tree limbs. This forces the soil into alternate depressions and hummocks and make mowing unpleasant, if not difficult. There isn't much you can do except to spread a thin dressing of black soil over the surface each season and then rake and roll it smooth. When spreading the dressing care must be taken not to cover the crowns of the grass plants. Also, be very careful when raking the dressing not to damage the plants or pull them loose. If the black soil is damp when spread and raked, let it dry sufficiently to prevent it from sticking to the roller. On sloping curbs or lawns it is often best to use a light top dressing of peat moss, cocoa-bean hulls or some similar lawn dressing rather than black soil which may wash away in a heavy rain.

Any of these dressings will help to "cushion" the bumps and depressions and make your mower more tractable. Of course, it may be possible to trim the trees in such a way as to break and disperse the streams that are causing the trouble, but this may be costly and difficult to carry out effectively.

Hide-a-fence planting

What plants can I use to conceal a chain-link fence? The fence is about 50 ft. long and, although quite new, I'd like to conceal it entirely.—J.L., Mich.

If the fence is located where the sun shines most of the day, a flowering vine such as clematis or climbing honeysuckle will do it in a season or two. However, you should consider that it also will contribute to the deterioration of the fence by opening the way to rust. Also, the weight of the vine eventually may cause the linkage to sag between posts.

A smoke detector may save your life

Sixty percent of fires in the home occur when people are sleeping. Smoke detectors can awaken you and give you a chance to escape before the fire spreads

By MORT SCHULTZ

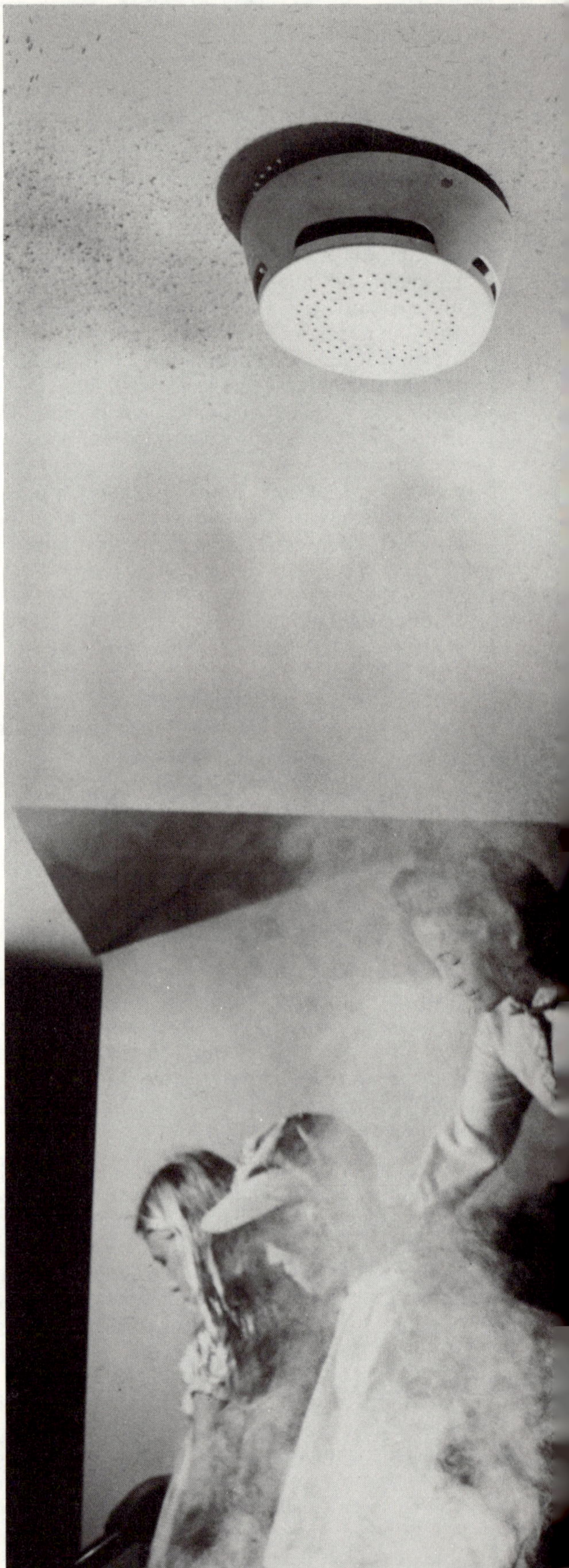

IN FAIRFAX, VA, smoke from a smoldering fire caused a family of five to suffocate as they slept in their expensive two-story home.

Commenting on the tragedy, Fairfax assistant fire chief William Bittle said, "It doesn't seem right spending $80,000 on a house, but not $50 for safety."

The $50 Chief Bittle was referring to would have bought the family an automatic warning device that would have sounded an alarm moments after the fire started, awakening them and giving them time for escape.

In Freehold Township, NJ, a 15-year-old boy and his grandmother perished when fire swept a two-story home during the night. The boy died in a leap from a second-story window trying to escape. The woman was asphyxiated by smoke.

"There is no doubt in my mind that if there had been a smoke detection device in the home we could have possibly saved the lives of two people," Fire Marshal Frank Wilgus says.

300 fires an hour

The dramas in Fairfax and Freehold are duplicated every day of the week. According to the National Commission on Fire Prevention and Control, statistically there is the likelihood that nationally within the next hour 300 fires will break out. This figure translates into a mind-boggling 2,628,000 fires a year.

The Commission reports that annually in this country alone fire kills 12,000—more than 6000 of them in home fires—injures 300,000 and destroys $11 billion in property.

SEE ALSO

Boating, safety . . . Fire extinguishers . . . Firewood . . . Ladders . . . Safety, workshop . . . Security, home . . . Wiring, electrical

Every day one fire official or another is reminding us that this terrible toll in lives and suffering could be substantially reduced if homeowners planned for fire as carefully as most do, say, for vacation.

But most people don't. Most of the nation's 70 million residences are presently without fire-detection devices. This is particularly tragic when you realize that 9 out of 10 deaths from fire occur at home, but that an estimated 8 of every 10 of them could be saved if homes were equipped with detection alarms.

Joe Erdmann and his wife and daughter today swear they owe their lives to such a device. About 2 a.m. Erdmann was awakened abruptly by a raucous blast from the smoke detector outside the bedroom area in his Neenah, WI, home.

A wisp of smoke from a fire smoldering in the kitchen had set off the alarm, giving Erdmann time to evacuate his family and extinguish the flames. "Thanks to that smoke alarm we were able to save our lives and our home," he says.

The two basic types of home fire detectors are smoke and heat. A smoke detector detects particles of combustion. A heat detector detects high temperature or a high rate-of-temperature rise.

inexpensive protection

When activated, both types emit a leather-lunged horn blast of at least 80 decibels for at least four minutes that will arouse the soundest sleeper.

Some fire experts suggest a system combining both heat and smoke detectors where maximum protection is desired and cost is no object. However, many now feel that the newer, more sensitive smoke detector that does not require heat buildup to function offers early-warning protection at a modest price—and should become just as common a household appliance as a toaster, food mixer or hair dryer.

For the average home, an elaborate setup is not needed. The National Fire Protection Assn. advises that "some very real protection is possible with one smoke detector on each floor or one smoke detector placed between the bedroom and the rest of the house."

smoke sensors work far away

The most important necessity when fire starts is to give a home's occupants ample warning of danger so they can escape. Smoke detectors do this.

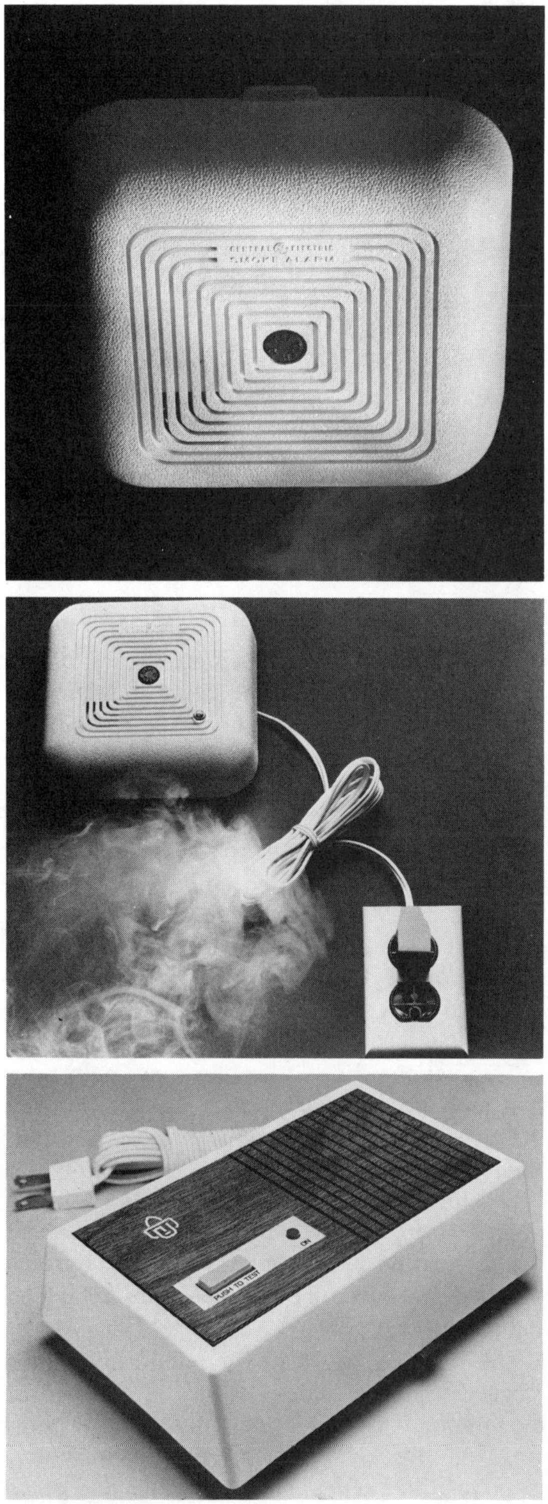

MANY DETECTORS come in a choice of battery or plug-in models such as the GE model shown in the top two photographs. The battery-powered type is handy for ceiling mounting where no power source may be near. The battery models also require a weak-battery warning indicator. The bottom photo shows the handsome Gillette photoelectric model. It's also available in battery and plug-in versions

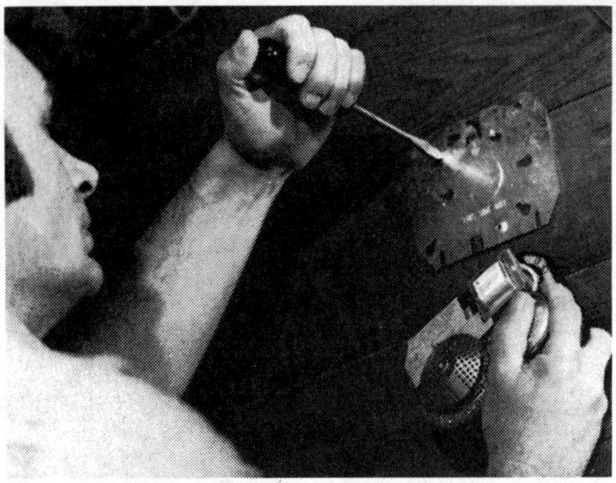

INSTALLATION IS easy, as typified by this Honeywell mounting sequence. The base plate is first screwed to the wall or ceiling

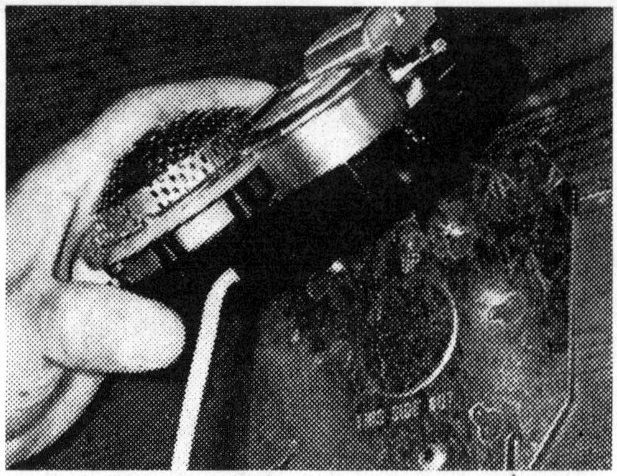

NEXT THE SENSOR unit is attached to the plate as shown in the photo above. Alarms are best mounted high on the wall or ceiling as smoke rises

"Smoke detectors by their very nature can monitor smoke far from the point of origin because smoke moves, rising up to the ceiling and up stairways," Richard B. Bright states. He is a senior research engineer concerned with fire-protection for the U.S. Bureau of Standards.

A reliable smoke alarm costs $15 to $50. If you deploy more than one, they can be wired together in series so if smoke activates one alarm, the alarms in other areas will sound off, too.

It is at night that alarms earn every penny you spend for them. Sixty percent of fires in the home occur when people are sleeping.

The National Fire Protection Assn. points out that most people who die in home fires are not the victims of flames, but inhale smoke and poisonous gases that rise ahead of the flames.

"Victims suffocate to death in the middle of the night, asleep, never knowing what happened," the association points out. "Many die upstairs from a downstairs fire that never burns a thing on the second floor."

The danger of death by suffocation has reached a point of crisis because of widespread use in homes of synthetic materials, such as polyvinyl chloride. Synthetics are used in furniture, carpeting, drainpipes, shower curtains and other furnishings. When they begin to smolder, deadly chemical gases are given off.

how detectors work

"Flame is the last on the list of killers during fire," the National Fire Protection Assn. informs us. "Most people die from lack of oxygen, hot air or gases, and from smoke—often before they can awaken."

Smoke detectors are designed to sniff out fumes and warn people of danger before they are overcome. There are two basic types of smoke detectors for the home: photoelectric and ionization.

Photoelectric smoke detectors contain a small light source. When smoke enters the enclosure that surrounds the unit, the light beam is disrupted by smoke particles, causing light to be reflected to a photoelectric cell. This triggers the alarm.

An ionization smoke detector employs a small amount of radioactive material, which is less than the amount used on luminous watch dials. The material ionizes the air in a small pocket, causing a faint electric current. This current triggers the alarm when it's disturbed by fine smoke particles.

Both types work well and are approved by fire safety experts. Many are made by well-known reliable manufacturers such as General Electric, Honeywell, Archer, Wells Fargo, Westclox, ADT, Fyrnetics, Statitrol, Norelco, Emhart, and Pittway. Whatever unit you select, it is important that it carry the UL (Underwriters Laboratories) or FM (Factory Mutual) label. This is your assurance the device has been tested by an independent agency and has met rigid standards.

battery or plug-in?

You have a choice of battery or plug-in power. Each has its advantages. Battery-powered alarms

THE FINAL STEP is installing the cover. This snaps on the sensor unit. The detector should now be given a thorough test using the self-testing controls

are handy where there is no nearby wall outlet to plug into, especially since such sensors should usually be mounted high—on the ceiling or near the top of a wall—to intercept rising smoke and fumes. They also eliminate the possibility that a chance power outage could cause the units to fail to sound off.

But batteries require periodic checking and replacement—a vital precaution to insure proper operation. Any unit you consider should have an automatic indicator, visual or audible, to warn when batteries are low and need replacement. Both battery and house-wired units should also have test buttons because frequent testing is important to insure that the devices are operating correctly.

House-powered alarms eliminate the need for battery changing but require a source of current. If there's no convenient outlet, or you don't want the power cord to show, you may want to connect directly into your house wiring—a neat though slightly more expensive installation.

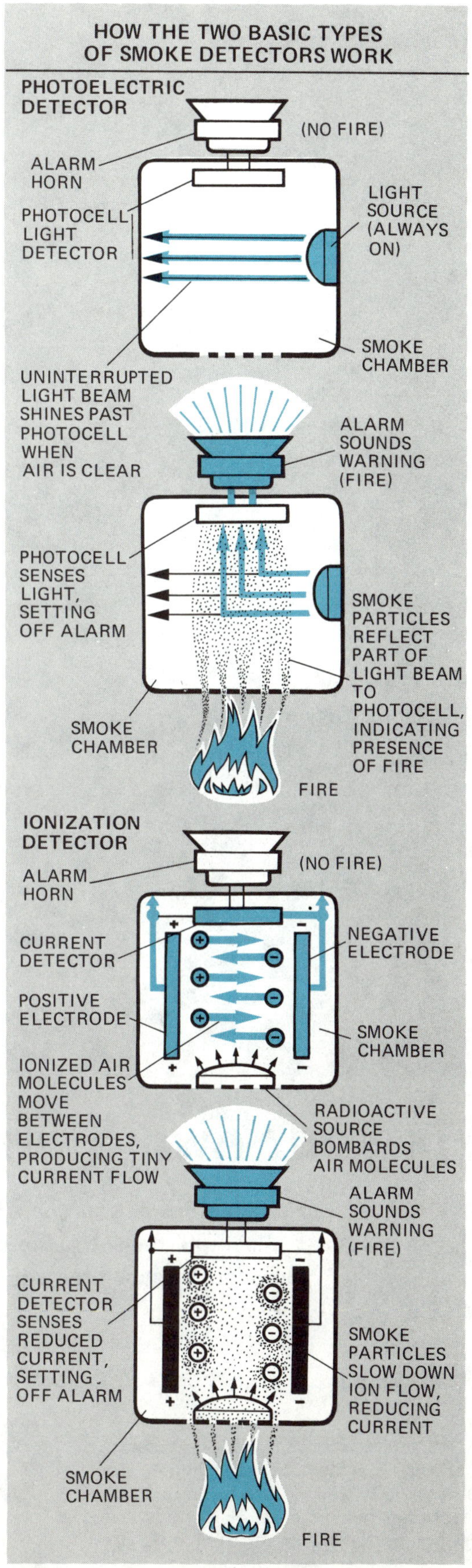

TWO BASIC TYPES of smoke detectors are diagrammed in simplified form at the right. In the photoelectric alarm, a small light beam, constantly on, shines across a darkened chamber. If fire occurs, smoke particles enter the chamber, act as tiny reflectors and divert part of the light to the photocell detector. The photocell senses the light and sounds an alarm. In the ionization detector, ionized air molecules gravitate toward oppositely charged electrodes, setting up a tiny current flow. Entering smoke particles slow the ion flow, producing a current drop that triggers the alarm. Units which combine smoke detectors with heat detectors offer maximum protection

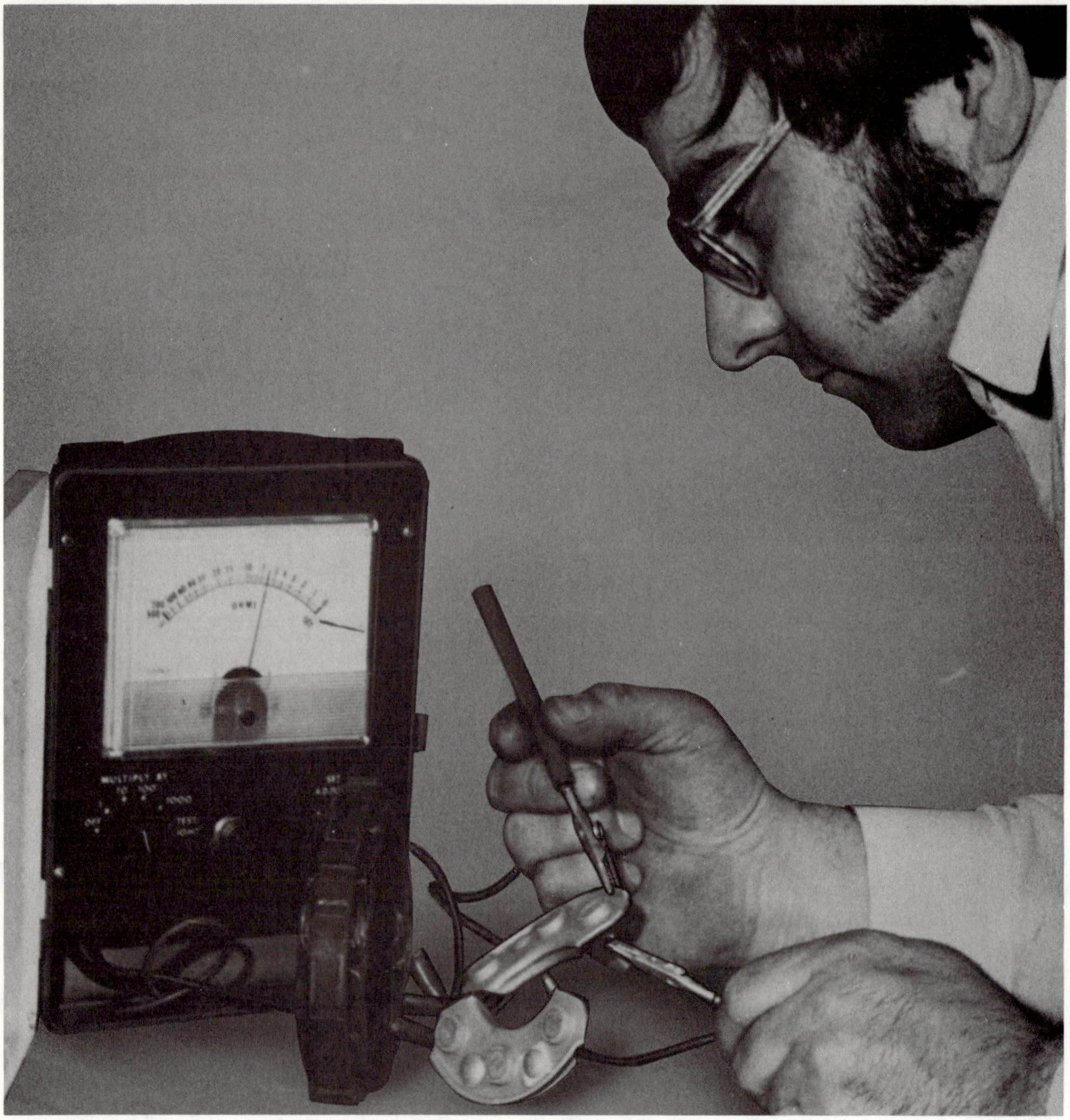

Fix your own alternator

These reliable power sources are blamed for more than their share of automotive problems. Most alternator trouble can be "fixed" by work on an associated component

By MORT SCHULTZ

SEE ALSO

Autos, maintenance . . . Battery testers . . . Carburetors, auto . . . Dieseling, auto . . . Differentials, auto . . . Distributors, auto . . . Electronic ignition, auto . . . Gaskets, auto . . . Ignition systems, auto . . . Tune-up, auto

ALTERNATORS HAVE been used in U.S.-built cars since the early 1960s. They're also called alternating current (a.c.) generators, Delcotrons (the GM trade name), or—more loosely—just generators. An older model U.S. car or an import may have a direct current (d.c.) generator instead. You should check. They're quite different breeds and the information here doesn't apply to d.c. generators.

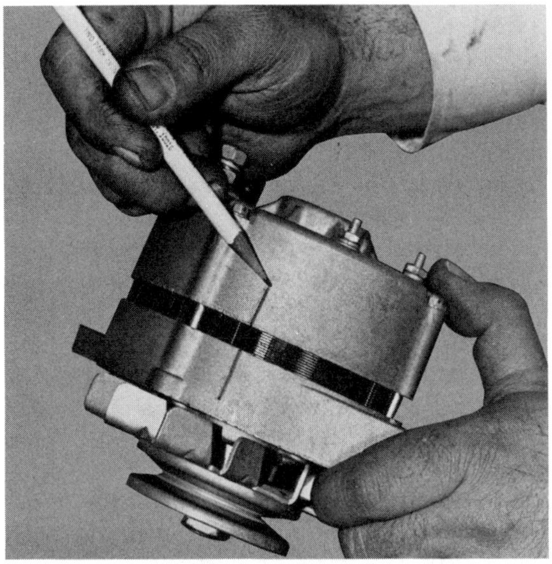

MARK the alternator before stripping it for bench tests; proper reassembly will be much surer.

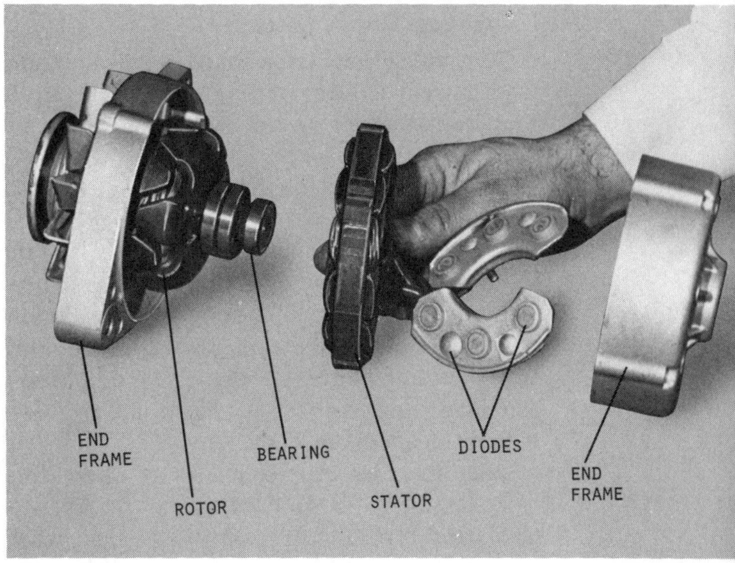

CHECKING INDIVIDUAL alternator components lets you limit replacement costs to those that are bad.

For decades, all cars had the d.c. version. But more and more electrical accessories—air conditioners, higher-capacity batteries, additional lights, AM-FM radios and tape decks, for example—strained d.c. generators' capacity. Alternators have greater output and weigh less.

The alternator is one of the most reliable, efficient assemblies in a car. So reliable, in fact, that a problem in the electrical system probably comes not from the alternator itself, but some part associated with it.

chart your solution

Notice the troubleshooting chart on page 72. It lists electrical problems and matches them to causes *not* part of the alternator. Before pulling your alternator from the car, follow the "what to do" procedures. The odds are good you'll solve the problem.

The drive belt is an excellent example of an alternator-associated component that causes problems often blamed unfairly on the alternator itself. In fact, in seven cases of electrical failure of every 10, that belt is the troublemaker.

A drive belt that is loose or worn or slips because it has become glazed costs you alternator output. Replace a glazed belt. Also replace a damaged belt with a new belt of proper size, properly adjusted. To adjust tension, a belt tension gauge is far more accurate than the "press-by-finger" method. It minimizes overtightening risk that can strain, maybe destroy, bearings.

Tighten a drive belt by using a pry bar against the stator support—never on the end frames. Hold the alternator against its belt and tighten the bracket nuts.

an alternator's components

All alternators consist of a rotor, a stator, and two end frames, one containing the diodes (rectifiers). They're necessary to convert or "rectify" the a.c. output to direct current, required by a car's electrical components.

Basically, the rotor is a field coil wound on an iron core that's mounted between two iron poles. It revolves inside the stator, mounted between the end frames. The stator consists of wire loops wound into slots of a laminated frame. Two spring-loaded brushes are on slip rings on one end of the rotor shaft. Rings are attached to leads from the field coil and brushes are connected through a voltage regulator to the battery.

With the voltage regulator closed, current passes through one brush, through the slip ring on which it rides, and through the field coil or rotor. Then it goes through the other slip ring and brush and back to the battery through the ground path.

The revolving rotor's moving magnetic field cuts across the stator's windings, inducing alternating current. The diodes let current flow in only one direction, to the battery, so they convert the a.c. to d.c.

Most alternators have six diodes—three negative and three positive—often contained in a heat sink. To replace a bad one, you must replace the heat sink and all its diodes. But in other cases, diodes are pressed individually into the end frame.

voltage regulator, a partner

The voltage regulator controls the alternator field current and regulates the charging rate in the alternator-battery circuit in response to the battery's state of charge. There must be enough electricity to do the job, but not enough to cause overcharging.

A major difference among alternators is in the location of the regulator. Early systems used electromechanical regulators outside the alternator. Solid-state or electronic regulators, also outside the alternator, were the first modification. The latest step has been the electronic regulator within the alternator body.

Domestic cars use six makes of alternators: Chrysler, Delco (GM), Ford, Leece-Neville, Motorola and Prestolite. Whichever you have, whatever its style, whether you plan tests of the alternator itself or its regulator, the service manual or service instructions are essential. Don't plunge ahead without them. They're available from the manufacturer's technical publications department.

where to get details

Be sure to supply the unit model and serial number; normally they're on a plate attached to the alternator end frame. Here are the addresses to which you can write:

Ford Parts Div., Ford Motor Co., Livonia, MI 48150; Mopar Div., Chrysler Corp., PO Box 1718, Detroit, MI 48288; Delco Remy, General Motors, Anderson, IN 46018; Leece-Neville Co., 1374 East 51st St., Cleveland, OH 44103; Motorola Automotive Products, Inc., 9401 West Grand Ave., Franklin Park, IL 60131; or Prestolite Co., 511 Hamilton St., Toledo, OH 43602.

For alternator or regulator tests, you also need a tachometer and a voltmeter/ammeter with carbon-pile rheostat to control voltage. If bench testing is required, you'll also need an ohmmeter.

On the alternator itself, it's wise to begin with an output test; you leave the unit on the car. Besides, if output is OK, the electrical trouble can't be blamed on the alternator itself.

You hook up test instruments according to the instructions and run the engine at the specified speed—say 1250 rpm. Adjust the carbon-pile rheostat so you get the specified voltage, perhaps 15 volts. The ammeter should now say you're getting electrical output to meet the manufacturer's specs.

moving quickly

Keep in mind that during the alternator output test, the regulator may be out of the circuit. If so, your system doesn't have its protection. So finish the test as quickly as possible and don't exceed engine speed the manufacturer calls for.

This troubleshooting chart deals with electrical problems that may make you believe that the alternator is malfunctioning. In most cases, what appears to be alternator-induced problem is traceable to some other component. Alternators are seldom to blame for electrical malfunctions in a vehicle.

PROBLEM	CAUSE	WHAT TO DO
Battery low in charge headlights dim at idle. (Note: recurrent unexplainable discharge of the battery suggests need for testing the entire charging system.)	1. Drive belt. 2. Battery cables or electric system wiring. 3. Drain on battery. 4. Battery is damaged or worn out.	1. Adjust or replace. 2. Clean battery cables and terminals. Clean and tighten all wiring connections. 3. Check for drain with ignition "OFF." 4. Test battery capacity. Replace battery if necessary.
PROBLEM	**CAUSE**	**WHAT TO DO**
Ammeter registers constant discharge or charging system light remains on; battery doesn't hold charge; low alternator output.	1. Drive belt. 2. Battery cables or electric system wiring.	1. Adjust or replace. 2. Clean battery cables and terminals. Clean and tighten all wiring connections.
PROBLEM	**CAUSE**	**WHAT TO DO**
Lights and fuses fail prematurely; short battery life; battery uses excessive water; resistor wire burns; coil damage; high charging rate.	1. Electric system wiring. 2. Regulator.	1. Clean and tighten all wiring. Replace damaged wires. 2. Replace a bad regulator.
PROBLEM	**CAUSE**	**WHAT TO DO**
Noise.	1. Drive belt. 2. Water pump.	1. Treat or replace a squealing belt. 2. Check the water pump with a sound detecting tool, such as a stethoscope, to assure that it's not to blame rather than the alternator.

Even if the output isn't up to snuff, the alternator may be OK. Resistance in the circuits can block the flow of enough electricity even if the alternator is trying to put it out.

So, before you remove the alternator for bench testing, conduct resistance tests of the field and charging circuits. You may well save yourself lots of work. High resistance is usually caused by loose or corroded connections.

If you must pull the alternator, first scribe a line across the end frames to ensure correct reassembly. Test diodes first for continuity and shorts, since they fail most often; then the stator and rotor for continuity and grounds. Identifying the culprit saves you the necessity of buying a complete new alternator, since you have to replace only the part that failed.

Here are some of the important general rules for alternator work. They'll prevent costly damage and protect you from injury:

- Be sure the ignition is off before you go near either the alternator or regulator.
- Use tools with insulated handles.
- Beware of the alternator's output terminal; it's always "hot."
- Always disconnect the battery ground before hooking up instruments, then double-check polarity (plus to plus, minus to minus), and reconnect the ground. Wrong polarity, even momentarily, may ruin the diodes.
- And never ground the field circuit between the alternator and regulator. It may damage the regulator and possibly burn out field windings. Many alternators are not fused.

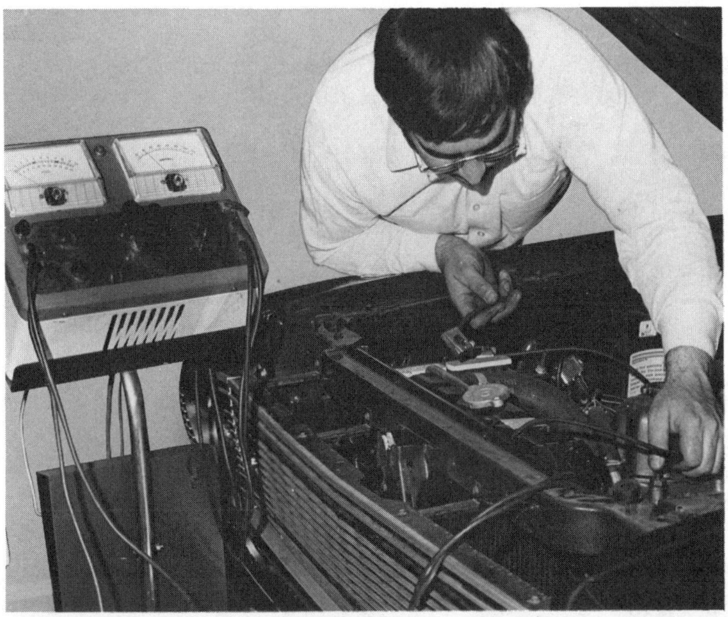

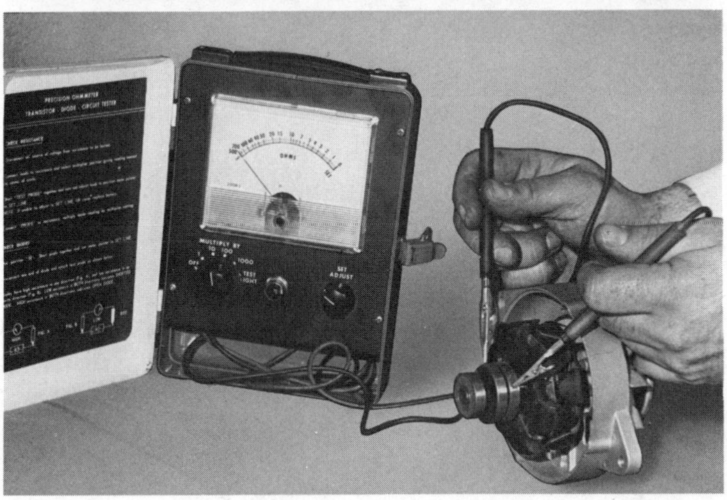

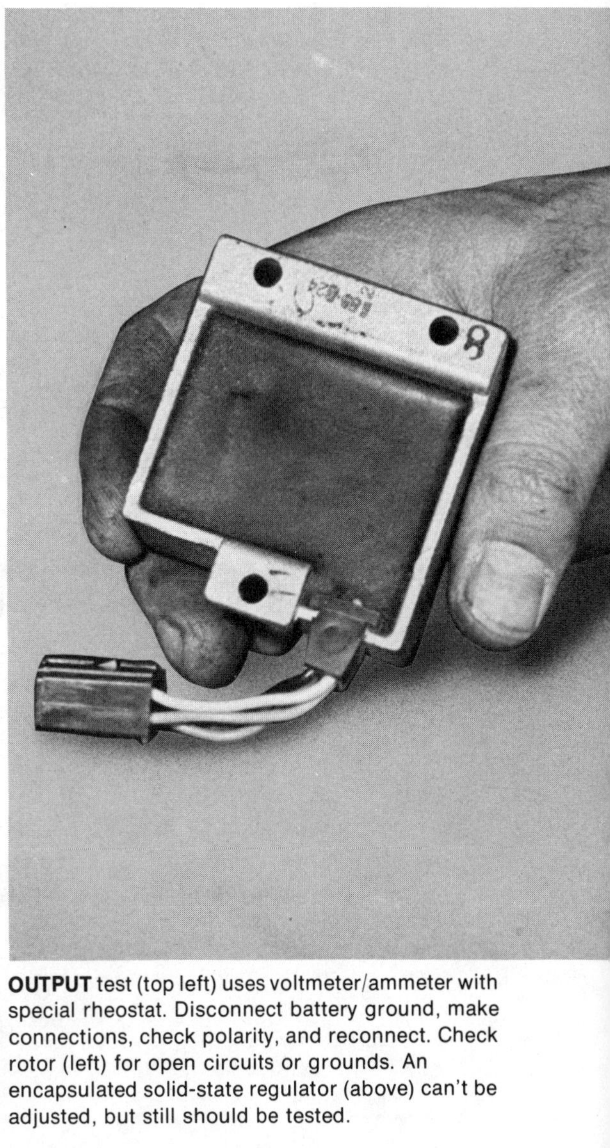

OUTPUT test (top left) uses voltmeter/ammeter with special rheostat. Disconnect battery ground, make connections, check polarity, and reconnect. Check rotor (left) for open circuits or grounds. An encapsulated solid-state regulator (above) can't be adjusted, but still should be tested.

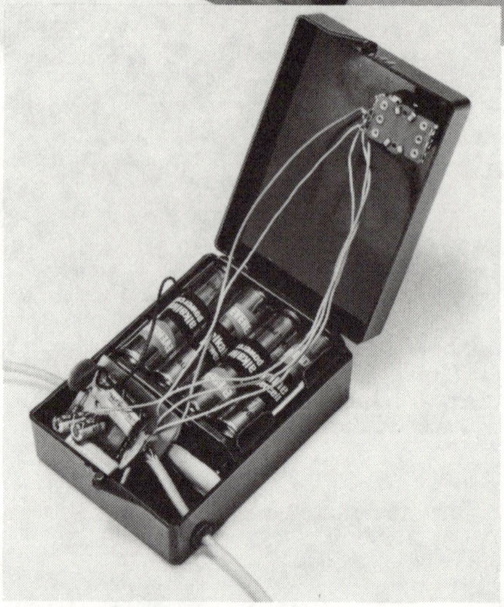

Big sound from a transistor radio

This easy-to-build circuit and a loudspeaker will turn your transistor portable into a take-along hi-fi system. You'll find it great for picnics or trips to the beach

By JEFFREY SANDLER

THERE'S BEAUTIFUL SOUND trapped inside your AM/FM transistor radio, but you might never know it. What starts out as a good signal is degraded as it passes through inexpensive amplifier stages, then loses still more quality fighting its way out through a 2-in. loudspeaker.

But with our booster amplifier, you can get hold of that clean, original signal, crank it up and drive speakers with all the volume you'll need, even outdoors. With highly efficient speakers like Poly-Planar P-40s, the sound quality is superb. In our tests, the booster amp performed just like a.c.-powered receiver-speaker combinations in the $100 to $125 price range. The sound is so good it has to be heard to be believed.

SEE ALSO
Cassette recorders . . . Cassette tapes . . . Citizens band radio . . . Hi-fi . . . Hi-fi centers . . . Mixers, audio . . . Speakers

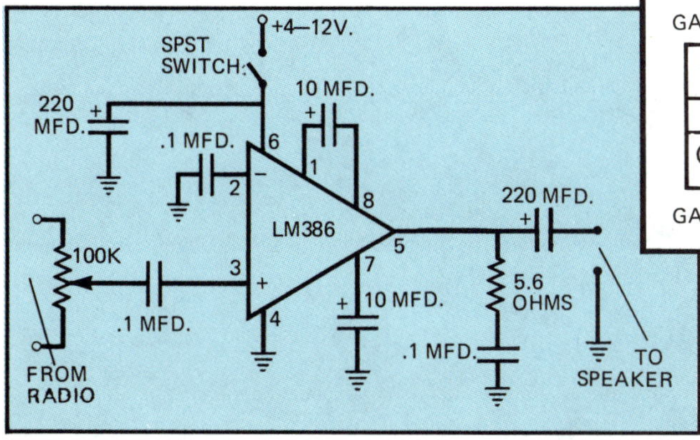

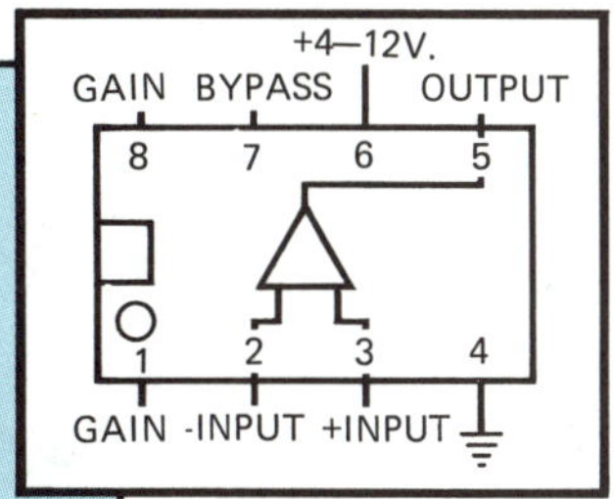

WHEN BUILDING the booster, be sure to observe the polarities for the electrolytic capacitors shown in the schematic. The diagram above shows the pin locations on the IC package.

But this booster amp is compact and battery-powered. It turns your transistor radio into a completely portable hi-fi receiver. It's not stereo, of course, and it's *not* intended for a.c. operation—using the amplifier with a non-battery power supply or with a line-powered radio could present a shock hazard.

how it works

The circuit is designed around National Semiconductor's LM386 chip, a low-voltage audio power amplifier that steps up a signal 20 to 200 times. Here the gain is set at 200 by means of the 10-mfd. capacitor between pins 1 and 8. The amplified signal appears at pin 5 and drives the loudspeakers.

The other circuit components set up proper IC operating conditions. One 220-mfd. capacitor filters the battery power supply; the other keeps d.c. voltage out of the speakers. The 10-mfd. capacitor between pin 7 and ground provides additional supply filtering. The 5.6-ohm resistor and .1 mfd. capacitor off pin 5 and the .1-mfd. at the minus input (pin 2) prevent instabilities. The .1-mfd. capacitor between the volume-control pot and pin 3 blocks d.c. from the input.

Build the circuit by following the schematic, or get the complete kit, including printed-circuit board. Power can be anything from 4 to 12 volts. With one 9-v. battery, the amp will drive a large (and relatively inefficient) acoustic-suspension speaker system with good volume. But a 12-v.—eight dry cells—supply will give higher undistorted volume.

The only tricky part is getting into your radio. You can simply plug into the radio's earphone output, but that won't give you the best sound and it will tie you to the radio's volume control. It will be much better for you to take your input from across the radio's volume control potentiometer.

In many radios, there's room enough in the case for an extra jack—use the open-circuit type (Radio Shack 274-297 or 274-251) and wire its terminals to the opposite sides (outer terminals) of the radio's volume-control pot. Otherwise you'll have to replace the earphone jack with an open-circuit jack and make sure you reconnect the radio's speaker so that it's not cut out by the jack.

Two types of AM/FM portables I've used successfully with the booster amp are Radio Shack models 12-666 and 12-662. The pocket-size 12-662 is shown in the picture on page 74.

Shielded cable between radio and amplifier is a good idea, though not always necessary. The speakers driven can be up to 16 ohms impedance; I've been quite satisfied with the quality and volume obtained driving two 8-ohm Poly-Planars connected in series.

The efficiency of the booster amp is at a maximum when it is driving a 16-ohm load, and you can overheat the IC by using too great a supply voltage with a low-impedance speaker—limit supply to 9 volts with an 8-ohm speaker, 8 volts with a 4-ohm speaker. Take care not to short the output leads together with power on; this can ruin the chip in seconds.

build from a kit

The amplifier is available as a complete kit including a drilled, etched and labeled printed-circuit board, all components, box, battery case, shielded cable—everything but batteries—from Circuit Craft, Inc., 10 Idell Rd., Valley Stream, NY 11580. Poly-Planar P-40 loudspeakers are available from the same source (these are bare foam speakers without the grille cloth or frame).

Secrets of cutting compound angles

By WAYNE C. LECKEY

Compound cuts are made with both the blade and miter gauge tilted the required degrees. The blade guard has been removed for picture clarity

■ GETTING THE FOUR CORNERS of a "hopper"-style picture frame to fit is fairly easy, but determining the degree of bevel for a simple four-piece box with sides that slope, say 35°, can be puzzling. For example, the butt joints of the box appear to be 90°, when viewed from the top, but when they're viewed in a true plane, you'll find the "square" edges are less than 90°—actually 70½°. That's the tricky part of compound angles: The bevel does not show in a plan drawing, and even when you study the completed job, the angles are not what they seem.

Compound angles are required when sawing the parts of any pyramidal shape of four, six or eight sides, and are made with the blade (or table, as the case may be) tilted to cut a bevel and the miter gauge swung to cut a miter. Thus both the miter and the bevel are cut in one operation.

The chart on the next page takes all the guesswork out of setting your saw to cut a number of common compound angles. It gives the required tilt for the saw blade and the swing (tilt) of the miter gauge in degrees.

The fastest and most economical way to saw parts for sloping box or flared frame is from a long board which has been prebeveled along both edges. This is called strip cutting. The miter gauge is left at the same setting and the board is flopped after each cut. When the parts are individually cut from scrap, the miter gauge is turned around and used backward for the second cut so wide side of work is always against the miter-gauge facing.

The upper drawings on this page show four standard miter-gauge positions for strip cutting—A and B for cutting miter joints, C and D for butt joints. Here the blade tilts to the right.

MITER-GAUGE POSITIONS FOR COMPOUND CUTS

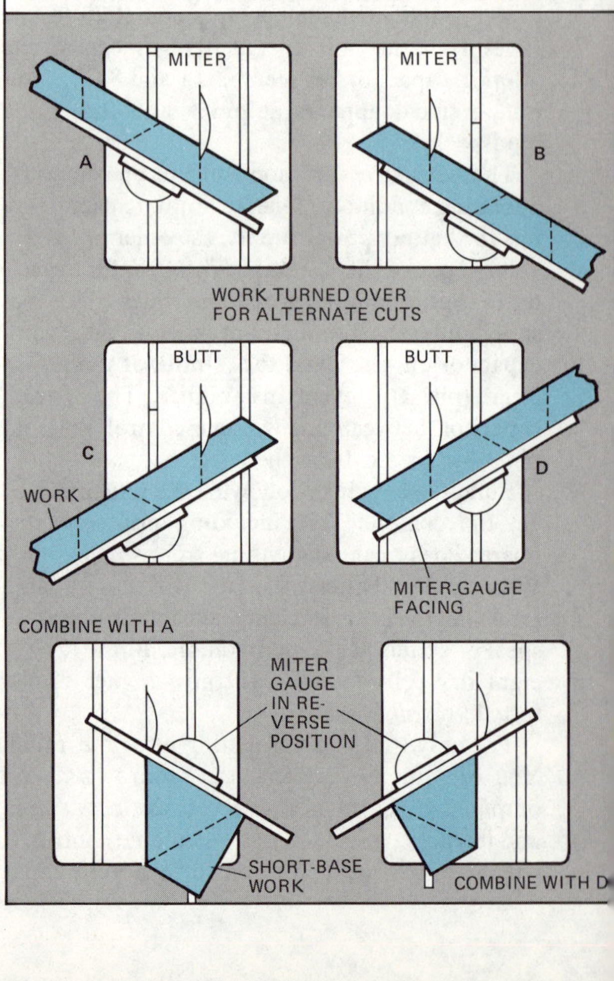

The two sets of positions are pairs worked by shifting the miter gauge from one table groove to the other. Prebeveling the edges is done so the top and bottom edges of the pieces will be on a flat plane when assembled. If the box sides slope 35°, for example, the top and bottom edges are beveled 35°.

You can use any of the four miter-gauge positions shown when the work is not prebeveled. However, only two of these positions can be used when the work is prebeveled and the job calls for mitered joints at all four corners, as the bevel must bear against the miter gauge with the sharp corner facing up. When a peak is to be formed like the roof of a birdhouse, and cut from individual prebeveled pieces, the long side of the work must be held against the miter-gauge facing for both cuts; the bevel must face up for both cuts.

In the case of rough work, compound joints are simply butted and nailed or, for greater strength, glued and nailed. However, in finer work, splines are used. These are thin strips of wood cut to fit saw kerfs made in mating members.

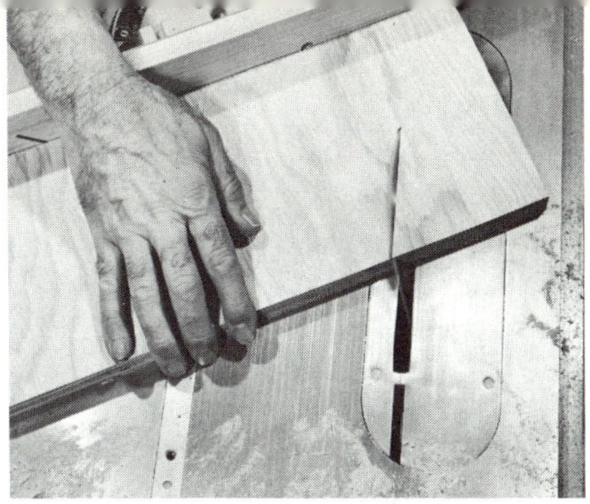

When parts are cut individually from separate pieces, the first cut is made with the work held in the position shown above

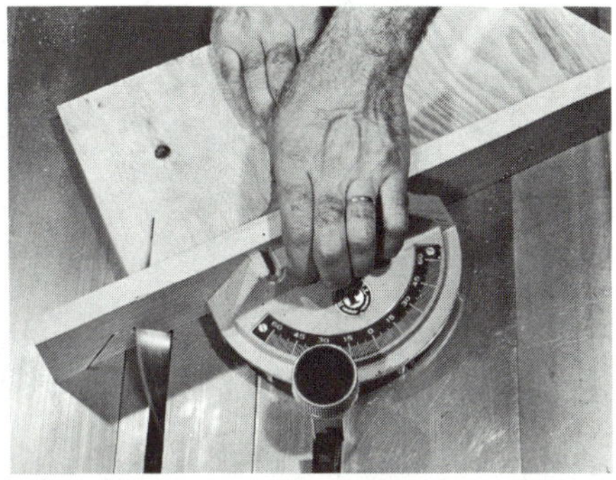

To make the second cut, the miter gauge is turned around and used backward. The same miter-gauge setting is used

SAW-TILT AND MITER-GAUGE SETTINGS FOR COMPOUND ANGLES

FRONT VIEW  ANGLE	 4 SIDES, BUTT JOINTS		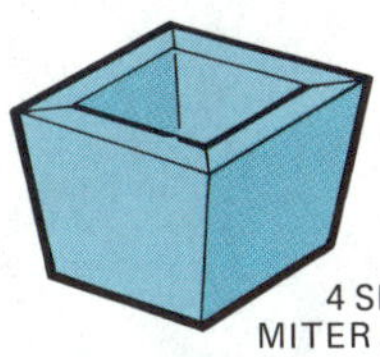 4 SIDES, MITER JOINTS		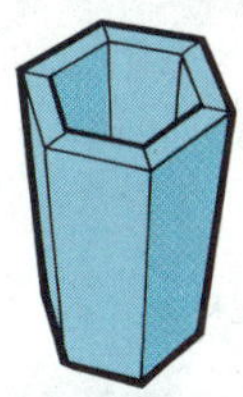 6 SIDES, MITER JOINTS		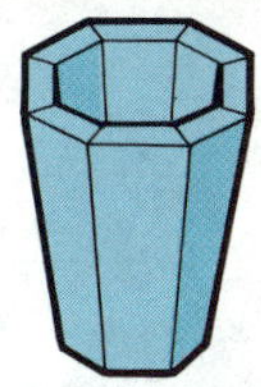 8 SIDES, MITER JOINTS	
WORK ANGLE	SAW TILT	MITER GAUGE	SAW TILT	MITER GAUGE	SAW TILT	MITER GAUGE	SAW TILT	MITER GAUGE
5°	1/2	85	44-3/4	85	29-3/4	87-1/2	22-1/4	88
10°	1-1/2	80-1/4	44-1/4	80-1/2	29-1/2	84-1/2	22	86
15°	3-3/4	75-1/2	43-1/4	75-1/2	29	81-3/4	21-1/2	84
20°	6-1/4	71	42	71	28-1/4	79	21	82
25°	10	67	40	67	27-1/4	76-1/2	20-1/4	80
30°	14-1/2	63-1/2	37-3/4	61-1/2	26	74	19-1/4	78-1/4
35°	19-1/2	60-1/4	35-1/4	60-1/4	24-1/2	71-3/4	18-1/4	76-3/4
40°	24-1/2	57-1/4	32-3/4	57-1/4	22-3/4	69-3/4	17	75
45°	30	54-3/4	30	54-3/4	21	67-3/4	15-3/4	73-3/4
50°	36	52-1/2	27	52-1/2	19	66-1/4	14-1/4	72-1/2
55°	42	50-3/4	24	50-3/4	16-3/4	64-3/4	12-3/4	71-1/4
60°	48	49	21	49	14-1/2	63-1/2	11	70-1/4

Figures are in degrees and are for direct setting to tilt scale and miter-gauge scale provided tilt starts at 0° and miter gauge at 90° in the normal position.

How to drill angled holes accurately

The biggest problem is to stop drill-bit wander. Next is to finish the hole without break-through, jamming or bit breakage. Here's how to handle these problems

By WALTER E. BURTON

■ DRILLING A HOLE at an angle can be a frustrating job, especially when you're drilling metal. Starting the hole is difficult because the drill bit tends to wander or grab. Finishing the hole is no cinch, either—breaking through can be ticklish, with jamming and bit breakage possible.

But there are tricks that can take some of the headaches out of angle drilling. First off, you must provide a surface perpendicular to the drill bit so it can start squarely.

The simplest way to do this is to start drilling with the bit at a right angle to the surface and then tilt either the workpiece or the drill until the desired angle is reached. The latter is done when you're using a portable drill in wood and other soft materials, but locating the hole at a precise point requires care. Another drill-starting trick is to make a center-punch mark at an angle, as shown in bottom, left photo on page 80.

When using a conical "crater" formed with a drill, start drilling as shown at the left. The width of the crater side (crater radius) should be nearly equal to the diameter of the hole to be drilled.

SEE ALSO

**Clamps . . . Drill press techniques . . .
Drills, portable . . . Lifters, drill press . . .
Metal-lathe accessories . . . Portable drills . . .
Power-tool maintenance . . . Power-tool stands . . .
Shop techniques . . . Shop tools**

ANGLE DRILLING (left) is easy when a "crater" is first made with a large twist drill held perpendicular to workpiece (see inset). Punch mark (below) is starter hole for lathe center drill; a twist drill finishes the hole. Wires (below, right) show angles of holes drilled through metal bars and blocks by author.

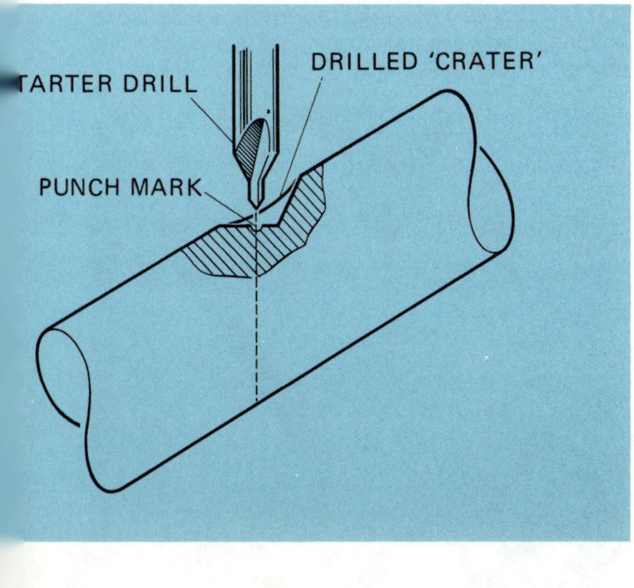

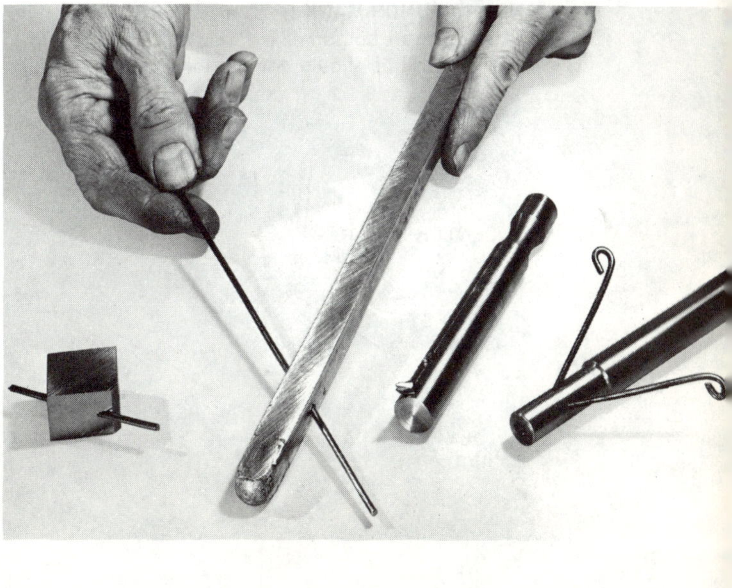

how to drill angled holes, continued

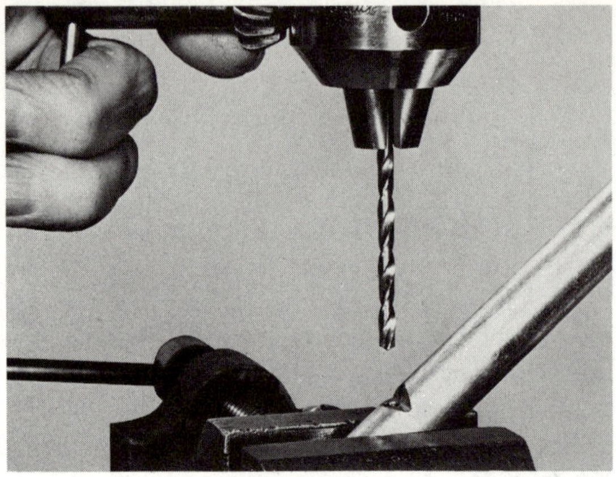

After making a punch mark at the desired location, begin drilling with a regular lathe center drill. Select a "stubby" one since a steeply angled surface may cause a twist drill to grab at the corners.

With the drilled-crater technique, it may be desirable to use initially a twist drill that is slightly smaller than the finished diameter of the hole. Best results with this method will be obtained when the hole is perpendicular or nearly perpendicular to the crater side.

The use of a machined groove for a starting land, shown below, right, is especially helpful when several holes are to be drilled at the same distance from the end of a rod and at the same angle to its axis. The groove can subsequently be removed by machining the bar to a smaller size, as was done with the one shown on page 79.

Although it is not practical to make too deep a hole with an end mill, it can be used to make a very neat starting recess, as shown on page 83.

If a number of identical workpieces are to be drilled, a jig can be made to speed the job of starting and drilling holes at the same angle.

The methods shown on these pages should produce accurate results if care is taken in locating the starting surface and in positioning the punch mark. Once started, drilling should go smoothly until the bit breaks through. The be-

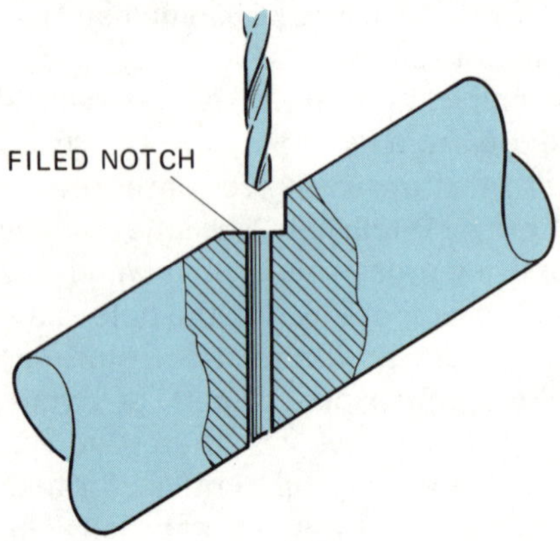

WHEN NOTCH IS FILED or sawed in bar with one side perpendicular to hole axis, it provides flat surface for drill. The technique works fine when finished look is unimportant. Punch mark and the use of lathe center drill give the most accurate start.

ANGLED PUNCH MARK helps start a drill when angle and hole size are both small. To keep the bit from drifting, the entire drill tip should contact the punch mark.

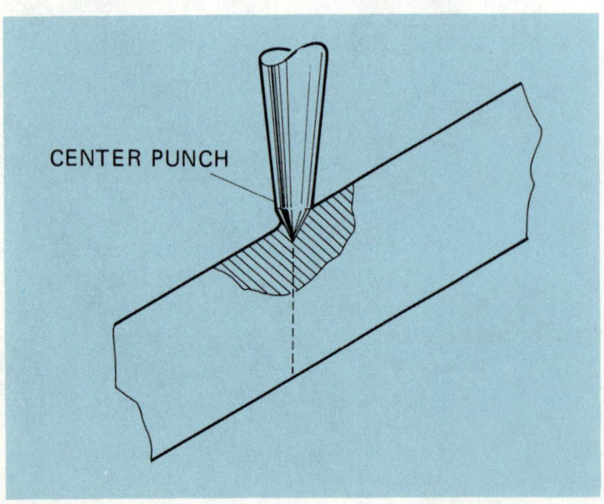

MACHINED GROOVE is a variation of the notch method. Starting surface can be turned at any angle, but groove must be wide enough for drill clearance.

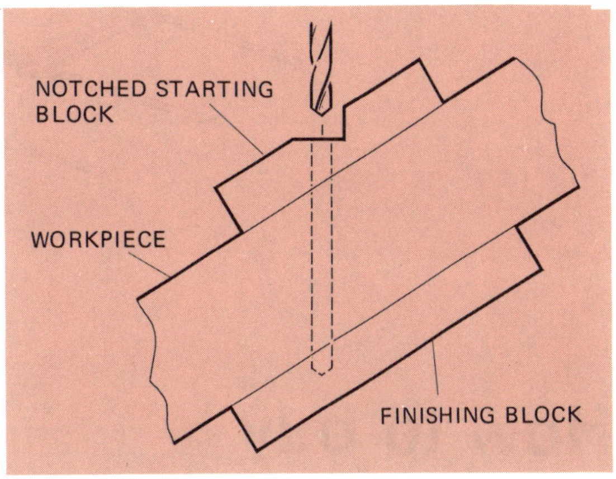

STARTING BLOCK of scrap material, notched to angle desired, is clamped to workpiece; a finishing block clamped underneath assures clean drill breakthrough.

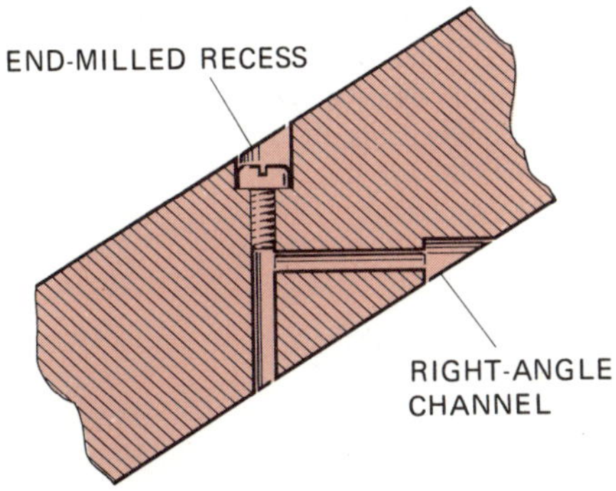

END-MILLING A RECESS is the neatest way to provide a starting surface for drill. When hole is to accommodate a pan-head screw, recess is milled slightly larger than diameter of head, which seats squarely against flat. Right-angled channel is typical use of method.

BORING BAR for lathe is made using the end-mill technique. Grind cutting bit from high-speed steel, tap hole to receive ¼-20 Allen setscrew for locking bit.

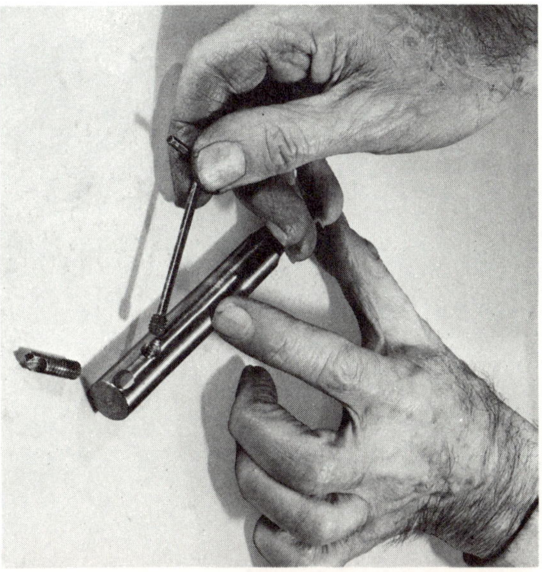

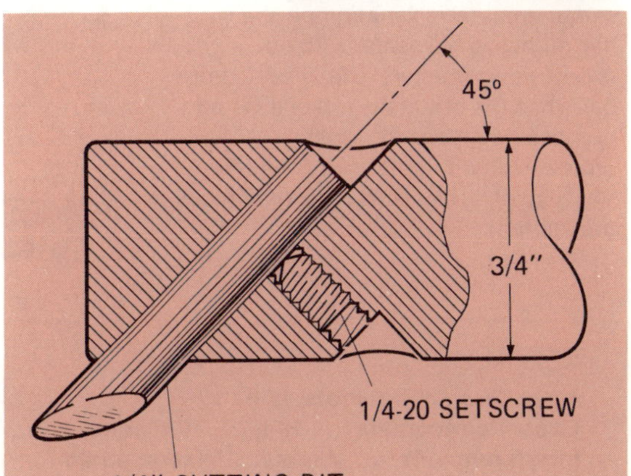

ginning of this moment can usually be felt and often heard. Feed slowly and carefully at this point, until the drill emerges completely and runs free. If bit jamming is a recurrent problem, clamp a piece of scrap material to the bottom of the workpiece for the drill to continue into, so that it will leave a clean-edged hole on the workpiece.

A scrap block can also be used to aid starting (top, right). When no finishing block is used, there are usually some irregular fragments (burrs) to trim away from the bottom of the hole.

Secure clamping of the workpiece is important in angled drilling, since bit pressure will tend to swing the workpiece downward. When using a progression of drills of several different sizes, start each drill carefully to prevent grabbing. Generous use of cutting oil is also helpful. And wearing a face shield or goggles for protection from flying chips is not just a good idea—it's a must.

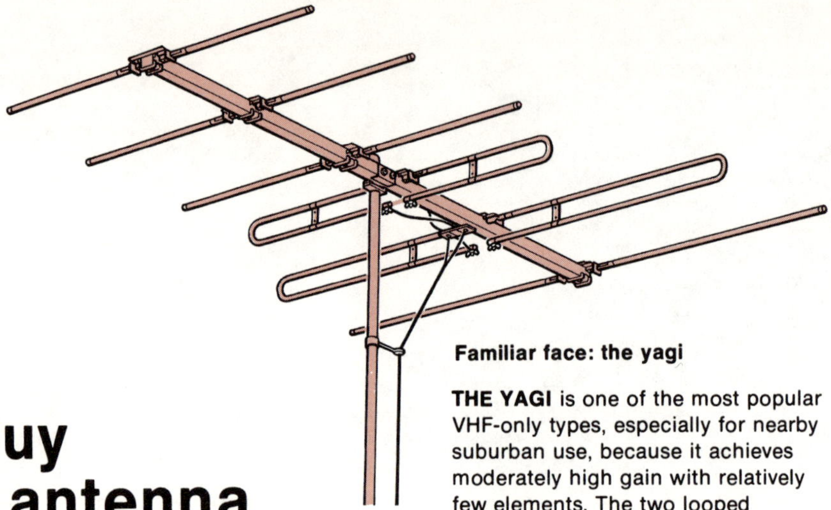

How to buy the right antenna

By LEN HILTS

Familiar face: the yagi

THE YAGI is one of the most popular VHF-only types, especially for nearby suburban use, because it achieves moderately high gain with relatively few elements. The two looped elements are active ones; others include three "directors" in front, one rear reflector, all to increase directivity. Single-channel VHF antennas are usually yagis, though most yagis cover whole VHF band.

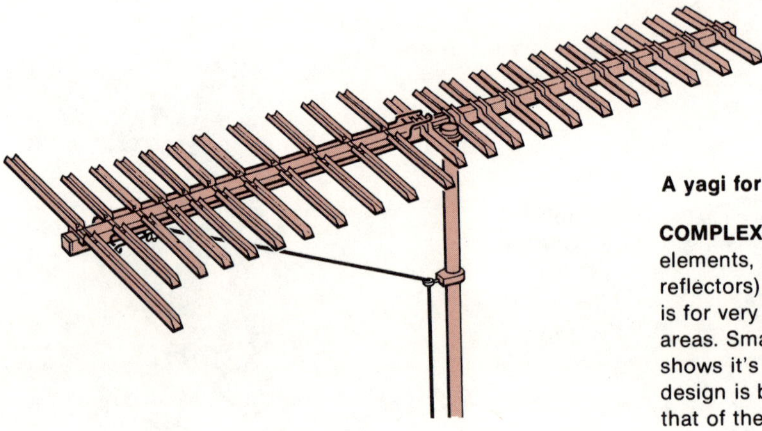

A yagi for UHF

COMPLEX DESIGN (10 active elements, 12 directors and reflectors) shows that this model is for very weak fringe signal areas. Small size of elements shows it's solely for UHF. But its design is basically the same as that of the VHF yagi above.

Swept yagi is all-active

DESIGNED for VHF and FM use in strong signal areas, this variation on the yagi has all active elements, with no reflectors or directors. That gives it more gain than the one at the top of this page, but less directionality; what directionality it has comes from the V-sweep of its elements (open end faces the station).

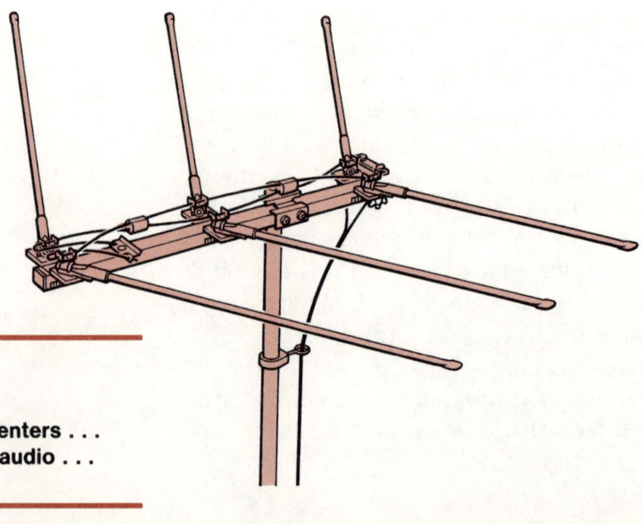

SEE ALSO

Amplifiers . . . Cabinets, hi-fi . . .
Cassette recorders . . . Hi-fi . . . Hi-fi centers . . .
Interference, tv . . . Masts . . . Mixers, audio . . .
Speakers . . . Television antennas

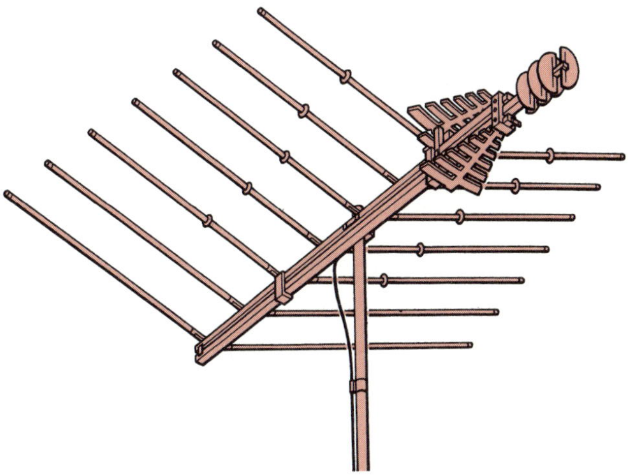

'Log-periodic' for all channels

CALLED "LOG-PERIODIC" because the spacing between its V-shaped active elements varies logarithmically, this model is actually two antennas in one: "Christmas-tree" cutouts at front form a second log-periodic section for UHF use; discs at front are UHF directors. A distant-cousin yagi, it uses many active elements, but no reflectors or directors. All-channel models usually require a "splitter" at the set (not shown) to direct signals to the set's VHF and UHF antenna terminals.

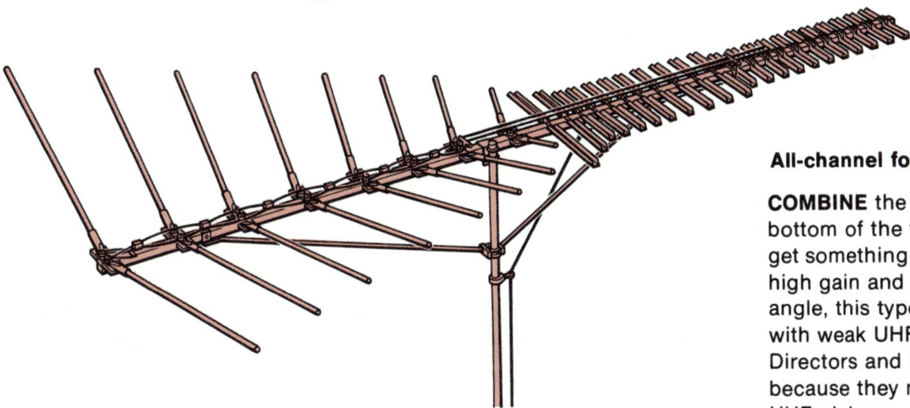

All-channel for weak signal areas

COMBINE the two antennas at bottom of the facing page, and you get something like this. Intended for high gain and a narrow reception angle, this type is used in areas with weak UHF and VHF signals. Directors and reflectors aren't used because they might interfere with UHF pickup.

■ TO GET THE BEST pictures on your TV set, you must have the right antenna for your reception area and it must be in good condition. If you are suffering from weak, fuzzy pictures, annoying ghosts, snow on the screen or poor color, the problem could be either in your TV set or in the antenna. Too often, people automatically assume that there is something wrong with the set and call the repair man. But it could be that a new antenna will revive the old set better than a dose of new transistors.

There are several reasons for this. First, rooftop antennas take a beating and actually wear out. They oxidize or become coated with grime, and parts are bent, twisted or misaligned. Second, if the antenna is very old, it was not designed for today's transmission and reception techniques. And third, the lead-in system may

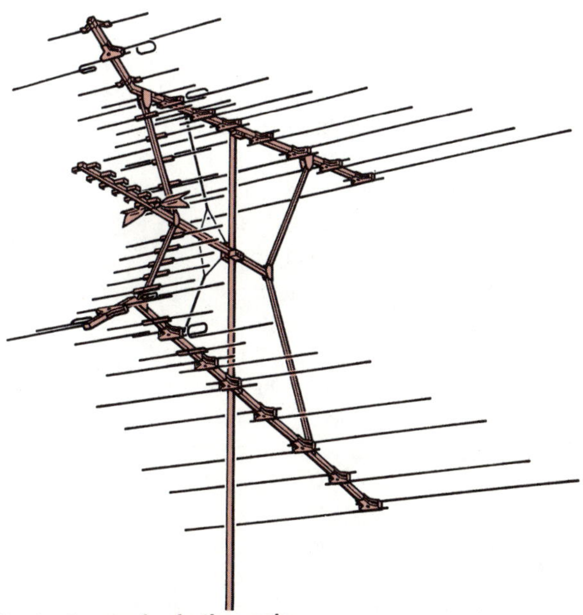

Stacked array for further gain

IN VERY WEAK signal areas, antennas can be stacked to increase gain. This setup came from the factory as a stacked array, but ordinary antennas can be stacked, too. Small UHF elements are mounted between the VHF sections.

have deteriorated badly, allowing moisture and interference to weaken the signal before it reaches your set.

If your antenna is relatively new and provided good reception when you bought it, check the lead-in cable for cracks and see that all the connections are tight before going to the expense of a new antenna. If you spot damage, install a new lead-in cable.

The most efficient lead-in system consists of 75-ohm shielded cable from the antenna to the set. This is much less subject to interference and deterioration than the flat 300-ohm cable. If your set has the 300-ohm lead-in and you replace it with 75-ohm, you will need to purchase two inexpensive matching transformers. One is installed at the antenna and the other at the back of your set, at each end of the 75-ohm cable. The signal from the antenna is stepped from 300 to 75 ohms by the transformer, travels down the cable at 75 ohms and, just before entering the set, is stepped back to 300 ohms.

selecting the antenna

If a new antenna is needed, be sure to select the right type. In the past, this has been difficult because of the variety of types available. Now the job is simplified.

The typical TV set needs three kinds of antennas: one for VHF reception (channels 2 through 13); one for UHF reception (channels 14 through 83); and one for FM reception.

You can buy three individual antennas, or a single combination antenna with elements for all three types of reception. In most reception areas the combination antenna is the best buy. Installation in simpler and total cost is lower.

Let's look at each type:

VHF antennas. These are swept-back yagi designs made to receive 88 to 108 MHz FM stereo and mono broadcasts all well as VHF channels 2 to 13. The boom lengths of these antennas range from 30 inches up to 160 inches, and the number of elements can go from 6 to as many as 34. The more elements, the longer the boom, and, generally speaking, the more elements, the greater the reception range.

Reception range is measured on flat terrain from the transmission tower of the station to your antenna. The smallest VHF antennas are good for reception 20 to 30 miles from the tower. The largest can range up to 185 miles.

UHF antennas. These antennas consist of much smaller yagi elements mounted straight rather than swept back. As with the VHF units, the more elements on the boom, the greater the reception range. In a typical antenna, an 80-inch boom with 25 elements might be rated at a 100-mile range on flat terrain. One with 16 elements on a 40-inch boom might have a 50-mile range.

You will see UHF antennas called "corner reflector" yagis. In this design, the boom is Vee shaped, with the open arms of the Vee pointed toward the transmission tower. Corner reflectors generally strengthen UHF reception. Most combination UHF-VHF antennas have corner reflectors built in.

FM antennas

If you own a hi-fi stereo FM system, a good rooftop FM antenna provides the strong, clean FM signal you need for good stereo channel separation, especially if you are a long distance from the FM station. The best FM antennas provide good reception up to 175 miles from the station. Other FM antennas are rated at 100, 50, and 30 miles. Buy an FM antenna according to your distance from stations you usually listen to.

Note that the sound accompanying TV programs is transmitted via FM, but the TV antenna itself is made to pick this up. You don't need a separate FM antenna for television reception.

Combined antennas. The most popular antennas today are a combination of VHF, UHF and FM units, mounted on one boom. These permit top reception on all channels, 2 through 83, and also provide strong FM reception. Note that only one lead-in cable is used for all three signals, so installation is simplified. The signal is divided by means of an inexpensive signal splitter just before it enters your TV set. Signal splitters usually are included with the antenna when you buy it.

Manufacturers specifications. Antenna manufacturers now generally label the product to indicate the range of reception for all elements. A typical label might indicate that VHF reception of an antenna is 120 miles, UHF reception is 90 miles, and FM reception is 90 miles. The most important thing to know when you head out to buy an antenna is how many miles you are from the stations you listen to most.

At one time, there were few UHF stations and most antennas received only VHF. But in recent years, more and more UHF channels have gone on the air, and many more will go on stream in the future. Thus, if you have no UHF channels now, or only a few of them, it still makes sense to mount an antenna that can receive them, since there is so much room for growth in this area.

special problems

Up to this point, we have been talking about reception over flat terrain and within easy range of station transmitters. There are other considerations for TV viewers located a long distance from stations, in hilly country, or in places where the signal can bounce off buildings and other obstructions.

TV sets located more than 60 miles from transmitting stations generally are said to be in the "fringe" area. The fringe area can be defined as that area where reception begins to degrade when a standard antenna is used. The fringe area varies, of course, according to the power output of the station and the type of terrain. In some places, the fringe area begins as far as 100 miles or more from the station.

Your own experience and that of your neighbors can tell you what to expect in the way of reception, and whether or not you are in a fringe area. Before buying a new antenna, find out how other people are receiving the channels you want, and what sizes of antennas are getting the best reception. If the biggest standard antennas are getting less than the best reception, you are in a true fringe area.

There are two solutions to reception in a fringe area. One is to install a "stacked array" antenna. A stacked array is nothing more than two or more antennas mounted together to increase the gain of the TV signal. You can buy ready-made stacked arrays from radio supply houses, or you can mount several standard antennas and bring the signal through lead-in cable from one to the next to the TV set.

An easier and often more effective solution is a signal booster or preamplifier, a small black box that amplifies everything the antenna feeds it. A booster provides an excellent signal where a single antenna of maximum efficiency doesn't give a good picture. It amplifies both the signal and interference, however, which may be a problem. Boosters can be mounted on the antenna or in the attic, half way between the antenna and the TV set. Antenna-mounted boosters have the advantage of not amplifying any interference picked up by the lead-in cable.

operating several TV sets

A booster is of particular value if you operate several TV sets from the same antenna. In most areas, the TV signal is strong enough to drive two or three TV sets without picture loss. However, in fringe areas, even the operation of a second set on one antenna may degrade the picture noticeably. If you have more than two sets in a strong signal area, or more than one set in a weak signal area, consider the use of a booster to improve your pictures.

Direction problems. You are lucky if all of your TV stations are located in one direction from your home. You can point your antenna at them and get good reception from all. Most antennas receive through a 60-degree arc. That is, if you pointed your antenna straight north, it would provide strong reception from any station located within 30 degrees to the left or right of its line of aim. Other stations would either be weak, snowy or not visible at all.

The best solution to this problem is an antenna rotor mounted on the roof to turn the antenna toward the station you want to receive. You dial the compass setting you want on a small box usually placed on top of the TV set. The antenna swings to that setting, assuring you of the best reception for stations in that direction. The rotor is great if you are located between cities because it allows you to bring in programs from both cities.

Ghosts. Ghosts in a TV picture are caused by a signal reflected off of a building or other object that arrives at your set a fraction of a second after the direct signal arrives. Ghosts are a problem in cities with tall buildings, mountainous areas and places with any kind of tall obstruction. Ghost problems can't be solved by a new antenna.

In some cases you can cut down on ghosts by aiming the antenna directly at the station transmitter, so an antenna rotor may be of help. But each ghost problem is different and must be solved by trial and error.

indoor antennas

The antennas built into modern sets give good reception in close-in areas, sometimes better reception than an outdoor antenna. The main problem with them is that you may have to change the position of the antenna elements for each station. You can buy indoor antenna units with tuning controls and built-in boosters. These may be better than the built-in rabbit ears but their rabbit-ear elements still have to be aimed for each station.

Videotape recorders. Many people do not realize that a videotape recorder records directly from the antenna, and not from the TV set sitting next to it. This means that the picture you record is only as good as the signal brought down from the antenna. So if you have a VTR, or plan on buying one, a good antenna becomes doubly important.

How to put up TV antennas

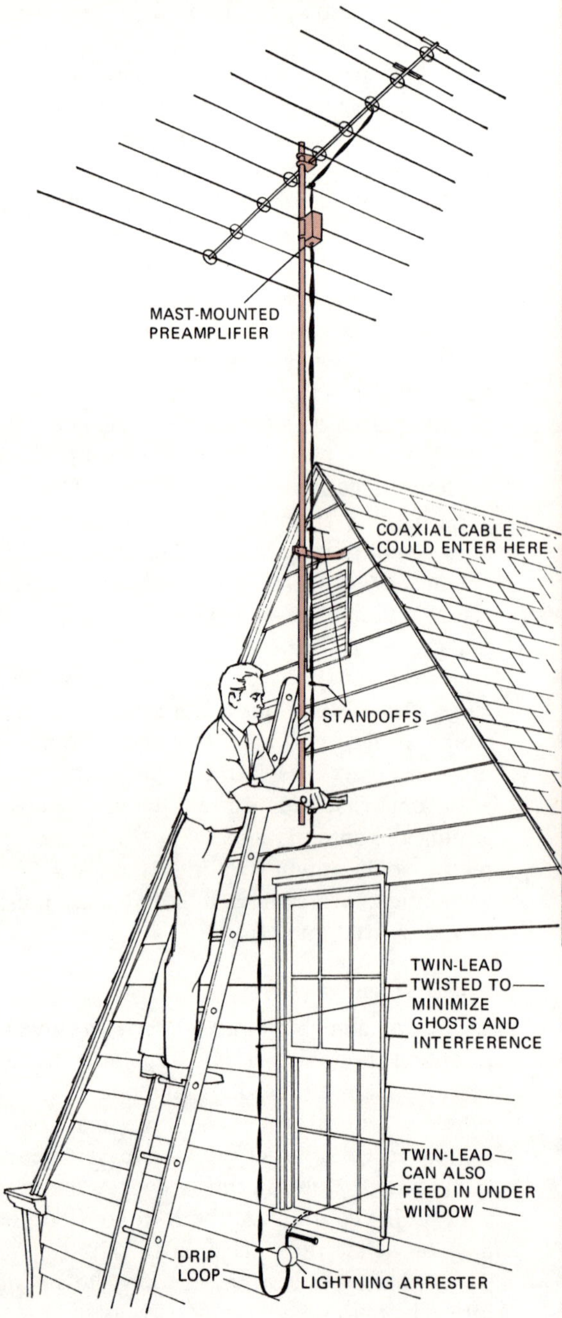

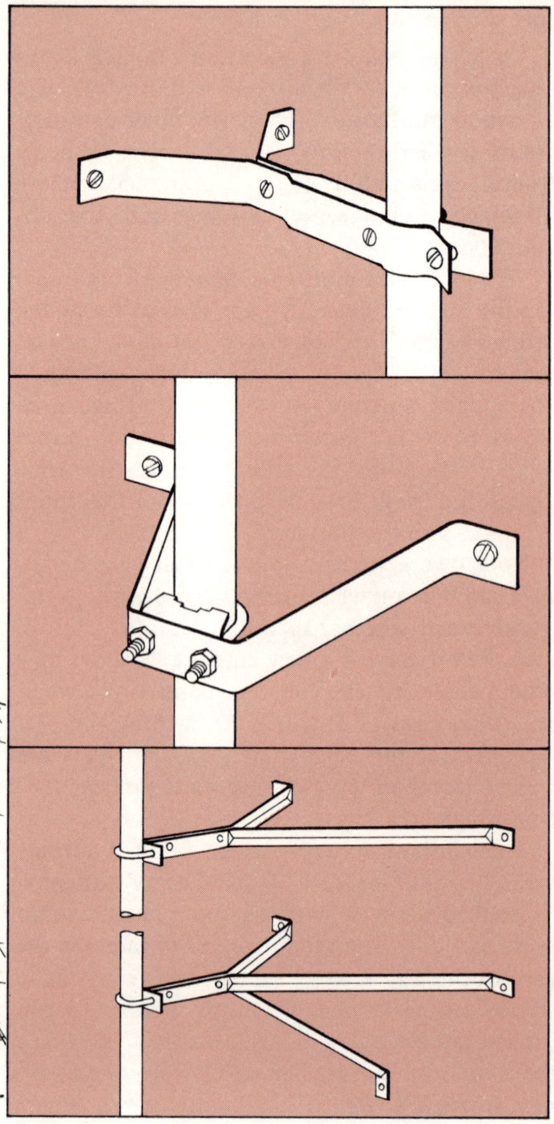

Gable mount must clear eaves

Techniques start with the right mount. Above: three types of wall mount; pick a pair deep enough to clear your eaves' overhang. Mount them at least 2 ft. apart for masts up to 10 ft.; for 15-ft. mast height, use three brackets, 2 ft. apart, and a 20-ft. mast. Coaxial cable is the best lead-in, unless you have very weak signals and no ghosts or interference; if you use flat twin-lead (it's cheaper), twist it once per foot to reduce ghost and noise pickup. Keep twin-lead well away from metal, or from surfaces which may get wet.

SEE ALSO

**Citizens band radio . . . Hi-fi . . .
Interference, TV . . . Masts . . . Storage ideas . . .
Television antennas**

Chimney mounts avoid roof-walking

Chimney mount is popular and easy, if the chimney's at least 3 feet high, made of real brick, and in good condition. Check for loose bricks and chipped mortar. Use sturdy mounts, with heavy-duty, rustproof hardware and brackets, stainless-steel straps. Smoke corrodes, so if chimney is active, use color-anodized steel masts, 75-ohm antenna with screw-plug coaxial connections. Straps should be near top and bottom of chimney, 2½ to 4 ft, apart—the farther, the sturdier. Line up straps with brick rows to level them, attach mast brackets loosely before raising antenna to roof, align antenna mast with a level before tightening straps. No chimney? Use vent-pipe mount.

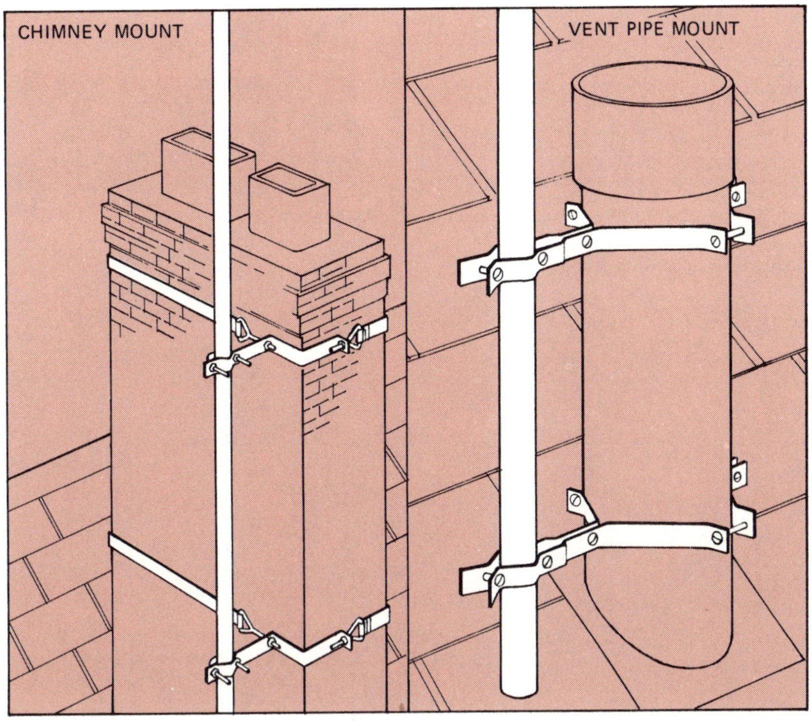

Tripods are the most rigid roof mounts

Tripod mounts, unlike other roof mounts, need no guy wires for masts up to 5 ft. high; for taller masts requiring guys, base mounts (next page) are easier to install, cheaper. Eave-mounting tripod (below, left) has swivel mast support, so mast can be attached, swung into place, then fixed. Tower type (below, right) adjusts for flat or peaked roofs. All roof (and wall) mounts should be attached to beams or masonry—never into unsupported roofing or siding, or into mortar between bricks. To locate beams, tap with hammer, drive test nails where your roof feels most solid.

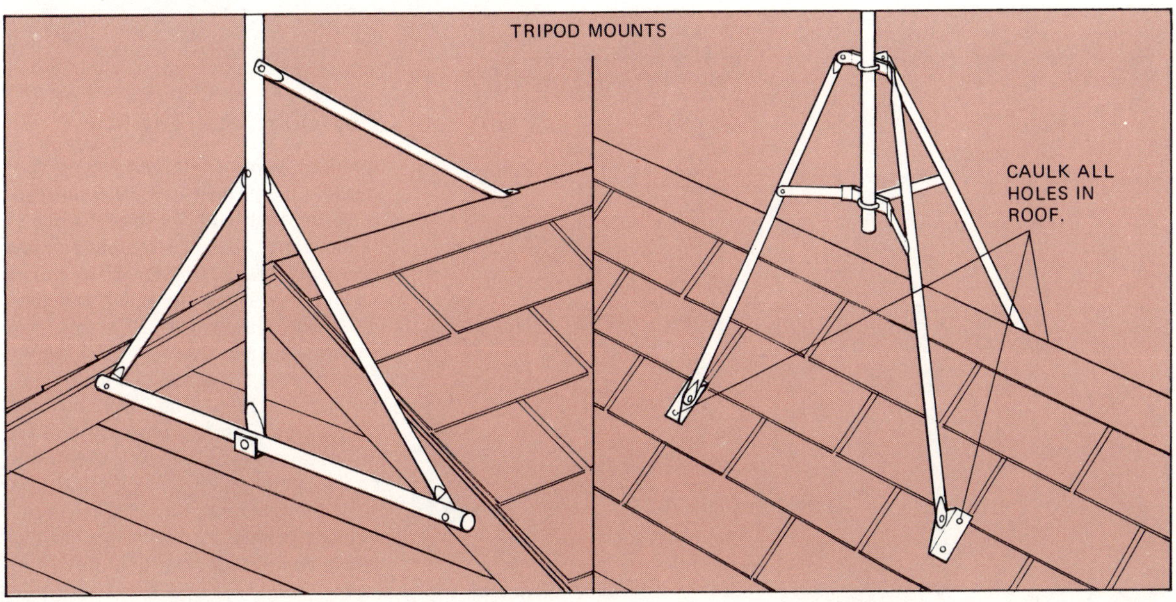

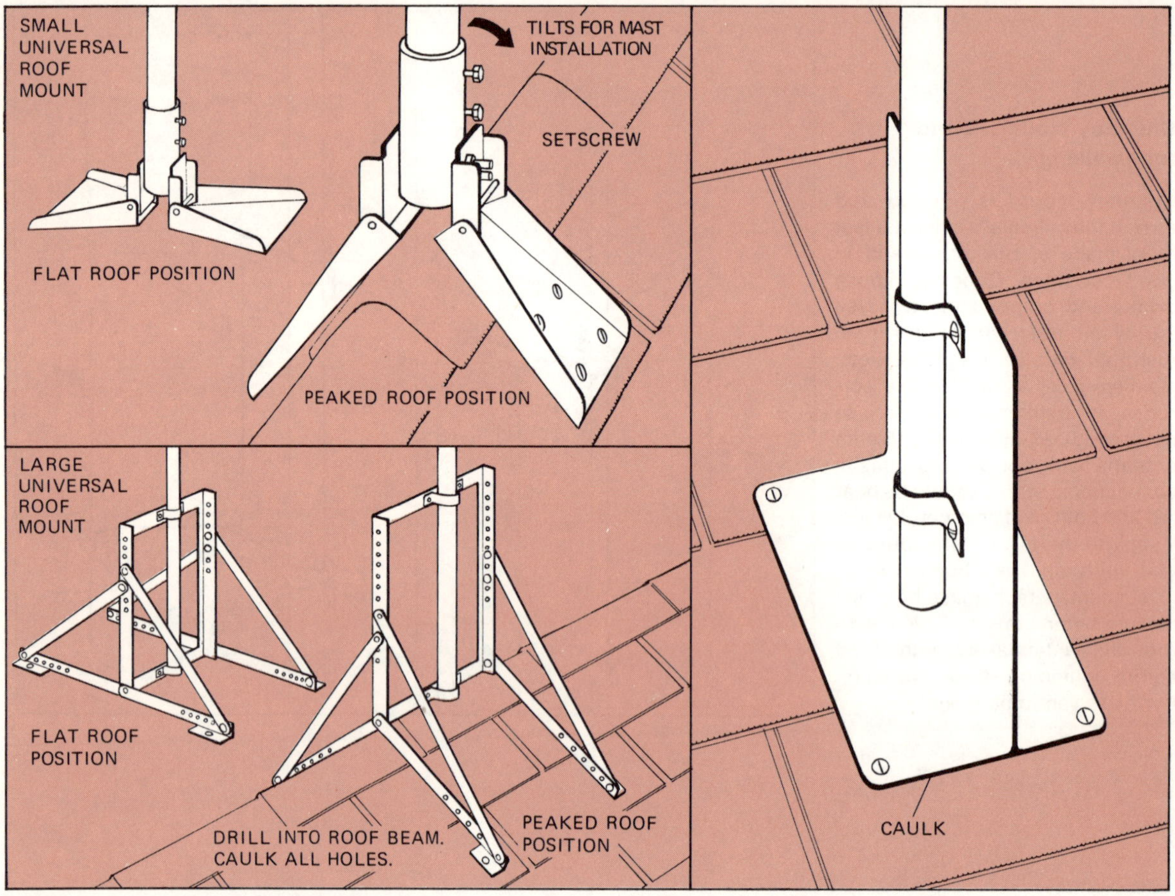

Three more types of roof mount

Saddle-type mounts for roof peaks usually adjust to fit steep or shallow roof pitches, flat roofs as well. Smaller type (top, left) tilts along roof ridge for easier mast installation; a lock screw holds it upright while you install the guy wires. Larger style (above, left) adjusts to peaks or flat roofs as shown, or to sloping roofs, can be used without guy wires if mast is short. T-girder roof mount (above, right) fits flat or sloping roofs, always needs guys. To avoid leaks, never let mast stub touch roof, and caulk with asbestos roof cement in all screw holes, under the feet of roof mounts, and under and over screwheads. Again, make certain that all screws go into beams and not into unsupported roofing, so that high winds won't peel roof when they pull at antenna.

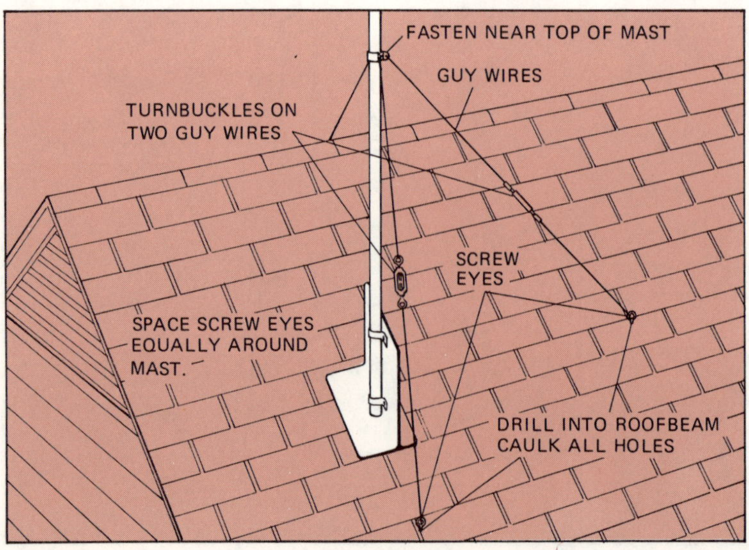

Guy wires: when and how

Use guy wires for all base-type roof mounts, masts over 10 ft. tall (one set of guys for each 10 ft. of mast), areas of heavy winds, snow, ice. Space screw eyes equally around mast, as far out as possible (ideal angle is 60° between mast and wires). On tall masts, use separate eyes for each guy, if possible. Anchor eyes in beams, caulk all holes. Don't guy to trees—they may bend and snap wires. Replace wires which kink during installation—kinks cause weak spots. Install one eye in direction prevailing wind comes from. Tighten turnbuckles evenly, so mast doesn't bow. Leave some slack; overtight guys may snap.

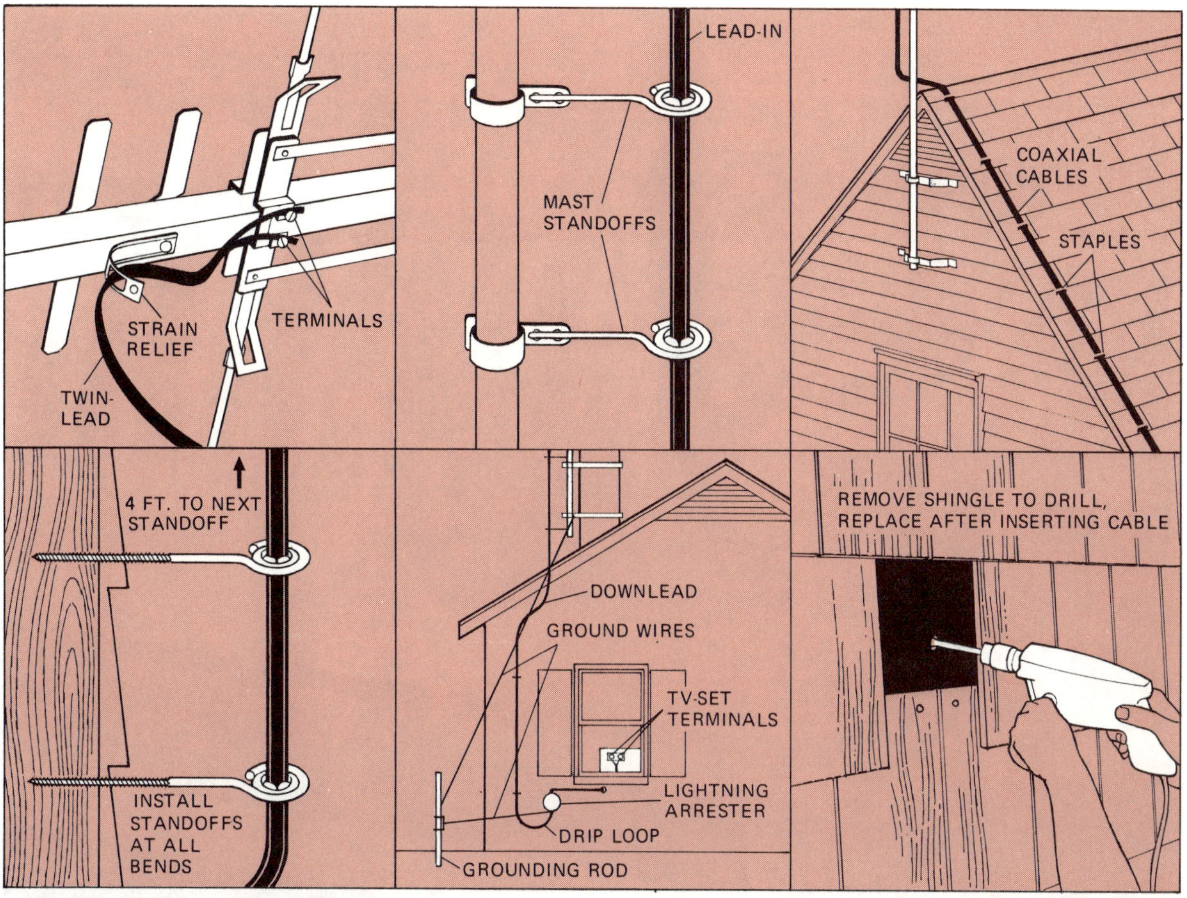

Wire it right for a better picture

Downlead should be wired to antenna and secured by a strain relief before antenna is raised. Flat twin-lead must be routed away from mast and building side with standoffs (leave enough slack between standoffs to allow for cold-weather contraction, wind, but not enough to let lead flap), and requires a lightning arrester where downlead enters house. Coaxial cables can be taped to mast, stapled to house (but be sure staples don't crush inner shield). Masts, lightning arresters, shield of coax must be grounded for safety. To keep wire entrance from leaking, form drip loop below it, drill hole slightly upwards. Holes around a coaxial cable can be caulked, but waterproofing of twin-lead entrances requires special feedthrough hardware. To conceal and waterproof a hole in a shingle house, remove one shingle, drill the hole, then replace the shingle.

MORE TIPS:

☐ To aim antenna: (a) Use a compass and a pilot's map which shows antenna tower sites; (b) have someone watch set and report to you by walkie-talkie or "people chain" (easier if set is near a window); (c) put your set in the yard, where you can see it from your roof (but make sure set is grounded); (d) Take a battery-powered portable set (preferably color) to roof with you.
☐ If putting antenna on a rotor, leave enough slack in leads at the top for rotor to turn without breaking the downlead.
☐ Coaxial cable and quality twin-lead can last 10 years; cheap twin-lead can go in 2.
☐ Coaxial cable can be led from attic or basement via heating or airconditioning ducts—handy if set is on an inside wall.
☐ For inconspicuous entry, bring leads into house at baseboard level, in a closet, or just below a window.
☐ If you must staple twin-lead indoors, drive staples parallel to conductors, as closely centered between them as possible.
☐ Leave slack where the downlead meets the set, so you can move the set for cleaning, or repair. The slack in coaxial cable can be coiled—but twin-lead should never be coiled, just left slack.

Build a handsome pine and maple bench

The original of this antique bench stood in the waiting room of Abraham Lincoln's law office. You can make this beautiful reproduction

By DAVID WARREN

SEE ALSO

Bars . . . Bridge tables . . . Butcher block furniture . . . Chests . . . Cupboards, china . . . Dining tables . . . Dry sinks . . . Finishes, wood . . . Hutch tables . . . Lowboys . . . Painting, furniture . . . Servers . . . Staining, wood . . . Wood finishes

■ BY THE EARLY 1840s, Abraham Lincoln had become a successful Springfield, Ill., attorney. His practice had grown rapidly, in recognition of his abilities in law, his quick grasp of argument, his sincerity and his lucidity of speech. Lincoln also possessed another attribute—he had a genuine appreciation of good design in furniture.

The bench he chose for the waiting area of his law office is a real beauty. It is constructed of pine and maple and is 19 inches wide by 78 inches long. We used the same woods to build the reproduction. Design features include a plank seat, Windsor arrow back and trestle leg assembly.

Before you begin construction, make several construction aids to assure accurate cuts and tight-fitting joints.

First, make a full-scale drawing of an end view, showing leg- and back-support angles and the spacing of the arm stays. Then make a full-scale drawing of the front and back of the seat ends. Next, draw a bottom view of the settee from the end to the center, showing legs, stretchers and angles. Save time by drawing only half, since the remaining half is a mirror image and locations and angles are merely flopped during construction. Finally, draw a full-scale top view of the same half, showing back-support and arm-rest locations and angles, and the spacing of arrow-back pieces.

Templates are also necessary for the Lincoln settee. On heavy cardboard, draw one for scooping out the seat area. Draw one of a back leg and one of a front leg. Also, make a template for the front and back corners of the seat. Then cut out the shapes using a utility knife.

Use the full-scale drawings as an aid to make sight guides that let you line up holes to be bored at proper angles. You will need a sight guide for each rear leg and for each front leg. Note that the borings for the corner legs are at compound angles. Cut the guides from 2 x 4 scrap, six inches long.

begin construction

Using the drawings, lay out and turn the arrow-shaped arm and back stays. Then plane the flat areas as required while the workpiece is held rigid in the lathe.

bending the stays

Make the bending jig as shown in the photo. It will bend two stays at a time. Soak them for four hours. Then place them in the jig and clamp

REPRODUCTION (top), is a ringer for the original (below, right) minus years of wear by clients who visited Lincoln's law office. Coves on legs (below) have been carefully duplicated.

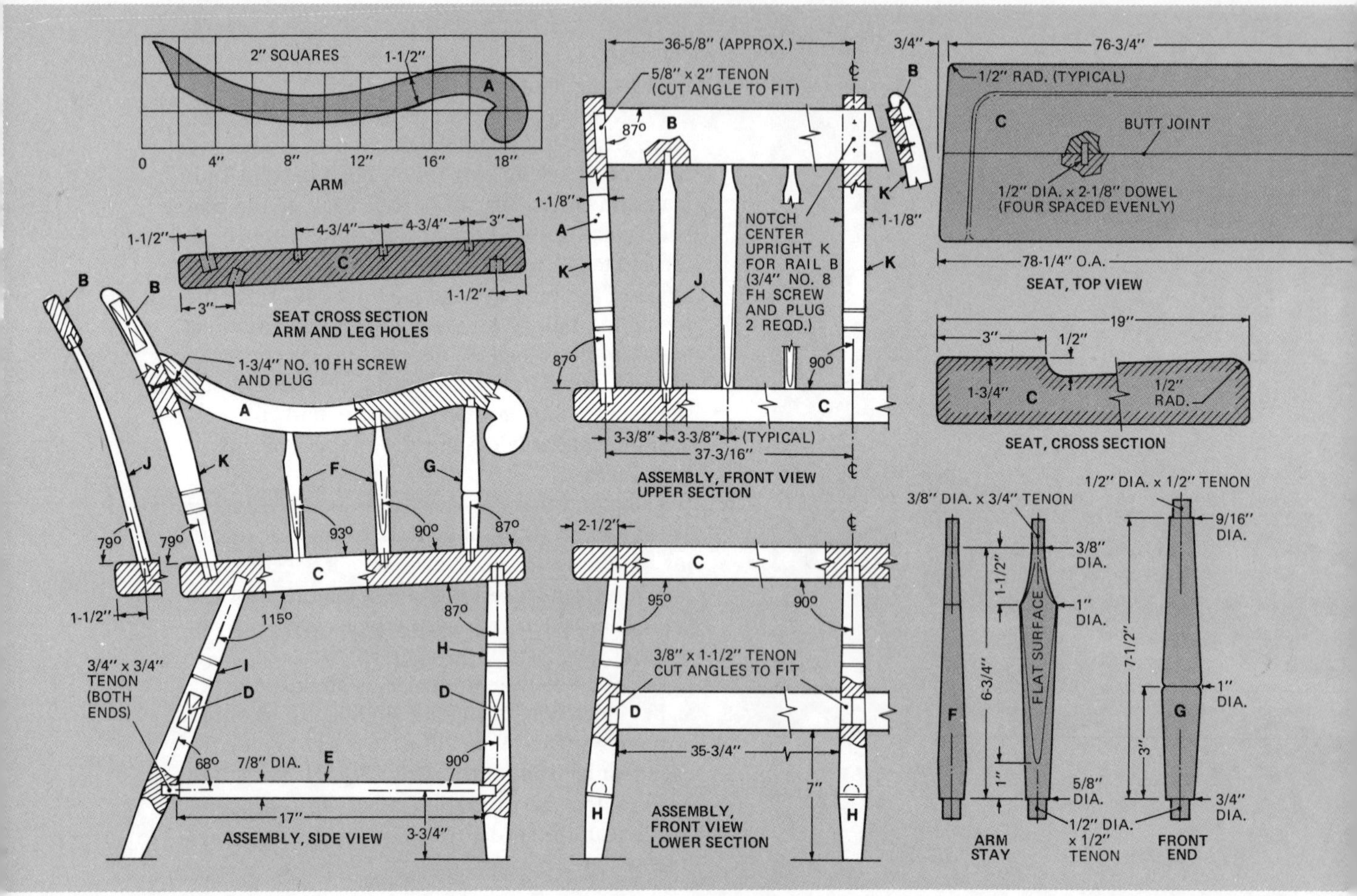

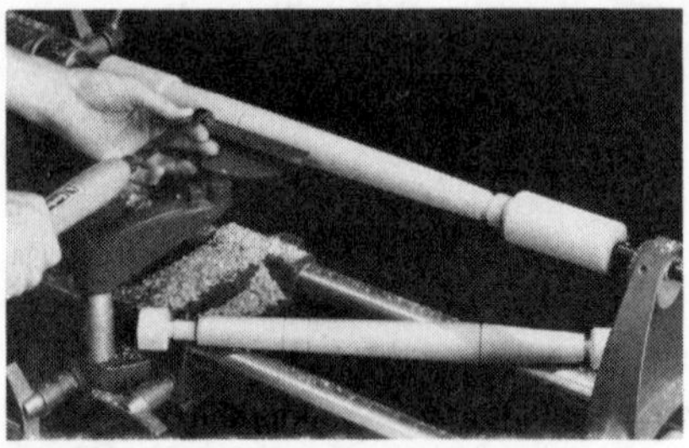

ROUGH SQUARE stock to round for arm stays with gouge. Use skew to turn to final diameters.

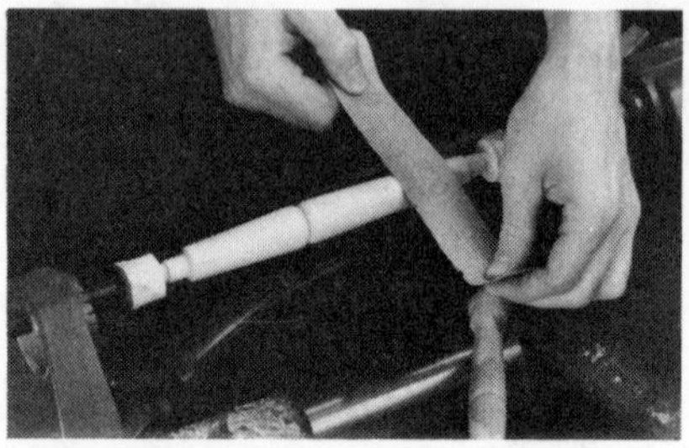

AFTER STAY has been turned and coves cut, sand smooth while workpiece turns in lathe.

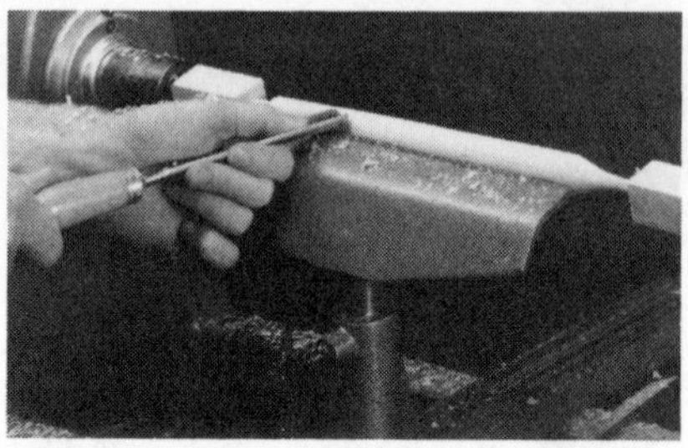

TURN 20 arrow-shaped back stays using template to check contour and to assure uniformity.

BEFORE YOU remove stay from lathe, plane two flats on opposite sides of workpiece as indicated in the plans.

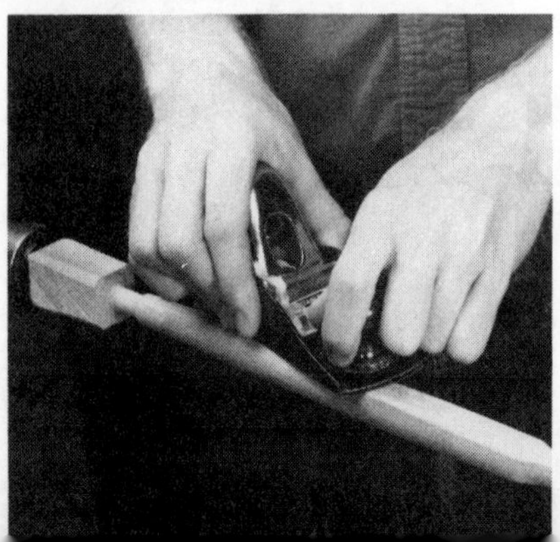

USE A SHOP-MADE jig constructed like one shown below to bend and clamp each water-soaked back stay until dry.

Jig should bend the curve slightly tighter than contour of back to allow for spring-back upon release from the jig.

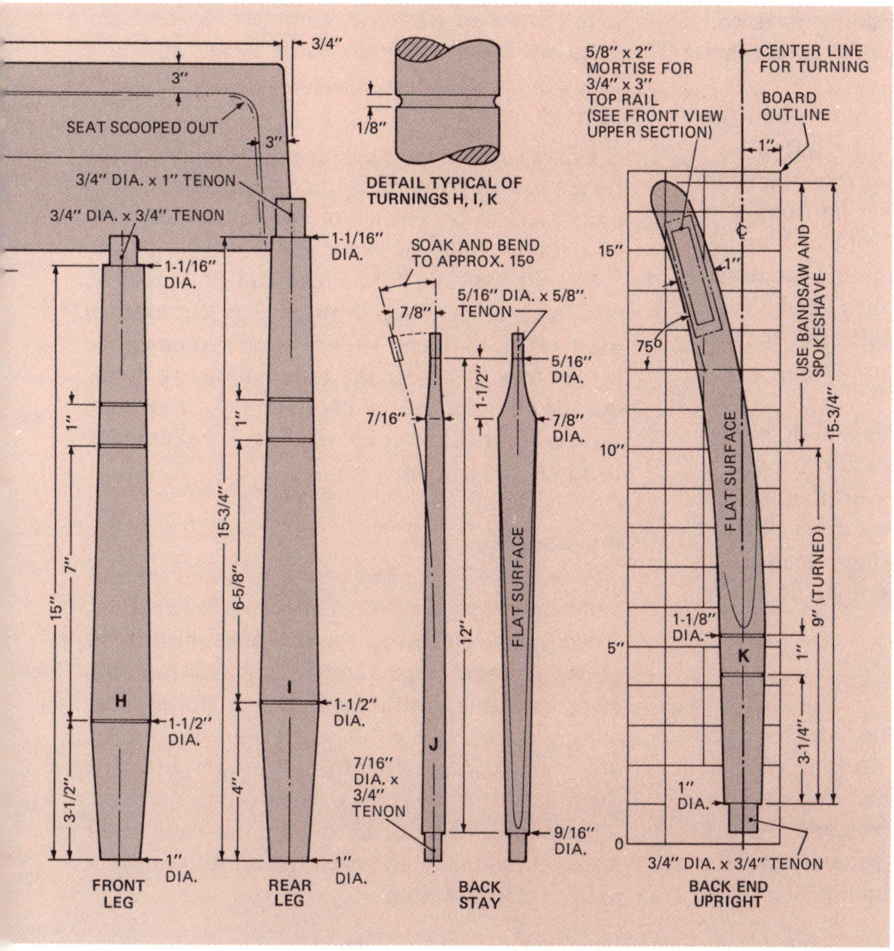

MATERIALS LIST—LINCOLN BENCH

Key	Pcs.	Size and description (use)
A	2	1⅛ x 6 x 18" maple (armrest) cut to shape
B	1	¾ x 3 x 73¼" pine (top rail)
C	1	1¾ x 19 x 78¼" pine (seat) glue-up from two boards
D	4	¾ x 2 x 36½" pine (bottom rail)
E	3	⅞"-dia. x 17" maple (rung)*
F	4	1"-dia. x 8" maple (arm stay)*
G	2	1"-dia. x 8½" maple (front end stay)*
H	3	1½"-dia. x 15¾" maple (front leg)*
I	3	1½"-dia. x 16¾" maple (rear leg)*
J	20	⅞"-dia. x 13⅜" maple (back stays)*
K	3	1½ x 3½ x 17" maple (back posts) cut to shape

Misc.: Plastic resin glue, paper for patterns, cardboard for templates, 2 No. 10 x 1¾" fh brass screws, 2 No. 8 x ¾" fh brass screws, wood plugs cut to suit, Minwax Ipswich stain, orange shellac, Carnuba wax.

*These are final dimensions Allow enough extra stock to facilitate turning.

pine and maple bench, continued

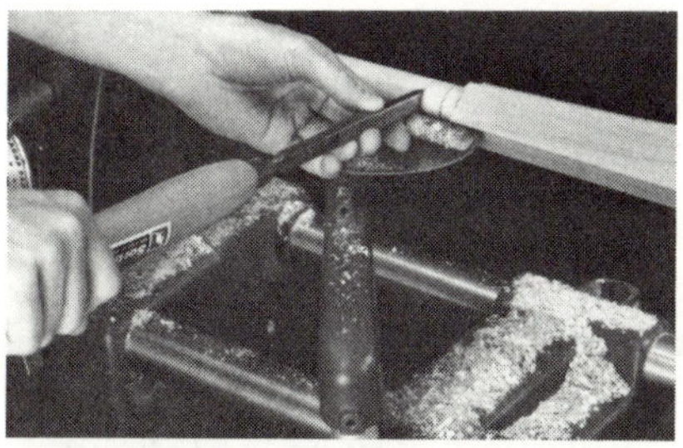

THREE BACK posts (K) are offset-turned. Then saw them to shape and use a spokeshave to round them off. Turning should be done at slow speed because of out-of-balance configuration.

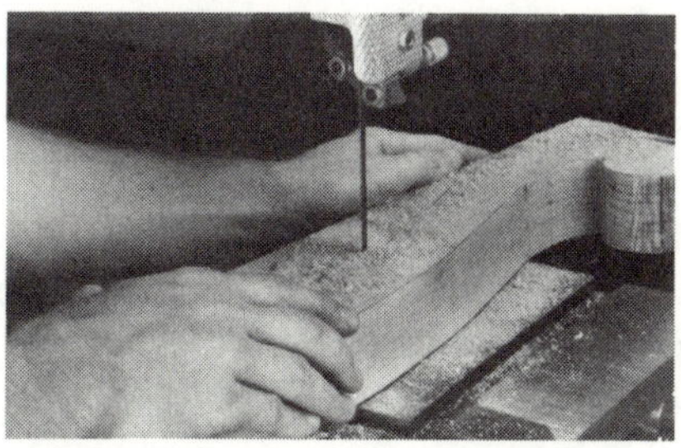

DRAW FULL-SCALE pattern for armrest, and trace onto board. Cut out shape with bandsaw, using a finetooth blade to shorten sanding time. Guard is raised for photo clarity only.

PLANK SEAT may be glue-and-dowel joined from several boards. Alternate direction of annual rings to prevent warping. Alternate bar clamps on both sides to prevent cutting.

YOU SHOULD use a piece of 2 x 4 with end cut to the proper compound angle as a sight guide for boring holes at the rear corners of the seat.

SINCE THE floor of a shop is rarely flat and level over a 4 x 8-ft. area, it's a good idea to shim a full sheet of plywood level with a long spirit level. This will provide a surface on which you can mark final length of the legs in order to prevent a wobbly bench.

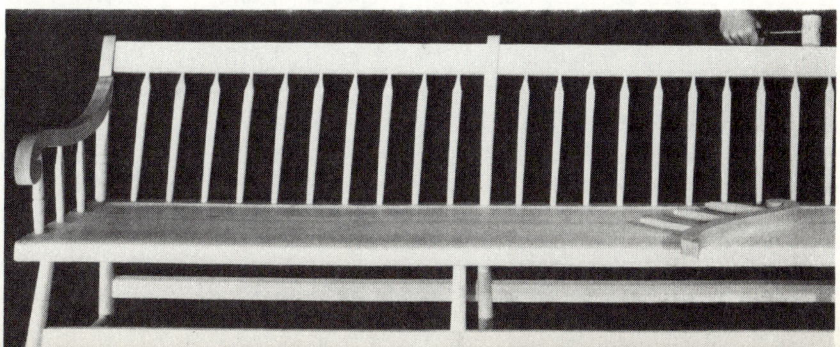

overnight, or until dry. Since bending stays will take at least 10 days, continue working on other parts in the meantime.

Turn the three back posts (K) next. Run the lathe at slow speed because of their out-of-balance shapes. Use the bandsaw and spokeshave to shape parts after turning the lower portions.

Using the full-scale drawing, proceed to lay out the two arms (A) and cut out on a bandsaw. Save the cutout waste pieces so they can be used to support the armpieces while boring the required holes later. Smooth the arms using a fine wood rasp.

We joined two boards with glue and dowels to make the seat (C). Each piece should be ripped ⅛ in. wider than necessary to allow for planing and joining. Plane the edges to allow a sliver of light to show at the center. When they have been glued and clamped, this will assure a tight fit at the ends.

shaping the seat

After the planks have been joined, cut the ends of the seat to conform to your drawing. Round the corners and scoop out the seat, using a 1-in. gouge and block plane. Test frequently with a cardboard template and use 80-grit sandpaper for the initial sanding. Finish the sanding step with 120-grit paper.

On the bottom of the seat, lay out the locations of the legs (H and I). Use the appropriate sight gauges to bore holes. Next, cut the rails (D). When you cut the tenons, pay particular heed to angles at the tenon shoulders to be sure you have a tight fit.

Mortises in legs can be cut with mortising attachment on your drill press, or by grouping bored holes to mortise dimensions and chiseling out the waste. Also bore the holes in the legs for the rungs (E). Trim the tenons to fit the mortises.

build bench from bottom up

To assemble the seat and legs, prepare plastic resin glue and glue legs to seat, rungs to legs, and rails to legs. Clamp to hold all parts in position and to square rails to rungs. Allow the completed assembly to stand for 24 hours before continuing. Then cut the leg bottoms at the proper angle and length.

With the bottom half assembled, proceed with parts for top half. Start by propping arm with cut-off pieces and make bores. A light pencil line on the side of the arm will help you to align the bit with the required angle.

Rest the assembled lower half of the bench on a full sheet of plywood, shimmed, leveled and fixed on the shop floor. Then locate and bore holes in the seat top, using a portable drill and sight gauge.

Cut away excess stock from the ends of the three posts (K). Finish shaping with a spokeshave and wood rasp. Then, sand with 100-grit, 150- and, finally, 180-grit paper.

Cut the top rail (B) to length and cut tenons on both ends as per shop drawing. Lay out and cut mortises on both end back posts. Then notch the center post to accept the rail. Follow by laying out the 20 holes for the back stays (J). The holes should allow the pieces to slip in and out easily to facilitate the assembly process later.

dry assembly

Next, round the arms with a rasp and scraper, and sand when the proper contours are reached.

You are now ready for dry assembly of the arms and back. Expect some filing and trial-and-error matching until a good fit is achieved in all mating pieces. While the bench is dry-assembled, hold each end post tightly to the arm and bore the holes for brass screws. Then counterbore, insert screws and tighten, drawing the arms to the posts. Do the same to fasten the centerpost to the top rail. Disassemble.

prepare for final assembly

Have a bucket of warm water and a cloth handy to wipe away excess glue. Begin by fitting and gluing the back posts and stays to the seat, then to the top rail. Secure with a band clamp. Glue and assemble the arms and their stays (F and G). Cover all screw heads with wood plugs cut to match.

finishing the bench

Allow the assembled unit to stand for 24 hours. Then, using the 180-grit sandpaper, sand all surfaces and break (round slightly) all sharp corners. Prepare all surfaces for staining by wiping with a tack rag.

We used Minwax Ipswich stain. Allow the first coat to stand undisturbed overnight before applying the second coat. Again, allow overnight drying. Then apply a coat of orange shellac. After four hours, rub all surfaces with No. 0000 steel wool and wipe down with a tack rag before applying a second shellac coat. Allow this coat to dry completely overnight.

Finally, rub gently with No. 0000 steel wool and wipe down with tack rag. Polish with a clean soft cloth and Carnauba wax.

New finish 'blooms'

After I refinished a chest of drawers with a stain, an undercoat of sealer and a top coat of brushing lacquer, the lacquer turned grayish-white. I removed the finish, did the job over and again discovered this grayish color. The materials I used were all new, right off the store shelves. Did I do something wrong?—D.T., Ga.

I suspect you did do something wrong—such as refinishing the chest in your basement where it was nice and cool and the humidity was very high. Or, you may have taken the chest outside and completed the refinishing in the shade when the humidity was also very high. Under these conditions, new finishings sometimes turn grayish-white. This is known as "blooming" and, although not common, it may happen under these conditions, especially with shellac and lacquer.

In your case there is no practical corrective measure except to start all over again. Make sure you get *all* the old finish, right down to the bare wood. Sand the surfaces and begin—and finish—the job in a well-ventilated room or do it outside when the humidity is low and natural drying conditions are at their very best.

Sow, yes; trap, no!

When I sow grass seed to patch my lawn, small, sparrow-size birds pick it up as fast as I can sow it. Evidently they are migratory as they only come in the spring and fall. Even though I cover the seed lightly they scratch it up. Do you have plans for a suitable trap that will enable me to get rid of the pests or thin them out a little?—P.R., Iowa.

This department does not supply plans. Besides, trapping birds is illegal in nearly all states. You might check with your state's department of conservation but I doubt if it would issue you a permit to trap what you describe as migratory birds. Actually, the birds never get *all* the seed in any given area and really do less harm than it may seem. However, a light covering of straw or grass clippings over the newly sown areas will cut seed consumption to a minimum.

Musty odor in chest

I have a fairly old chest with lid which is painted. Paint is still good but the interior has a musty odor. How can I "sweeten" it?—A.R. Parks, Boston.

Washing it with a mild to medium detergent solution, and drying it in the sun for several hours usually will do it. When it's thoroughly dry treat the interior with several fine coats of a spray lacquer.

Removing moss from brick wall

Moss is appearing on the brick walls of my home in several shaded areas. How can I remove it?—Edward Lassiter, Charleston, S.C.

Try to eliminate the condition that encourages growth of this objectionable plant, perhaps by removing or pruning shrubbery to let air circulate more freely and sunlight penetrate to the wall.

You can usually remove the existing moss by a vigorous scrubbing, first with a wire brush and then with a stiff-bristle scrubbing brush dipped in full-strength laundry bleach. Then hose the wall to remove all residues of the bleach. Wear rubber gloves when applying the bleach; also protect your eyes from spatters.

Spreading lawn 'weed'

A patch of what appears to be a new "weed" is spreading in my lawn. No one seems to know what it is and I seem to be the only victim. The leaves are shorter than lawn grasses and light green in color. The stuff pulls up easily, but eliminates the lawn grass where it's growing. What is it and what will kill it?—Bert Phillips, Bloomington, Ind.

Without a sample, I'll guess it's a variety of "creeping bent" grass. To kill it, cover it with a sheet of opaque or translucent plastic, or just pull it up, taking care to get all the root systems. Then spade the soil, rake out all remaining debris, add peat moss and a little sand, and reseed with a lawn grass. Keep the seeding well watered, but not too wet, until growth is well along into the season.

"Footprints" in the rug

My wall-to-wall wool carpeting is several years old and when I move the furniture about, the imprints of the furniture legs are unsightly. Is there a way, short of taking up the carpeting and dry-cleaning, to make these impressions less noticeable?—M.E., Colo.

Buy a small suede-shoe brush—the kind with stiff brass bristles. Scrub the impressions lightly in several directions with the brush and then in short strokes at right angles. Brushing too hard can damage the nap. Usually this treatment works; but if not, work the depressed nap with an upholstery shampoo, using the applicator made for the purpose. Follow the instructions on the container. After the area is partly dried, work it over with the suede brush, making light strokes at right angles. Or, if cost is not a factor, have the rug cleaned on the floor by a professional with special equipment.

by W. Clyde Lammey

Fast fixes for small appliances

■ LABOR COSTS being what they are, it is often impractical to have small, kitchen appliances repaired by a professional. It's a different story if you can do it yourself, because you can usually replace defective parts for a few dollars. The important thing is to know what you're doing, so you don't waste time or further damage the appliance.

Safety note: If you decide to attempt the repair of one of your appliances, keep in mind that the power cord should be unplugged from the power outlet while the unit is disassembled and while making tests with the ohmmeter.

SEE ALSO
Appliances . . . Coffee percolators . . . Food mixers . . . Food processors . . . Irons . . . Kitchens . . . Ranges . . . Toasters . . . Vacuum cleaners

The two types of kitchen appliances that you will be dealing with are those that heat and those that don't. The former predominate, and include toasters, toaster ovens and fry pans.

Appliances that heat have two of three major components in common—a power cord (either the attached or the detachable kind) and a heating element. They may or may not have the third common component, a thermostat. When an appliance doesn't get hot, barely gets warm or overheats, the trouble is usually with one of these three components. Before examining the components, however, check for loose connections or a defective outlet or plug.

TO TEST or replace a power cord, disassemble the appliance to get at the terminals (shown by arrows).

IF OHMMETER reads infinity (∞) with leads connected one way and 0 when the opposite way, cord is okay.

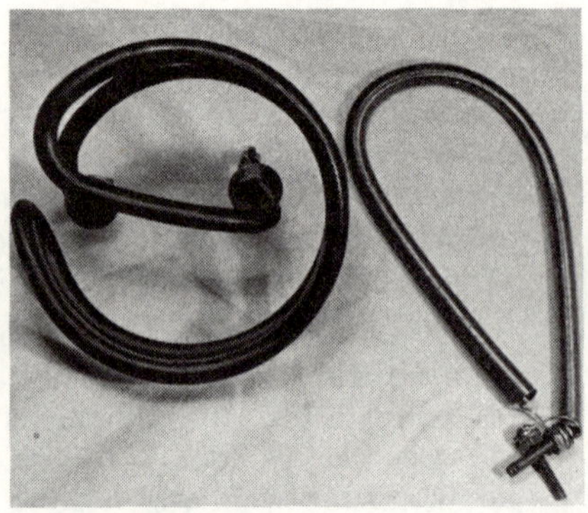

THERE ARE two basic kinds of resistance heating elements—a closed element (left) and an open element (right).

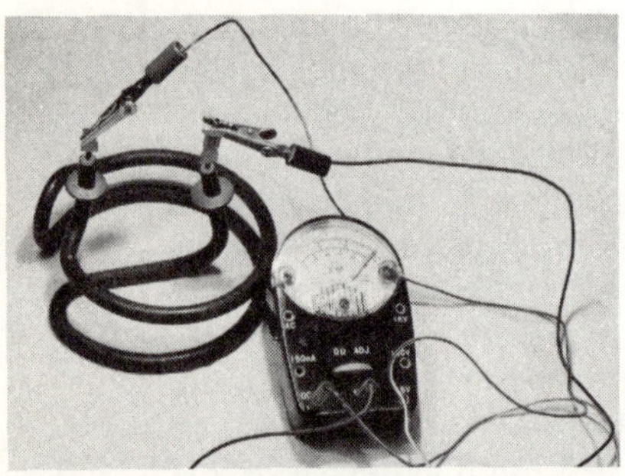

TEST a closed element by connecting ohmmeter to terminals. A zero reading indicates a sound element, a ∞ reading a bad element.

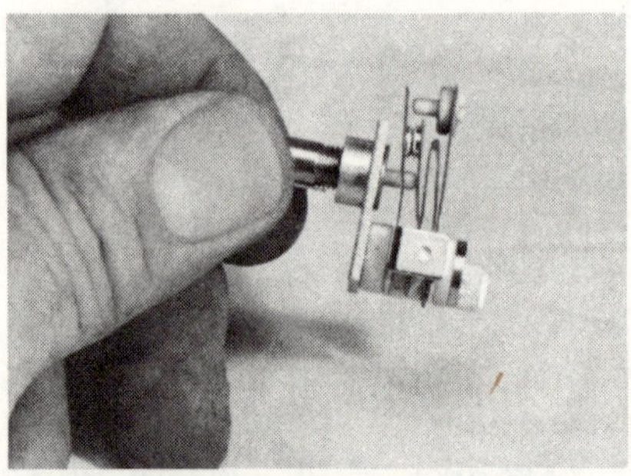

THERMOSTAT (shown removed) is a switch which opens and closes to disrupt or permit current to flow—depending on need to produce heat.

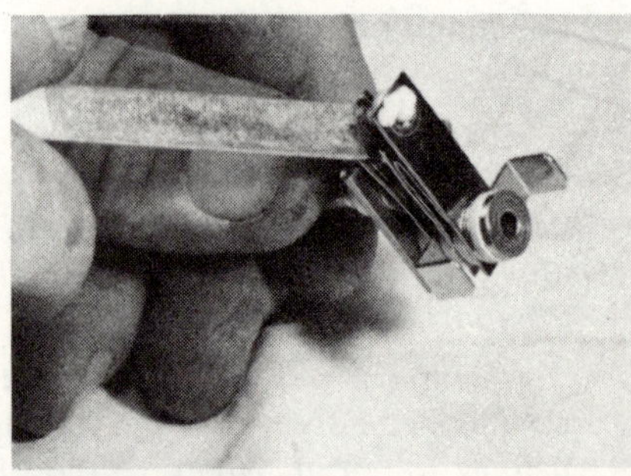

SOMETIMES dirty or pitted points hamper thermostat operation. To clean the points, stroke lightly with an ignition point file. Brush away dust.

Test the outlet by disconnecting the appliance and plugging in a lamp. If it doesn't light (and the bulb isn't defective), either the fuse or circuit breaker serving the outlet has flipped, or circuit wiring is bad.

To test a detachable power cord, connect another power cord (of the same gauge and known to be good) to the appliance. Does the appliance work now? If not, the problem may rest with the thermostat and/or heating element. Testing these components will be discussed later.

To test an attached power cord, *unplug it from the wall outlet* and open the appliance to reveal the other end of the cord. Now check to make sure a terminal hasn't come off a connector. If it has, you have discovered the problem. If a terminal is corroded or burned, or if the power cord is frayed at either end, replace the cord. It is in danger of failing and starting a fire.

Power-cord terminals are normally held to contacts by spade connectors, which are slide-on, slide-off parts, or by small nuts and bolts. To test a power cord for internal failure, once again make sure the appliance is not plugged in and disconnect one of its terminals.

Attach an ohmmeter lead to one of the cord plug prongs. Attach the other ohmmeter lead to either the disconnected or attached power cord terminal. The ohmmeter (set on the R x 1 scale) will either show continuity (0 or a slight rise off 0) *or* resistance (an infinity reading, identified on the ohmmeter scale by the symbol ∞). Now, transfer the ohmmeter lead to the other power-cord terminal. The ohmmeter needle should swing to the opposite end of the scale from where it was, reading 0 if it had shown ∞ or ∞ if it had shown 0. If it doesn't, the cord is defective.

To satisfy yourself further, connect the ohmmeter lead to the power cord terminal which gave a meter reading of 0. Then keep your eye on the ohmmeter as you pull, bend and twist the power cord over its entire length. If the ohmmeter needle suddenly swings to infinity, there is a power-cord break. Replace the cord.

There are two types of heating elements: open and closed. Open elements are visible. They are spring-type components, which are stretched over the appliance and held by ceramic insulators.

A closed element is a coil inside a metal housing. The element is separated from the housing by manganese, which acts as an insulator.

Open elements are tested by unplugging the appliance, disconnecting one terminal and at-

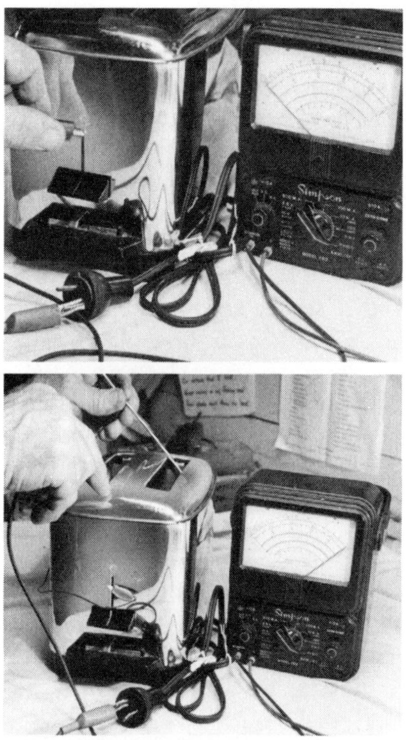

OHMMETER in top photo shows that this toaster does not have a short. In photo above, however, we created a severe short to show that ohmmeter needle will swing to 0. *Any* movement of the needle indicates a short.

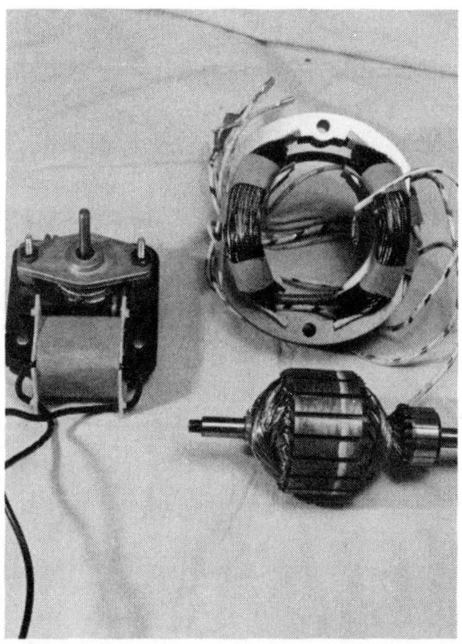

THE TWO most common types of small-appliance motors include shaded-pole motor (left), used in can openers and electric knives, and a two-part universal motor (right). Universal motor consists of an armature (bottom) and field coil. Appliances need not be discarded when motors go bad, since motor or components are available.

MAZE of gears and wire becomes clear once you know what you're looking for. With the backpulled off this can opener, the motor and power cord are easy to spot for testing.

taching an ohmmeter (set on the R x 1 scale) to it and to the other end. If the ohmmeter doesn't show 0 or a slight rise, but goes to ∞, replace the element.

The open element you get as a replacement may have to be stretched to fit the appliance. Do this by holding one end in a vise and pulling the element until it's the same length as the old element. Don't stand directly in front of the element as you stretch it; it can come loose from the vise and spring back toward you.

Examine ceramic insulators. Replace those that are broken, along with those that are loose and can't be tightened. If an insulator fails to hold the heating element securely, the element may loosen and become grounded against the appliance case, causing a short and creating a safety hazard to the user.

To test a closed heating element, remove the element, set the ohmmeter on the R x 100 scale and connect ohmmeter leads across the element terminals. The meter should show 0 or a slight rise above 0—not ∞.

rating the thermostat

A bad thermostat can prevent an appliance from heating or cause erratic heating (overheating or not hot enough). Check by unplugging the unit and carefully spreading the thermostat points apart to see if they are pitted or dirty. If they are, run an ignition point file (available at automobile parts counters) over the points. Make two passes. If points require more than this amount of filing to be cleaned, replace the thermostat.

To test for a defective thermostat in an appliance with an attached type of power cord, place a jumper wire across the prongs of the power-cord plug. The jumper wire should have an alligator clip on each end to keep the wire securely in place on the prongs. Connect the ohmmeter leads across the thermostat terminals. Then, with the ohmmeter set on the R x 1 scale, turn on the appliance on-off switch. The meter should show 0, or a slight rise above 0. Now, turn the on-off switch off. The needle should swing to infinity (∞). If it doesn't, replace the thermostat.

If you are testing the type of thermostat that is part of a detachable power cord, such as that used with skillets, fry pans, hot trays and the like, place a jumper wire across the prongs of the power-cord plug. Insert the ohmmeter test lead prongs into the two holes in the thermostat housing. The meter should show continuity (0 or a slight rise above 0).

When you have completed repairs and reassembled the appliance, check for grounds (shorts). This is important. Do the same if someone using the appliance gets a "tickle" shock. A short occurs when a wire touches the appliance case.

With the appliance disconnected from the wall outlet, set the ohmmeter at its highest scale (R x 100, R x 1000 or R x 10,000). Attach the positive ohmmeter lead to one of the power-cord plug prongs and press the common lead firmly against the appliance housing. Turn on the on-off switch. The ohmmeter needle should *not* show any deflection from ∞. If it moves off ∞, disassemble the appliance, locate and fix the short.

motorized appliances

Small kitchen appliances that do not use heat have motors that do the work. In this category are blenders, can openers, mixers, knives and food processors. If a motor runs (hums), but the appliance doesn't work, look for mechanical damage, particularly a broken gear or a binding bearing.

The most common problem when it comes to motorized appliances, however, is a motor that doesn't run and makes no sound. The cause is a defective a.c. outlet or power cord, a faulty motor, or a loose connection. If the a.c. outlet and power cord test out okay (as described earlier) and connections have been checked for tightness, turn your attention to the motor.

A damaged motor is no reason to discard an appliance. New motors cost about $10. In some cases, you don't have to replace the entire motor—just a part of it. Universal motors, for instance, have two separate components—armature and field coil. Either can be replaced at appliance part dealers.

The field is the more likely of the two units to fail, but to make a sound diagnosis inspect the armature, especially the commutator end. If the commutator is not burned or dirty, the armature is probably okay and you can replace the field coil. If the commutator is burned, examine the brushes. They are two independent units that sit on either side of the commutator. Replace brushes if they are worn (less than ¼ inch long). Dress the commutator by rubbing it lightly with emery cloth.

Another type of motor widely used in small kitchen appliances is a shaded-pole motor. It usually comes as a complete unit, so if it seems to be the cause of appliance failure, check with an appliance store and get the correct replacement.

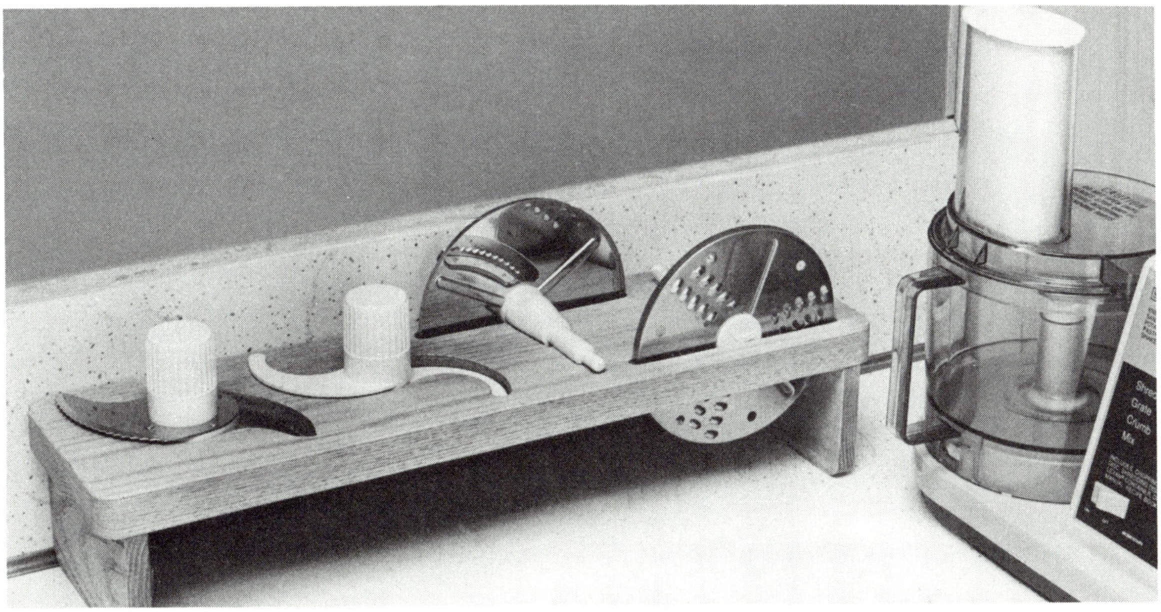

A handy rack for food-processor parts

■ STORE FOOD-PROCESSOR parts neatly and conveniently on hand in this accessory rack. Since the rack shelf consists of two pieces glued together, you can make the odd-shaped cutouts with a saw rather than carving or routing them. Make sure you select perfectly flat wood to facilitate joining.

Cut the four pieces needed. Use your processor parts as guides to outline the cutouts. Then bore entry holes for the saw blade in the cutouts: six in the top piece and four in the bottom one. Position holes for the long slots at the cutout ends.

Use a jigsaw or coping saw, making the cutouts slightly larger than the accessories to assure an easy fit. Use half-round and flat wood files, then sand smooth.

Glue shelf sections together and secure parts with finishing nails from below. When the glue has dried, cut the shelf corners round, break the edges with a plane and sand smooth.

Attach the legs with glue and finishing nails. Set the heads below the surface and use plastic wood filler. Apply polyurethane varnish.

SEE ALSO

Cabinets, kitchen . . . Food mixers . . . Food processors . . . Mixers, food

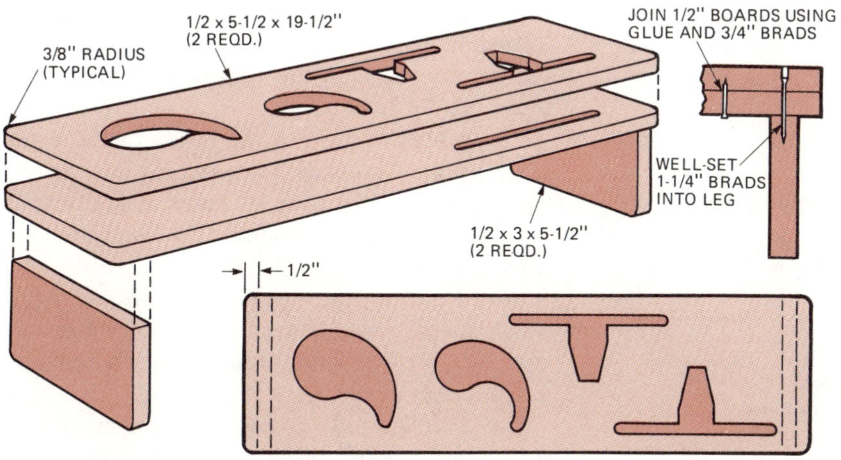

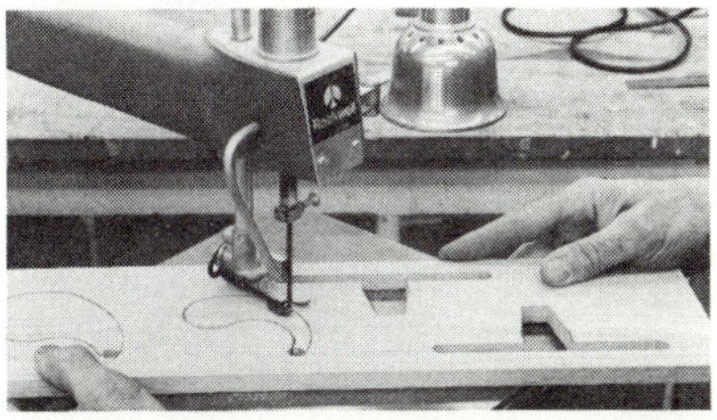

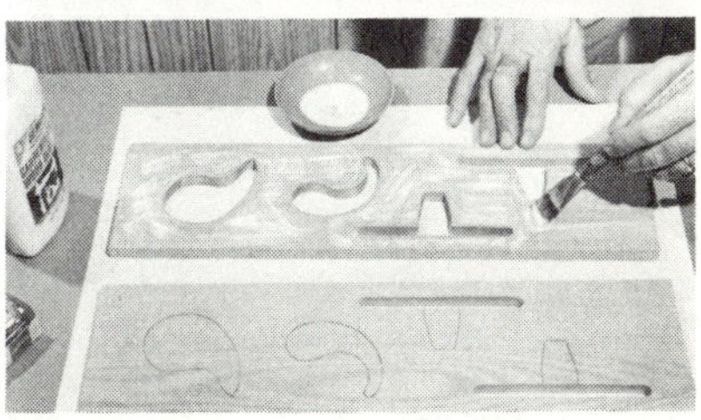

FOR PRECISE cutouts (right, top photo), use set-tooth blade. For parts fit, remove line when cutting. Use two nails (lower photo) to align parts. Apply glue sparingly, and then nail.

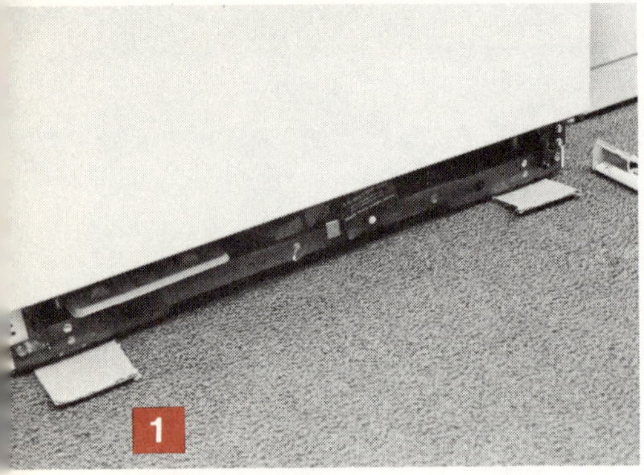

REMOVE the front grille and slide cardboard strips under leveling legs or rollers to move the refrigerator.

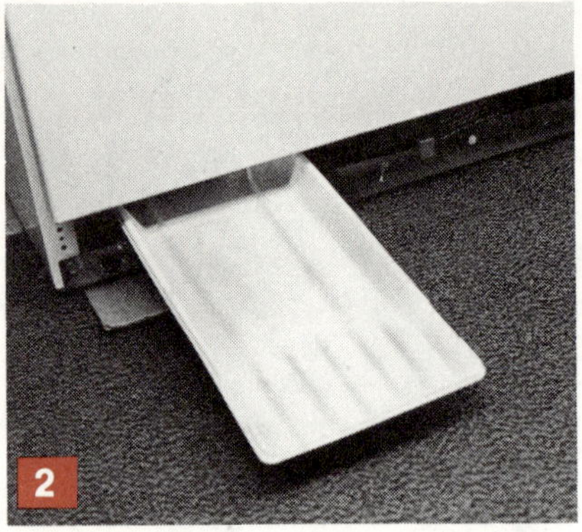

REMOVE drain pan; wash, replace. Vacuum the condenser coils under the refrigerator in a forced-draft system.

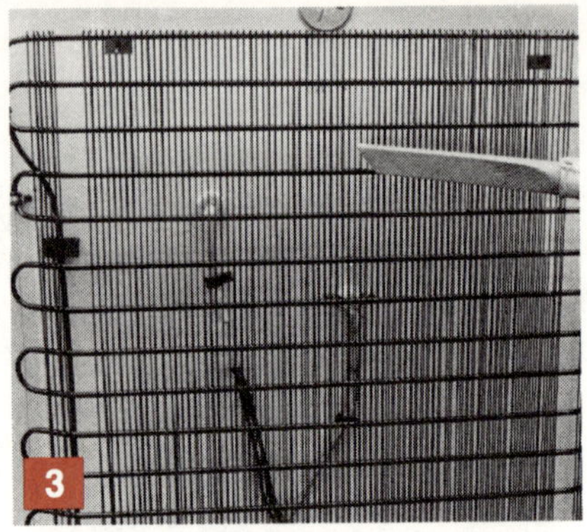

VACUUM the coils on the refrigerator back in a natural-draft system. Remove debris under the coils.

Refrigerator tune-up cuts operating costs

By C. J. LINDO

PREVENTIVE MAINTENANCE on domestic refrigerators is a safe and simple job. It helps keep the unit in good working order and cuts down on electric costs.

Before you start work, pull the plug. Nothing is more upsetting than shooting off fireworks in the refrigerator, winding a shirt sleeve in a condenser fan blade, or worse.

In most cases you will have to move the refrigerator to get at the plug. Start the move by grabbing the top front corners and rocking the refrigerator back and forth, then side to side. While rocking, pull it forward until you have enough room to reach behind it and pull the plug.

After pulling the plug, check to see if you have a natural- or forced-draft condenser. If you see black coils attached to the back, you have a natural-draft system. Forced-draft condensers are tucked away underneath, where a fan forces air over the coils.

Natural-draft condensers are easy to clean. Use a narrow nozzle on your vacuum and a dust brush. Carefully brush off dust and hair clinging to the condenser and vacuum it up.

Forced-draft condensers take a little more work to clean. Remove the front grille. With the help of a flashlight and a narrow nozzle, carefully vacuum out the condenser coils underneath the refrigerator.

The back cover is usually black cardboard with a strip of fiberglass insulation attached inside. Older models may have a black metal cover. Simply remove screws holding the cover.

Carefully vacuum the condenser fan motor and fan blade. Don't bend or warp the blade, or it will tend to wobble and wear out the fan-motor bearing.

If the fan blade is made of plastic, replace it with a metal one. Plastic fan blades tend to warp or become brittle and fall off due to the temperature in their location.

Vacuum out the rest of the dirt underneath. You should see clearly from back to front of the refrigerator, *through* the condenser coils before replacing the back cover.

The rubber seal along the inside of the door keeps heat and moisture from seeping into the refrigerator when the door is closed. A faulty seal or torn door gasket have almost the same effect as leaving the door open all day.

Wash accumulated dirt off the gasket with warm soapy water and carefully inspect it for rips. Also wash around the door frame where the gasket closes against it.

Use a dollar bill to check for proper gasket seal. Close the bill between the door and door

SEE ALSO

Appliance repair . . . Clothes dryers . . . Energy, saving . . . Freezers . . . Kitchens . . . Washing machines

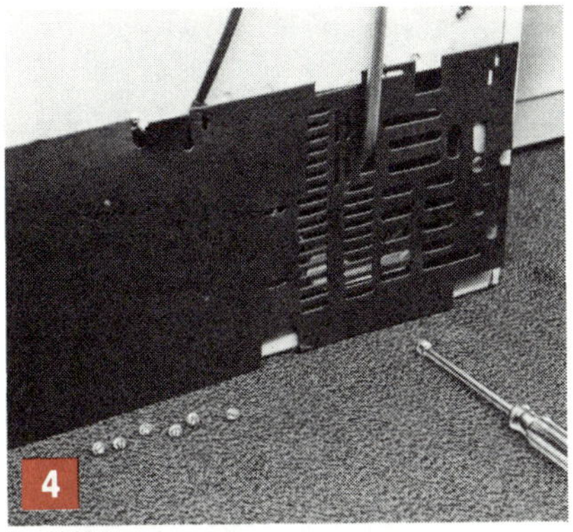

UNSCREW and remove the back cover; clean it with a vacuum. The cover is often cardboard, sometimes metal.

CAREFULLY VACUUM the condenser fan and the fan blade. Remove all dust and debris from the area.

LOOK FOR worn or torn door gaskets which let heat and moisture enter even when the door is closed.

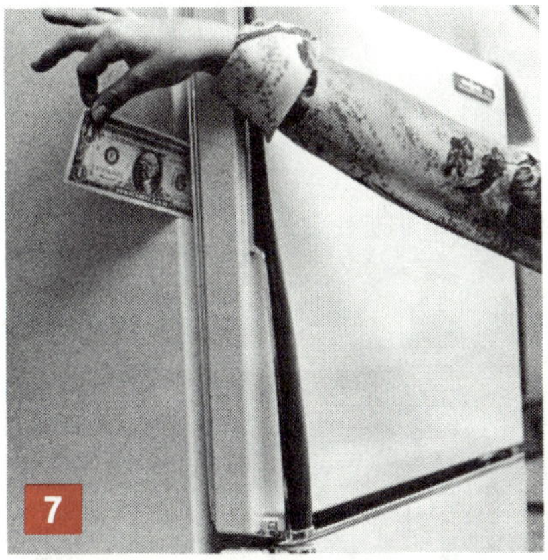

USE A DOLLAR bill to check proper gasket seal. You should feel tension when you pull on the dollar.

USING a hair dryer and a towel, carefully defrost the freezer. A dishpan can be used to collect melting ice.

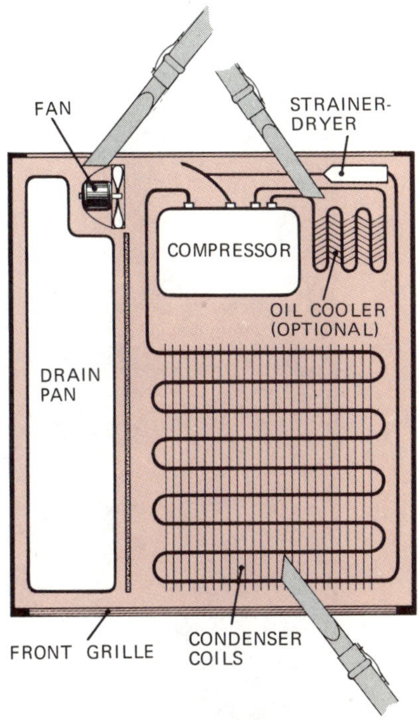

DRAWING OF REFRIGERATOR locates condenser coils, fan and motor. Make certain that these parts are thoroughly vacuumed.

frame. Slowly pull it out. If you feel tension, the seal is okay. Do this all around the gasket.

There are several ways to correct a seal leak. Fix small leaks by gently heating the gasket with a hair dryer and stretching it to fit. Lift the gasket and check to see that it is screwed in place. Larger leaks can be remedied by adjusting hinges so the door fits evenly.

Cracks in plastic door liners are among the easiest things to seal. While it is not good in places that must be rigid, an instant rubber caulking compound such as GE Silicone Seal adheres well and keeps moisture from soaking into the insulation between the liner and outer door shell.

Frost buildup in the freezer acts as an insulator and reduces the freezer's ability to absorb and disperse the heat of the food inside. Defrosting used to be a messy, time-consuming job. Today you can defrost an inch of ice in 15 minutes using a hair dryer—if you elect to consume the needed electricity.

Move food to the refrigerator section. Place a towel on the freezer bottom to absorb water and put a dishpan on a convenient spot on the floor. Turn on the dryer to its hottest setting and melt a spot of ice on the top of the freezer, holding the dryer at a 45° angle so water won't drip back into it.

As the ice melts, gradually work the hair dryer in widening circles. Don't let hot air hit the plastic directly. Use your fingernails to loosen slabs of ice gently. *Never* use metal or hard plastic to scrape off ice.

Wash the freezer with warm, soapy water and ammonia, rinse and dry. Plug in the unit, turn it on and the tune-up is complete.

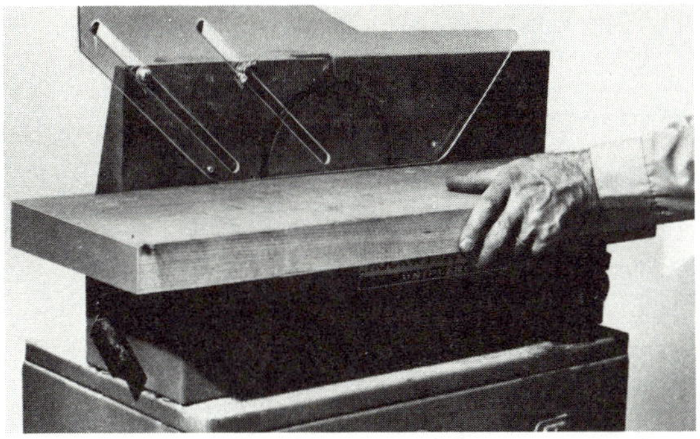

THE TURNING BLOCKS for the legs have square edges and are jointed smooth. Cut them from the 2-in. stock.

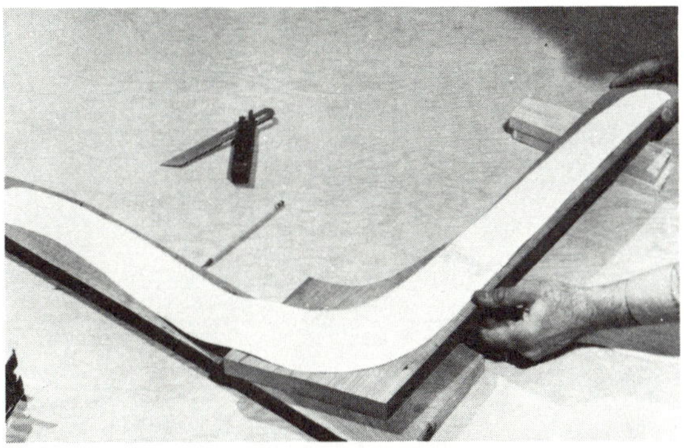

USE A PATTERN as a guide for positioning the side sections before you mark off the lap-joint limits.

THE LAP JOINT is cleared with a dado blade. Notice the end portion is left as a temporary support.

A LARGE LAP joint like this is extremely strong. Be sure to reverse the position for left and right sides.

A colonial chair in solid cherry

Authentically crafted in solid cherry, this family heirloom is a challenging shop project for any do-it-yourselfer. It calls for use of many different shop skills

By RO CAPOTOSTO

■ HERE'S A PROJECT to involve you in a number of shop skills, including repeat turnings, spokeshave shaping, lap-jointing and angle drilling. And, since this handsome cherry chair is planned for standard-size, ready-made cushions, you needn't worry about upholstering procedures.

This chair is sturdy, despite its trim lines and somewhat delicate appearance, and its legs, with 1¼-in. tenons, won't loosen in a lifetime. Lumber requirements are minimal: 12 ft. of $^5/_4$ x 8-in. and 8 ft. of $^8/_4$ x 8-in. cherry, plus three lengths of ¾-in. hardwood dowels.

Start with the side panels. Make over-size, rough-cut sections as shown in the diagram. Fit pieces closely to save lumber. It's wise to position sections one atop the other in proper relationship, then lay a full-size paper pattern of the side in place to double check proper angular placement. Remove the pattern and scribe lines to indicate lap-joint limits.

For safety when cutting wide laps, leave a bit uncut at the outside end until all inner portions are cleaned out. This can avoid a nasty accident, such as the workpiece dipping too deeply into the blade.

Make right and left sections for each side for symmetry of joint lines. Glue the pieces, using a few nails in the waste areas to prevent sliding during clamping. Then bandsaw sides to size and smooth. When rounding edges, don't shape the juncture of the armrests and the inside back corners.

SEE ALSO

Caning . . . Chairs . . . Clocks . . .
Cupboards, china . . . Dry sinks . . .
Furniture, care of . . . Gossip benches . . .
Hutch tables . . . Joinery . . . Legs, furniture . . .
Lowboys . . . Servers . . . Serving carts . . .
Stools . . . Upholstery . . . Wood finishes

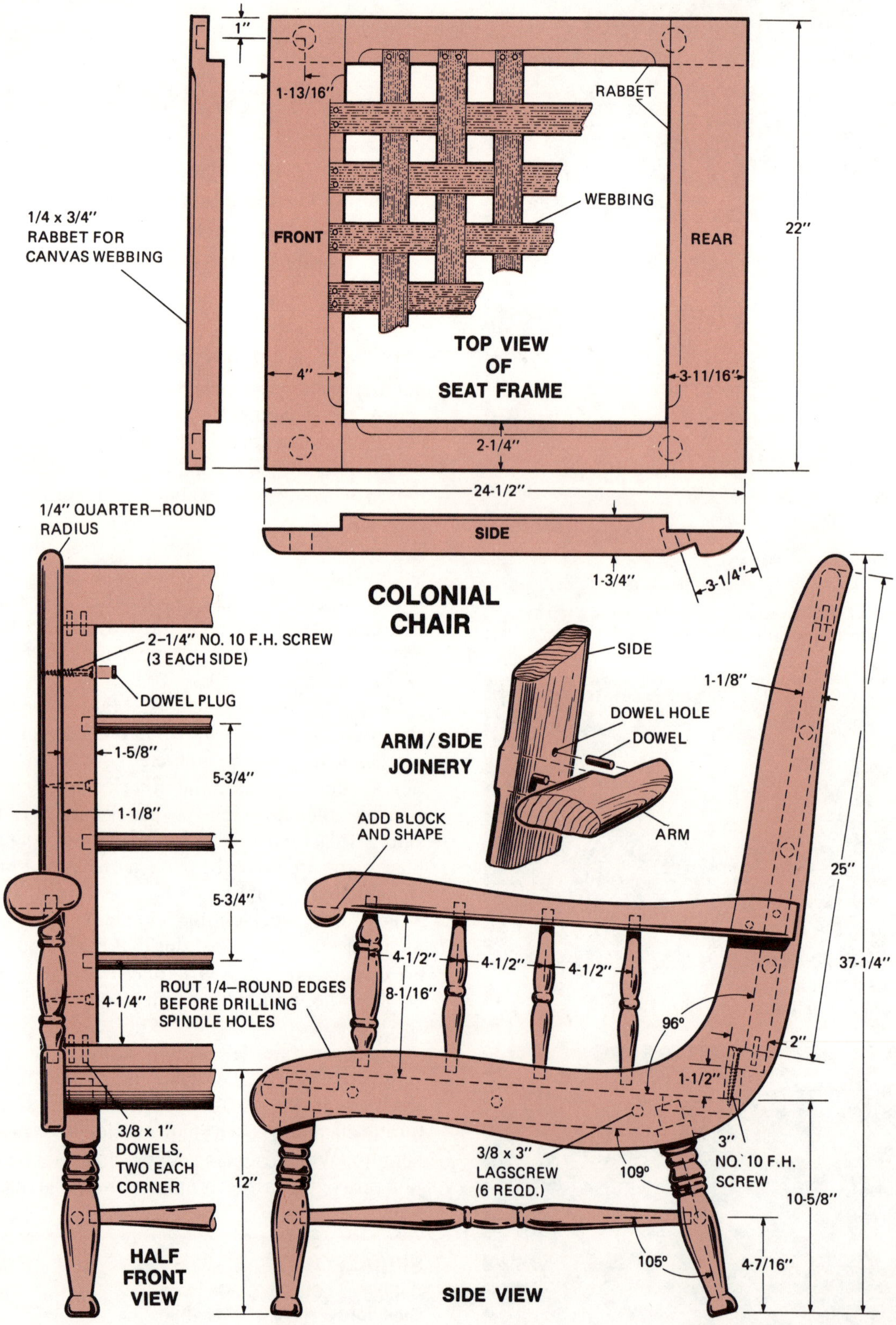
1"
1-13/16"
RABBET
WEBBING
1/4 x 3/4"
RABBET FOR
CANVAS WEBBING
FRONT
REAR
22"
TOP VIEW
OF
SEAT FRAME
4"
3-11/16"
2-1/4"
24-1/2"
SIDE
1-3/4"
3-1/4"
1/4" QUARTER–ROUND
RADIUS
COLONIAL
CHAIR
2–1/4" NO. 10 F.H. SCREW
(3 EACH SIDE)
DOWEL PLUG
SIDE
1-1/8"
DOWEL HOLE
DOWEL
ARM / SIDE
JOINERY
ARM
1-5/8"
5-3/4"
1-1/8"
5-3/4"
ADD BLOCK
AND SHAPE
25"
37-1/4"
4-1/2"
4-1/2"
4-1/2"
8-1/16"
4-1/4"
ROUT 1/4–ROUND EDGES
BEFORE DRILLING
SPINDLE HOLES
96°
2"
1-1/2"
3/8 x 1"
DOWELS,
TWO EACH
CORNER
12"
3/8 x 3"
LAGSCREW
(6 REQD.)
109°
3"
NO. 10 F.H.
SCREW
10-5/8"
105°
4-7/16"
HALF
FRONT
VIEW
SIDE VIEW

Due to the bottom curve on side panels, you need a simple jig to bore perpendicular holes accurately for the armrest spindles. Clamp two 2x4 pieces to the work to hold it in the proper plane as indicated in the drawing. Clamp assembly to the drill-press table and bore the holes. Cut armrest pieces and bore spindle holes before contouring the top surface so the pieces will rest flat and true on the table.

After boring the holes in armrest bottoms, screw on a piece of 2x4 to serve as a temporary clamping block to hold the work in the vise while you shape it with a spokeshave. Before shaping, remove some waste with the bandsaw. Note that the cross section of the armrest takes on varying curves. You can shape the pieces by eye but if you need guidance, cut some cardboard templates from a full-size sketch of the contours.

I erred slightly by not boring the dowel-joint holes between chair sides and armrests before cutting the slanted side of each armrest. Thus I had to glue on a temporary wedge to get a solid, square purchase with clamps between the two pieces for precise drilling. Anticipate this and bore the dowel holes after you notch out the back of the armrest, but before cutting any curves.

While the chair legs are angled (in one plane, front to rear), the construction and assembly is novel because of its simplicity. Front legs are driven straight into the seat frame, but achieve

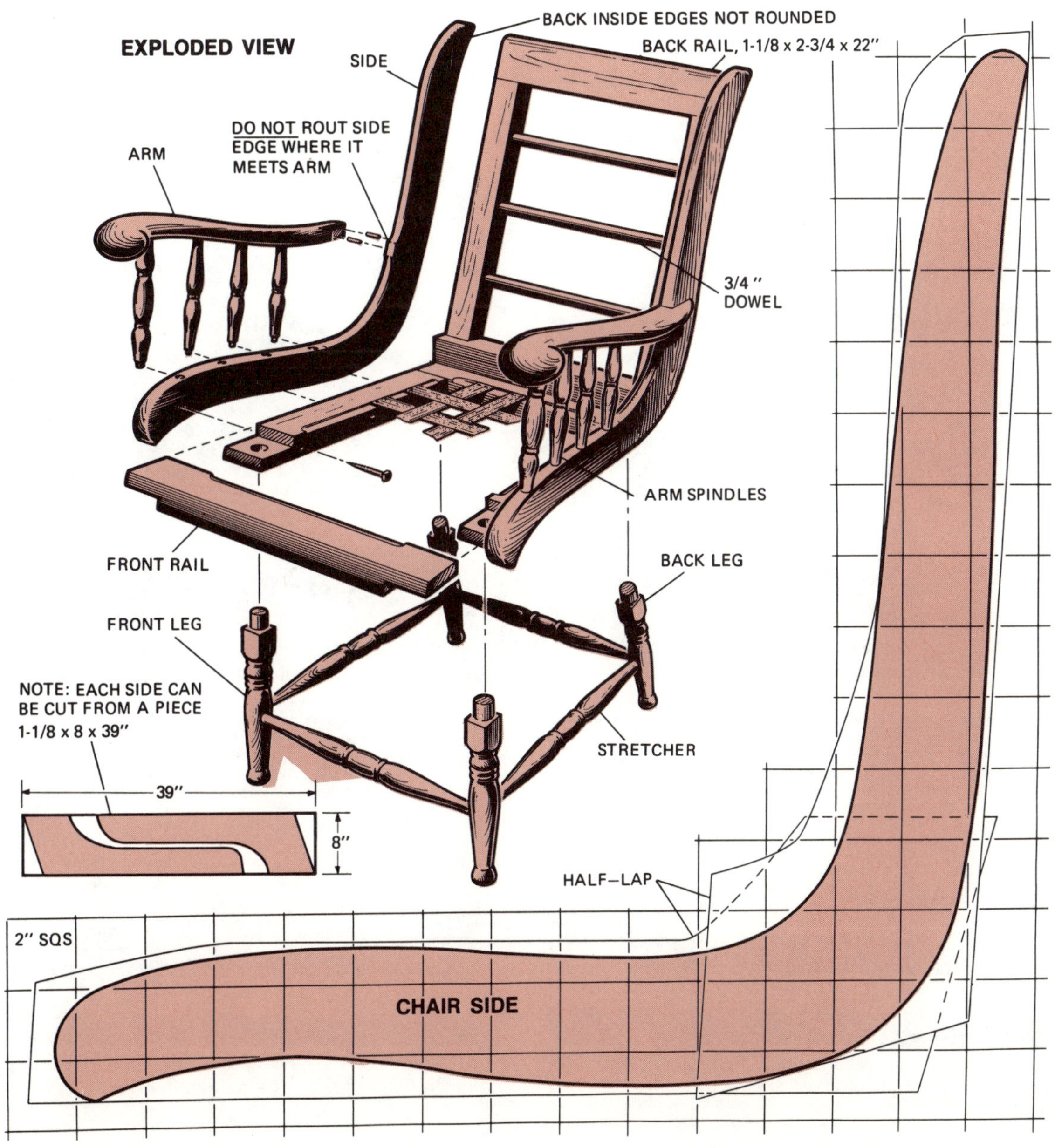

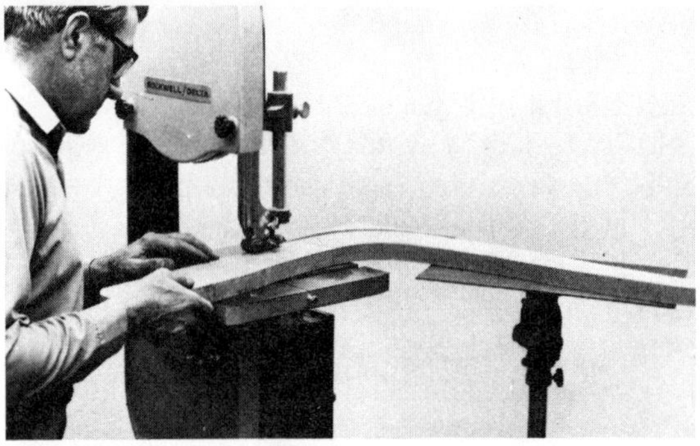

AN AUXILIARY work-support platform is a handy aid when bandsawing awkwardly shaped pieces like this.

RIPPLES made by the bandsaw blade can be smoothed out with a spokeshave as shown, or a plane and sander.

A ROUTER with a ¼-round bit will cut round edges on the side panels. *Don't* shape where armrest meets panel.

AN ORBITAL finishing sander with high o.p.m. lets you do an excellent smoothing job with little effort.

TO DRILL spindle holes accurately, sandwich the side between two blocks to hold it true and steady.

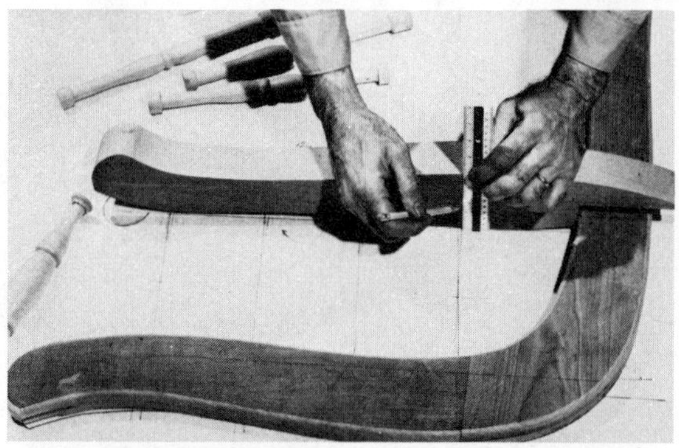

A FULL-SIZE SKETCH offers the easiest way to locate the exact position for holes in the armrests and sides.

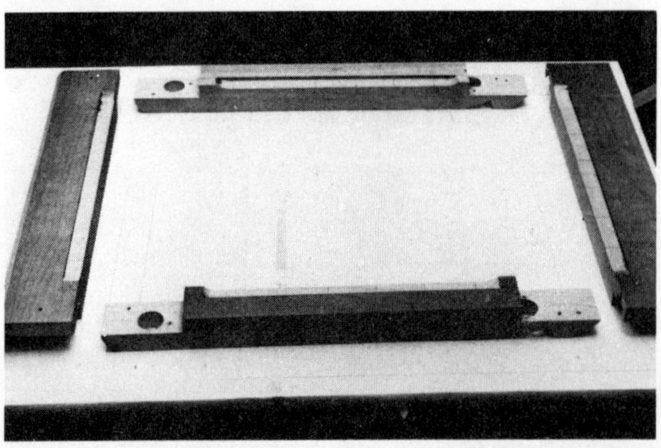

AN EXPLODED VIEW shows how the seat frame is made up. This view of the seat is from the top side.

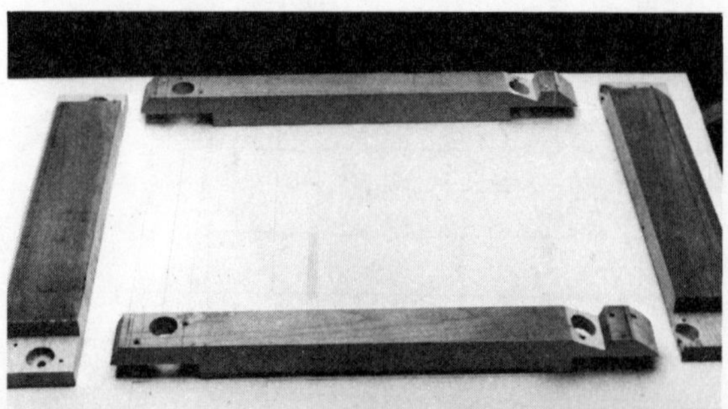

BOTTOM VIEW OF FRAME: Holes are predrilled for illustration. They can be bored after the piece is glued.

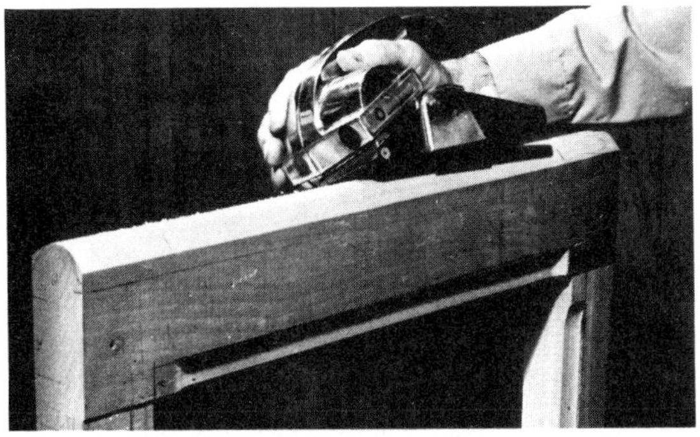

A POWER BLOCK PLANE, used to trim the assembled seat frame to the desired size, saves muscles.

THE SEAT FRAME must be propped up when you bore the angled rear holes. *Don't* try this without clamps.

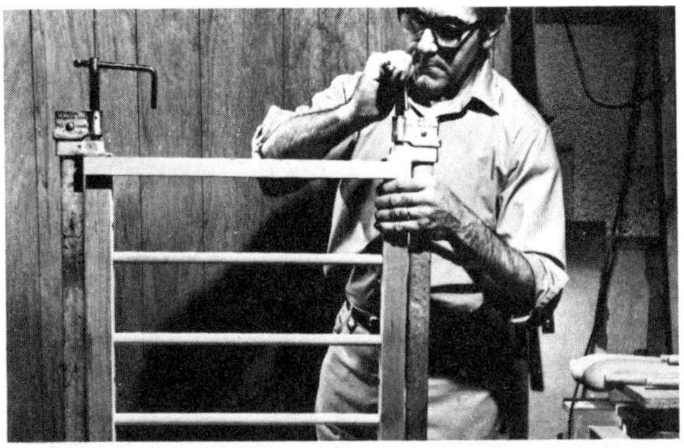

THE BACK FRAME is butt-jointed and doweled. Insert the long dowel spindles before assembling the frame.

THE BACK is joined to the bottom frame with screws and glue. Use a damp cloth to wipe off the excess glue.

their angle because the frame slants down toward the back.

The seat and back frames are made up as separate subassemblies and then joined together. Make the necessary cuts on the seat frame parts before assembly, including the angled notches below and wide rabbets for the webbing on the top side. The broad area of the lap joints supports a lot of glue so you need no doweling here. Besides, the leg tenons serve as huge dowels. Back framing members are butted, so paired dowels are called for at corners.

You'll need a simple jig, consisting of a large plank clamped to the drill-press table, to support the seat frame at the proper angle for boring holes for the rear legs. Round the front end of the seat and the top edge of the back frame, thoroughly sand all the exposed surfaces, then screw and glue the back to the seat. The side panels are glued on next. Use flathead, countersunk screws through the sides of the back frame and 3/8 x 3-in. lag screws to secure the seat framing.

You are now ready for the fun part of the project: turning the spindles. If you do not own a lathe attachment for making duplicate turnings, it will take you a little longer to do the work. The

FOR ACCURACY, holes for the screws are drilled on the spot with the members clamped in their final position.

A SPOKESHAVE will let you do a slick carving job on the armrests. The various contours are shown at right.

DON'T RUSH the shaping. Use full-size drawings of the contours, plus calipers, to make frequent checks.

job will take some patience and frequent checking.

Start by making a full-size sketch of each of the turnings for reference. Rip the turning blocks for the four legs and the two leading arm spindles out of 8/4-in. stock; the 5/4-in. material will take care of the rest of the spindles. Since the legs have squared ends, you'll have to smooth-finish these blocks. Because you will occasionally have to remove the turnings from the lathe, put a reference mark on one facet of the spur center and mark each block accordingly so that the pieces will always go back on the lathe in their original orientation.

Rough-turn all the blocks into cylinders, except for the leg blocks. These must be turned with squared shoulders not only at the top, but also in the waste area beyond the bottom. This is important because the two flats will later provide the only means of *successfully* drilling the holes for the spindles with *ease* and precision.

To prevent the corners of the square sections from splintering, first make nicking cuts with the toe of the skew. Now you can proceed to make sizing cuts with the parting tool on all of the roughed-in cylinders. It's desirable to keep all diameters a bit oversize to allow for the finishing cuts.

Complete any one of the turnings and then tie it to a shop-made hinging board that's mounted

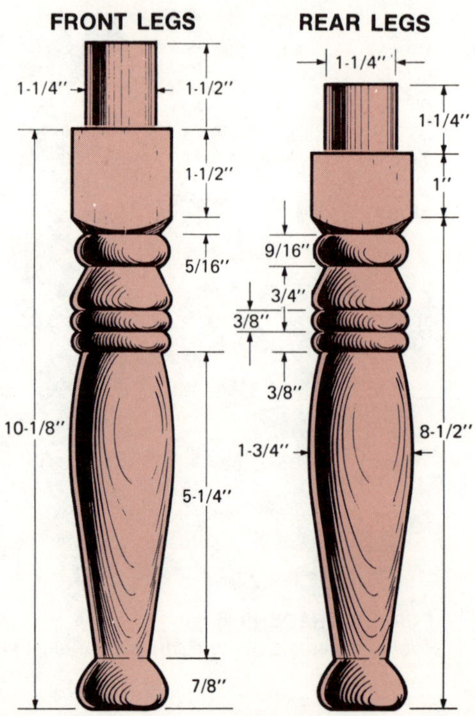

SHOP-TURNED SPINDLES used in the chair test your duplicate-turning skills, a task that is simplified if you make full-size patterns first. The turnings are even easier if you own a duplicating attachment for your lathe.

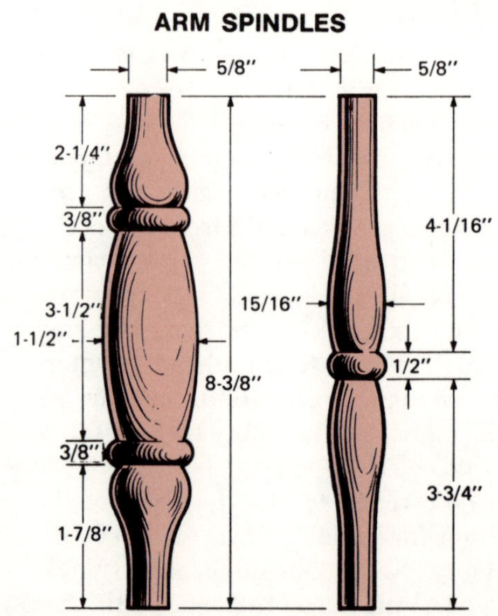

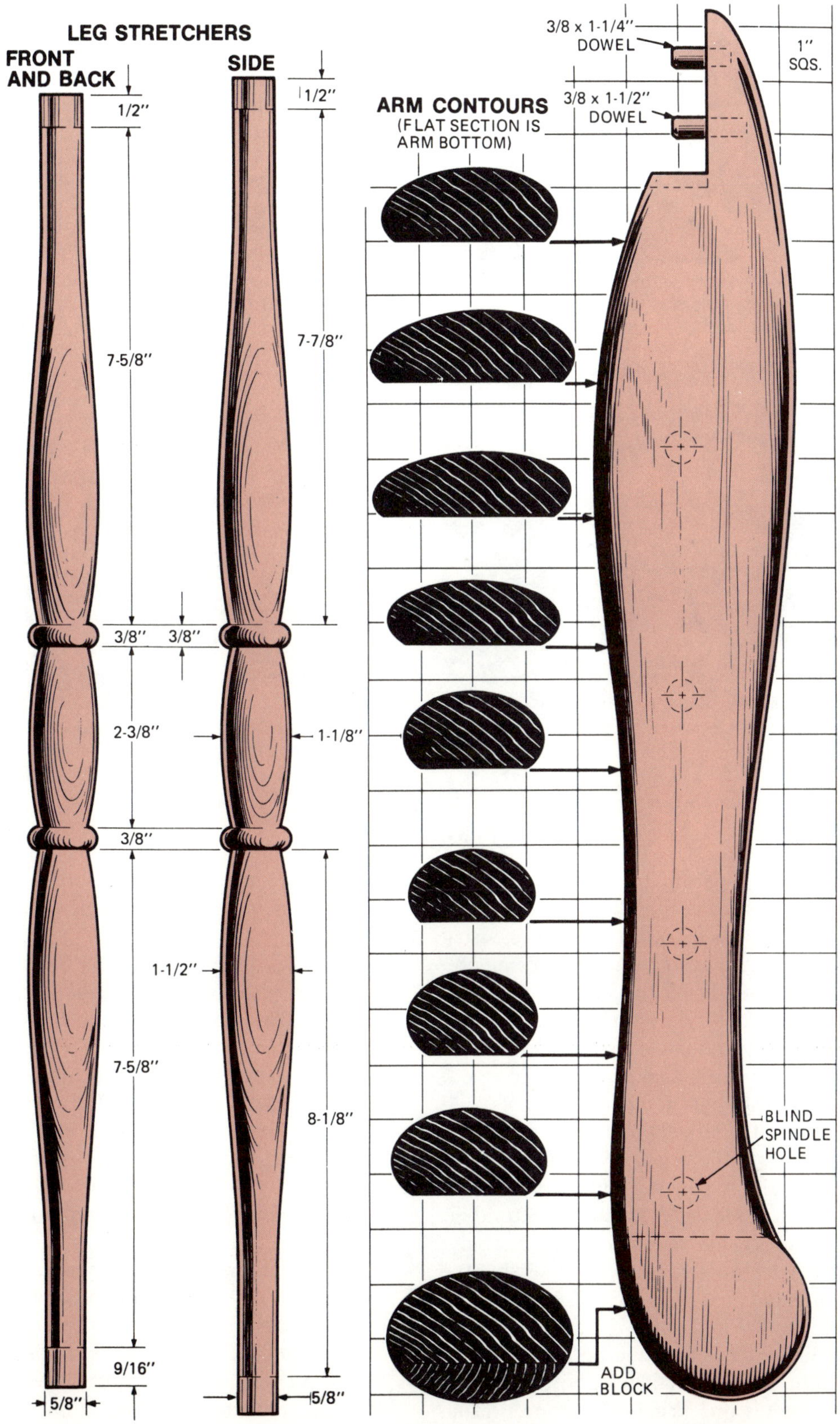

LEG STRETCHERS
FRONT AND BACK
SIDE
1/2"
7-5/8"
3/8"
3/8"
2-3/8"
3/8"
1-1/2"
7-5/8"
9/16"
5/8"
1/2"
7-7/8"
1-1/8"
8-1/8"
5/8"
ARM CONTOURS
(FLAT SECTION IS ARM BOTTOM)
3/8 x 1-1/4" DOWEL
3/8 x 1-1/2" DOWEL
1" SQS.
BLIND SPINDLE HOLE
ADD BLOCK

A DISC SANDER is the handiest tool for rounding off ball end of the arm. Added block is required here.

THE SIDE and arm must be rigidly clamped precisely in position when you bore the holes for the joint-dowels.

THE MASTER SPINDLE can be brought up close to workpiece for comparison to make repeat turning easy.

A HOMEMADE steady-rest is used to cut down vibrations that occur when you turn long, slender spindles.

behind the lathe to permit it to serve as a master spindle. Thus you can bring the master forward (up close) to the new workpiece for quick visual matching of the duplicate you are working on.

I also found it advisable to use a steady-rest to eliminate vibrations when turning the slender base spindle. If you don't have such a lathe accessory, you can easily fashion one out of wood. Simply cut a right-angle notch in a piece of wood and clamp it to the lathe bed. The corner of the angle is then set at the height of the lathe center.

It's a good idea to turn the ends of all legs and spindles just a shade under the drill size for their respective holes to allow a slight amount of play, or wobble, which is necessary to assemble the parts. When satisfied with each turning, sand it to completion before cutting off the waste.

However, don't cut off the bottom waste of the legs until the spindle holes are bored. Each of the legs requires one spindle hole bored at an angle (see drawing). This can be done simply by propping up a flat board on the drill-press table—set at the required angle—and clamping it solidly.

For clean, positive results I strongly recommend the use of spur drill bits for all boring. Rockwell Manufacturing Co., 400 North Lexington Ave., Pittsburgh, Pa., makes them, and they should be available at your local hardware store.

Final assembly is not difficult, but do make a nonglue dry run to permit any adjustments necessary, such as shaving off a bit here and there on tight-fitting spindles.

While you're doing this, don't forget to whittle a couple of flats on all leg and spindle ends so the excess glue can escape. If you don't allow for such glue ooze-out, you'll soon discover that some of the pieces just won't bottom, but they will spring out as soon as you release them.

Plastic resin glue is a good type to use. I prefer to make a mixture that's a bit on the heavy side so it won't become too watery, thus runny.

A SIMPLE DRILL-PRESS jig is necessary for boring holes in the legs. Flat ends make this trick possible.

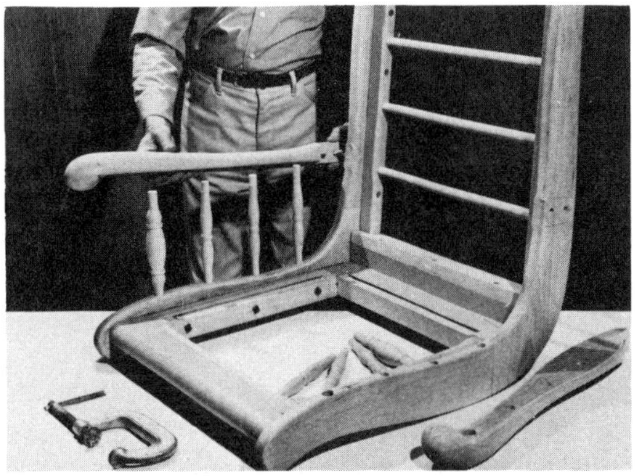

INSTALLING THE ARMREST requires a little give and take. Thus, it is best to use thick—not runny—glue.

IF SPINDLE ENDS and leg tenons are a bit smaller than the holes, the angled assembly will fit effortlessly.

WEBBING, with the ends doubled over, is nailed into the rabbeted recess. Use large-head carpet tacks.

Insert the armrest spindles into the sides and then add the rests. The two dowels projecting from the rear of the arms should be sanded to a slight taper to permit some flexing of the arm so it can be worked into place over the spindles. After assembly, wipe off all excess glue; stains and finish can't penetrate a skin of glue (which actually becomes a sealer coat).

Next comes the base. Insert the spindles into the four legs. While the assembly is right-side up, apply glue to the tenons and the shoulders and also to the holes in the frame.

If possible, have a helper give you a hand to turn the assembly upside down and insert the front legs first. Then, while he holds the front legs in the right position, with a bit of twisting you can work the rear legs in place. Use one bar clamp on each leg. Since there is no place for them to go, the spindles will take care of themselves.

The finish on the chair shown consists of a few coats of sanding sealer lightly sanded with 6/0 paper. Next, to a matte-finish lacquer, add a bit of analine stain (cordovan was used here). Spray on a number of coats. (Editor's note: At least three or four.)

Be mindful that the stain color builds up with each pass, so don't get overzealous when you add the stain. To be sure of getting exactly the shade you want, test it on a scrap of the lumber used for the chair.

After the finish has been applied you can install the seat webbing. Using large-head upholstery tacks, double up on the ends and pull them taut. Weave each strand over and under.

To equip the chair you'll need foam cushions of the following dimensions: Seat, 4½x22x23 in.; back, 4x21x22 in. If you can't get them locally, they are available as stock items through Sears Roebuck. You'll find them listed under "Replacement Cushions for Colonial Style Furniture."

How to resurface your asphalt drive

By KEN KAISER

■ THE WARM MONTHS are the best time to repair and rejuvenate your asphalt driveway. As a do-it-yourself project, it is entirely practical—one that will save you money and prepare the drive for the ravages of the coming winter as well as add many useful years to its life.

the basic problems

Before getting into the actual repair of the surface, it would be well to understand the causes of the problems in the first place and what may be done to improve the situation in the future.

Basically, there are three categories of problems that lead to cracks, ruts or deep depressions, heaving and broken pavement or edge-cracking. Obviously, there is ordinary wear and tear. Asphalt tends over a period of time to dry out and lose resiliency. Refurbishing will help correct this problem to a large extent.

If the drive was improperly laid originally—for example, not a thick-enough layer of asphalt or improper crowning to provide for water runoff—the drive will develop cracks, the first step in a moisture/seepage/freezing/upheaval sequence. Also, if proper forms were not used at the edge of the drive, it is only a matter of time before edge cracking occurs. Though a little larger in scope, this can also be handled as a part of the refurbishing job.

The ground-water problem that eventually leads to asphalt driveway defects has two aspects of its own: One is rainwater that sinks into the ground along the drive and then flows under it; the other—more serious and consequently more difficult to combat—is a high water table.

In the first instance, a partial solution is to provide a shallow channel on each side to direct the runoff water down the sides of the drive. These channels need to be slightly pitched to give the water a downhill run.

SEE ALSO
Concrete . . . Snow-melting systems

Since water will follow a path of least resistance if it is not given direction, it will sink into the ground and spread under the drive.

A construction note: Since asphalt is flexible, any trough or channel that is constructed (particularly along the sides of the drive) must be held in position at the edges by a permanent form such as metal or wood impregnated with a preservative.

The water-table problem is more serious because if the ground on which the driveway was installed has an abnormally high water content, there is little that can be done to eliminate or remove the water.

Since the problem here arises when the ever-present water freezes and forces the drive to heave and crack, the solution is to give the freezing and expanding water an outlet—room to expand in a harmless manner, thereby relieving the pressure on the drive itself.

installing a 'relief valve'

To create this "relief valve," cut a hole in the middle of the drive, using a post-hole digger. Dig down two to three feet deep, fill the bottom with loose gravel or stone and place an ordinary bell drain pipe and cover in the hole, level with the drive surface.

It is important to remember that water from below the drive is generally not the major problem. Rather it is water that has penetrated the surface of the driveway itself. The result is the same action that breaks rocks into pebbles—small amounts of water start a fine crack in the surface, then continually enlarge it until it eventually succumbs to pressure from underneath.

For this reason, you should establish a continuing maintenance program for the drive and pay particular attention to the last part of the job when a top coating is applied as the final sealer for the surface.

the importance of cleaning

Any patch, sealer or coating seals or attaches

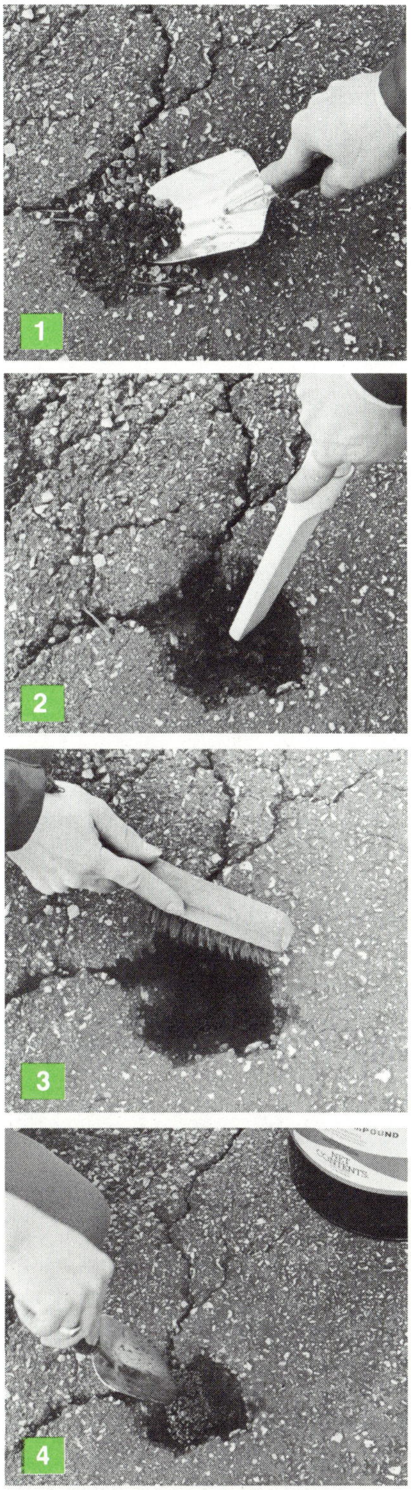

HOW TO FILL SMALL HOLES
1. Clean out the hole, removing any grass or weeds. Dig down to a solid base. 2. Blow clean with your vacuum cleaner. 3. Wire-brush the hole to dislodge any loose particles. 4. Fill hole with cold patch, mound slightly and tamp to compact solidly. Fill and tamp deep holes in one-inch layers. Do not try to fill them all at one time.

HOW TO PATCH 'CRATERS'
1. Use cold patch as it comes from the bag or can. Spoon it in holes or pour it over large depressions. 2. If area is deeper than 1 inch, apply and compact the patch in 1-inch-thick layers. 3. Place a board over the patch and use your car to compact it. 4. Use a lawn roller to compact sizable areas, rolling lengthwise, then crosswise.

IT'S IMPORTANT that drive be dry and clean before applying top dressing. Sweep surface with stiff broom (1). Use industrial paint roller to apply dressing (2); throw away when finished.

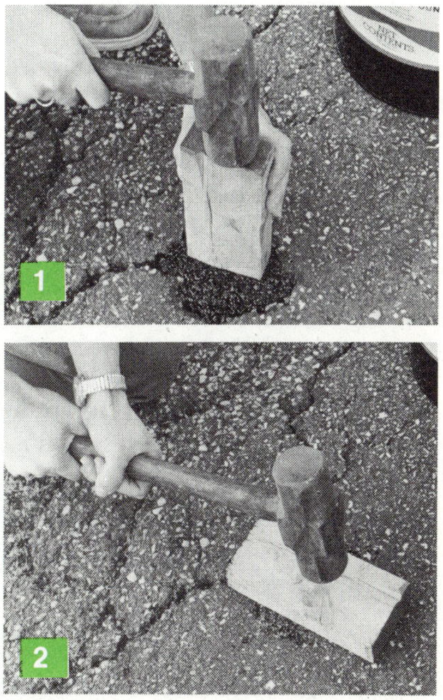

SCRAP 2 X 4 BLOCK and sledge are used to tamp cold patch in small holes and long, wide cracks. Place block on edge (1) or use flat (2). The more the patch is compressed, the stronger will be the bond.

HOW TO FILL LARGE CRACKS

Rake cracks with a screwdriver (from left) to remove old asphalt and gravel. Wire-brush top edges to remove loose particles. Blow out cracks with shop or canister vacuum. Overfill about ⅛ inch with crack filler, using a caulking gun. Smooth filler with trowel dipped in mineral spirits. Avoid applying filler when temperature is 40° F. or below as it may not set.

only to what it touches. If the area is dirty or if there is loose gravel or bits of loose asphalt, you will get a less-than-strong bond. For this reason, surface preparation is most important. Make sure the area you are working on is as clean as possible, even if it means going over it with a shop or household vacuum cleaner.

hairline cracks

The first step in the repair of a hairline crack is to make sure it *is* truly a hairline and that you aren't looking at only the narrow top edge of a wider, deeper wedge-shaped fault. Take a knife or screwdriver and try to rout out the crack. If it's nothing more than a hairline, meaning 1/16 inch wide or less, it will be sealed by a well-applied layer of top coat, the last step of the job. If the crack is larger than 1/16 inch, proceed with the next step.

repairing larger cracks

For this type of repair, you use a rubber-extended, asphalt crack filler. The rubber allows for flexibility and expansion after the material has cured. The crack filler is supplied in cartridges (like caulking compounds) and is used with an ordinary caulking gun.

Before filling the crack, make sure the area is clean and dry. If the crack filler will come into contact with metal drains or metal expansion joints, those surfaces should be wire-brushed of rust before applying the filler.

Crack filler should not be applied below 40° F. The material becomes highly viscous below this temperature and, when used with a gun-type applicator, it's more difficult to work with. Because of higher viscosity, the sealer will not fill the cracks completely, and since frost begins to form below 40° F., there could be a loss of adhesion later.

Crack filler is ready to use as it comes from the tube. Never thin it, even if it is stiff from having been stored outdoors. Bring it inside for 24 hours to warm it. Never apply direct heat to the cartridge with a torch or by heating in a pan of hot water. Crack filler contains a solvent which may, under direct heat, reach its flash point. In addition, direct heat may drive off the solvent, thereby destroying the cartridge.

Put the nozzle as far into the crack as possible to prevent any air entrapment and pull the gun toward you as you squeeze. Let the filler build up ⅛ inch above the crack. After the crack is filled, go back with a trowel or similar tool dipped in mineral spirits (not linseed oil) and tool the surface smooth. Make sure the crack is completely filled and sealed at the edge. You want to keep moisture out now that the crack is clean and dry.

Crack filler will cure in about 24 hours depending on temperature and humidity. The lower the temperature and the higher the humidity, the longer it takes to cure.

While the filler is curing, cover it with waxed paper to keep from tracking it into the house. The paper is easily removed the next day and any remaining traces will soon disappear with usage.

larger holes and depressions

Cold-patch driveway-patching compound is used for repairing big holes, depressions or ruts. Because it is made for filling and covering comparatively large voids, cold patch is a combination of hard aggregate (gravel, pebbles) asphalt, resins and wetting agents.

In your selection of cold patch, it is important to know that compounds are generally available two ways: in large 50 to 75-pound paper sacks or in 5-gallon cans. The paper sacks are usually less expensive, but have disadvantages. Many times the filled sacks are shipped and stored in tiers on pallets. This means that the lower sacks in the stack are being progressively more compacted than the upper ones before the material is used. Also, material stored in sacks may have a tendency to begin to oxidize, which leads to premature setup.

Again, surface preparation is all important. The area to be patched should be dry and free of dust. I used Gibson-Homans cold patch, which can be applied on a damp, puddle-free surface so the area can be made dust-free by hosing it down.

Cold patch is ready to use as it comes from the can or sack. It can be "spooned" or "ladled" into a hole or poured into a larger depression. If the area to be patched is deeper than 1 inch, it should be patched in 1-inch layers.

After pouring and spreading the cold patch, you must compact it, which is an important step. The more the patching compound is compressed, the more tenacious it becomes and the better the bond you get.

There are several ways to compact cold patch. If the area is a narrow hole, a good compacting tool is a 2 x 4. Place it on edge or side depending on area and then put a lot of muscle into a sledge hammer. If the area is large, such as a lengthy depression, a good compacting tool is an ordinary lawn roller. Roll it back and forth several times, then at right angles and back again.

Another good method for compacting a large patch is to lay a ¾-in. board over it and roll your car wheel back and forth over it.

If the area to be patched is along the edge of your drive, use a No. 1 grade, creosote-treated wood form to contain the patch. If the form is then left in position, it will help resist "creeping" which is inherent in all asphalt. Be careful when working with creosote. It is a registered poison and should be handled with sensible caution.

The newly cold-patched area can be driven over in three to four hours—but don't let your car stand on the patched spot for at least a week. This will give the patch ample time to set. The same holds true for the top coating. Usually you will patch one weekend, top coat the next.

top coating the surface

Now that all the cracks, holes, ruts and depressions have been repaired, it is most important that you seal the entire drive surface with a good quality top coat or dressing. It not only will provide a moisture-tight seal and give the drive a finished look, but it will rejuvenate the dry, brittle or deteriorated asphalt, literally adding years to your driveway.

Basically there are two varieties of top coating available: A Gilsonite base and a tar-emulsion base. There are advantages and disadvantages to each. Of the two, tar emulsion is generally a little less expensive per gallon, but requires two coats. Gilsonite requires only one coat. On the average, Gilsonite will cover 100 square feet per gallon, while tar emulsion covers between 60 and 75 square feet per gallon.

Tar emulsion is highly resistant to gasoline, oil and similar corrosives over long periods of exposure. Gilsonite, though less resistant, will stand up well to the occasional spill or drip.

application

Tar emulsion cannot be applied below freezing (if it freezes before it is applied, it loses its chemical qualities) and really should be applied above 45 ° F. Gilsonite can be applied near or above freezing. Tar emulsion requires thorough mixing before being applied; Gilsonite does not.

Tar emulsion requires about 2½ hours to dry to the touch versus about one hour for Gilsonite. The Gilsonite coating should be ready for traffic in about 12 hours (depending on temperature and humidity), while at the same temperature and humidity tar emulsion would require about 24 hours. In addition, since tar emulsion is a water-base compound, if it gets wet during the first 24 hours wait another day for it to dry completely.

tracking

During warm weather, tar emulsion has a tendency to become tacky. If the drive serves as a home basketball court or other playing surface, the coating may be picked up on shoes and tracked into the house. Gilsonite, on the other hand, is unaffected by the hot sun and remains tack-free once it has set.

Again, surface preparation is extremely important. With the Gilsonite base, the drive must be clean and dry. A true hairline crack will be sealed with an application of Gilsonite base coating. Anything larger than a 1/16-inch crack should be filled with crack filler followed by a five-day wait for proper curing.

Give the drive a good sweeping followed by vacuuming. If there is oil on the drive, wash the area well with detergent. Gilsonite top coating may be applied with a large squeegee, stiff brush, broom or roller. I used a long-handled industrial paint roller.

The coating is ready to use right from the can. Dip the roller to saturate it, then spread the coating over the drive surface. Apply it liberally to make sure the surface is well covered and sealed, but at the same time use as thin a coat as possible consistent with good coverage. Be sure there are no puddles, and don't try to cover less than the recommended 100 square feet per gallon. In this case too much is worse than too little.

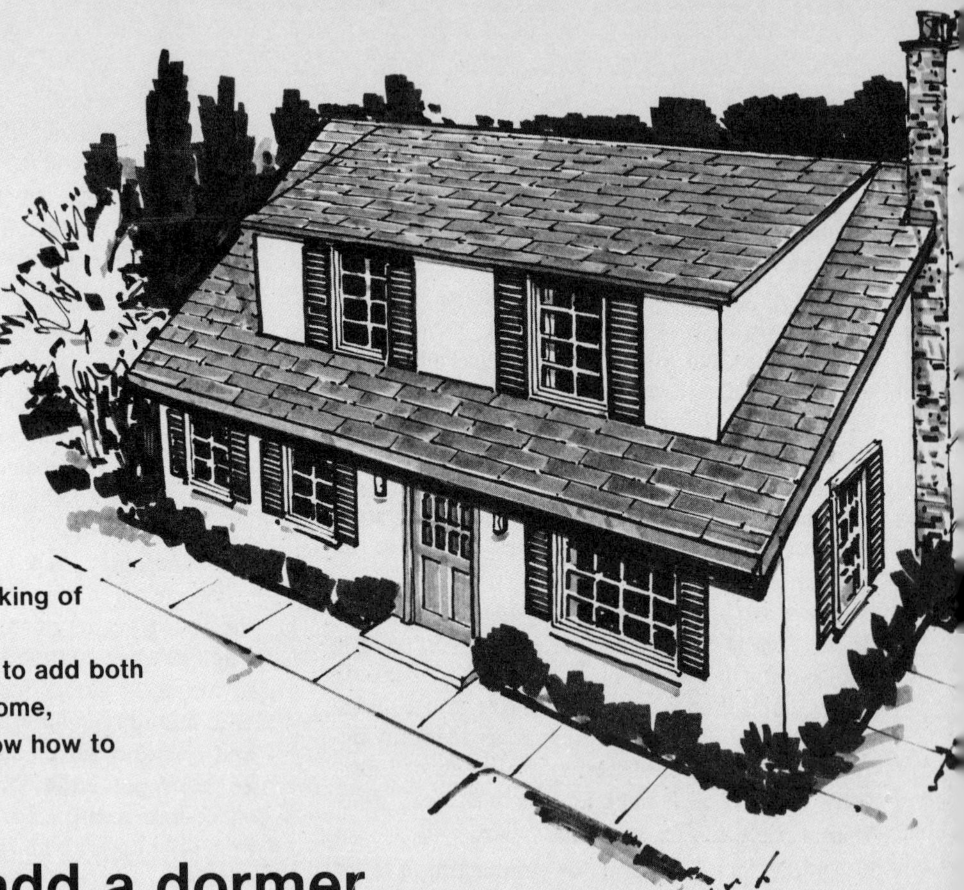

If you are thinking of converting attic space to an extra bedroom to add both light and space to your home, you'll need to know how to frame a dormer

How to add a dormer

WHEN A FAMILY starts outgrowing its house, moving to a larger one is not always the smart thing to do, especially if you have attic space that could be converted into the extra room you need.

Dormers play an important part in converting attic space into a bedroom or two. They provide not only added headroom that's often required but light and air as well. Dormers can also do a lot to perk up an uninteresting roof line.

Whether you can take on the job of framing a dormer yourself depends a lot on how handy you

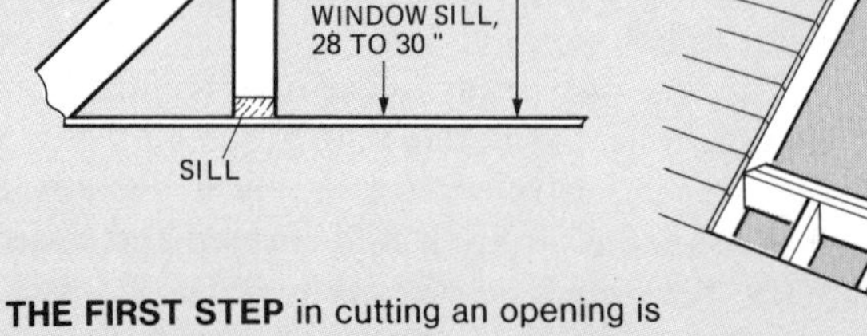

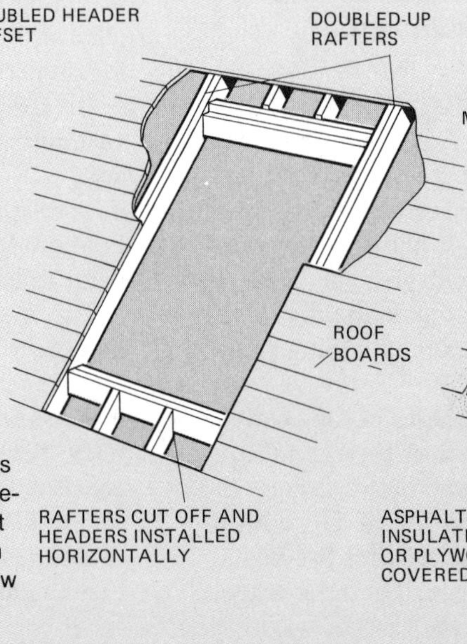

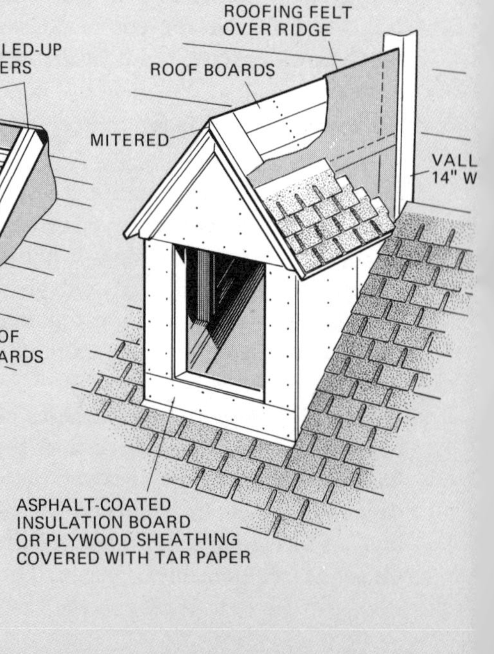

THE FIRST STEP in cutting an opening is to mark it with four nails, then carefully remove each row of shingles. Cut away felt paper and saw through roof boards flush with the existing rafters using a saber saw or handsaw.

IF FRAMING a dormer is too much for you to tackle even with the help of a friend, yet your attic remodeling plans require a dormer or two for adequate light and air, you can have this part of the overall job done while you take on the work inside. In seeking outside help, get bids from at least three contractors and compare prices. Ask each one for names of recent customers so you can get recommendations on their work. Insist on a comprehensive written contract with a complete description of the job, materials, timetable (especially important in this case) and payments.

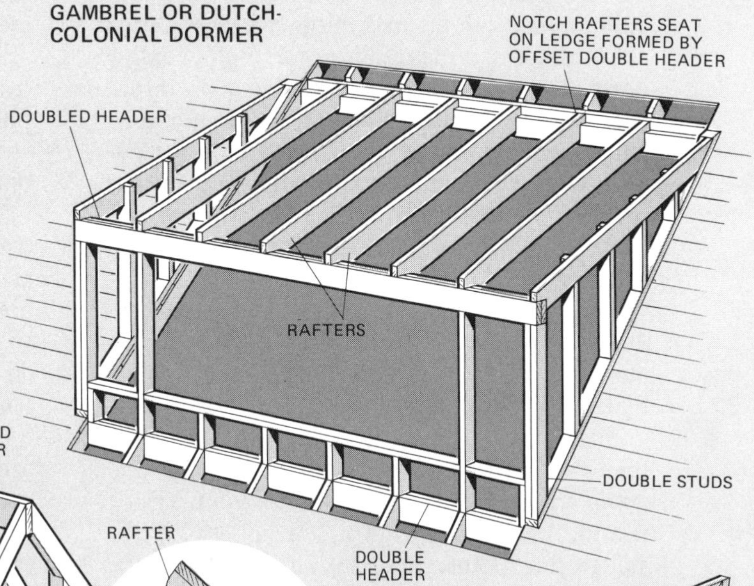

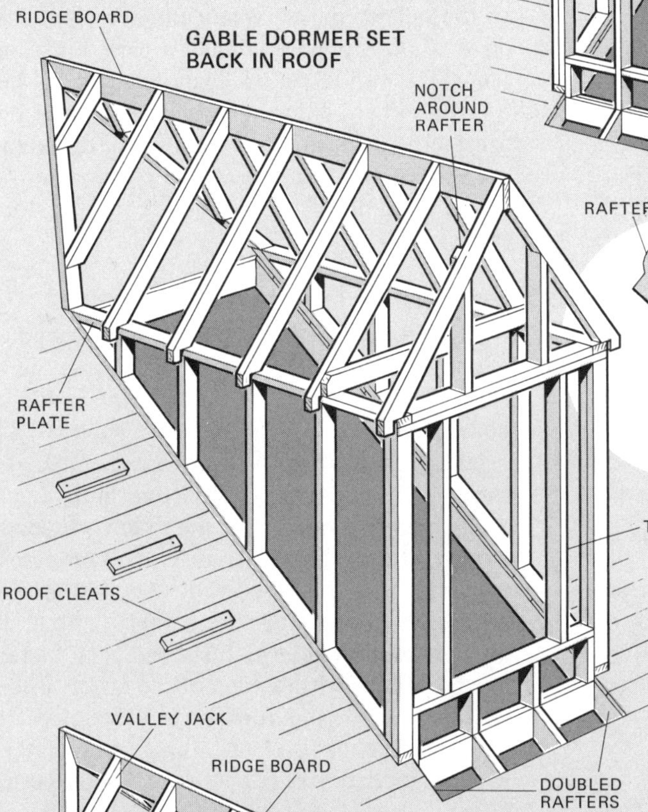

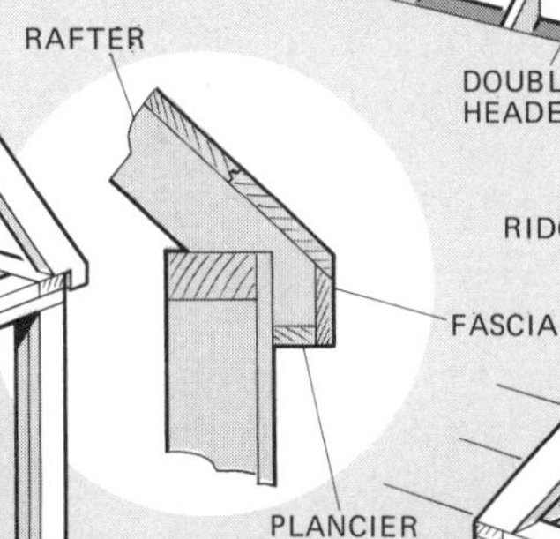

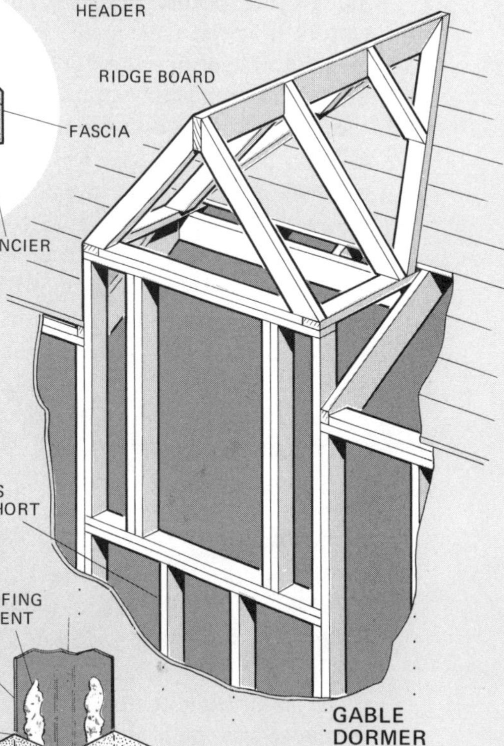

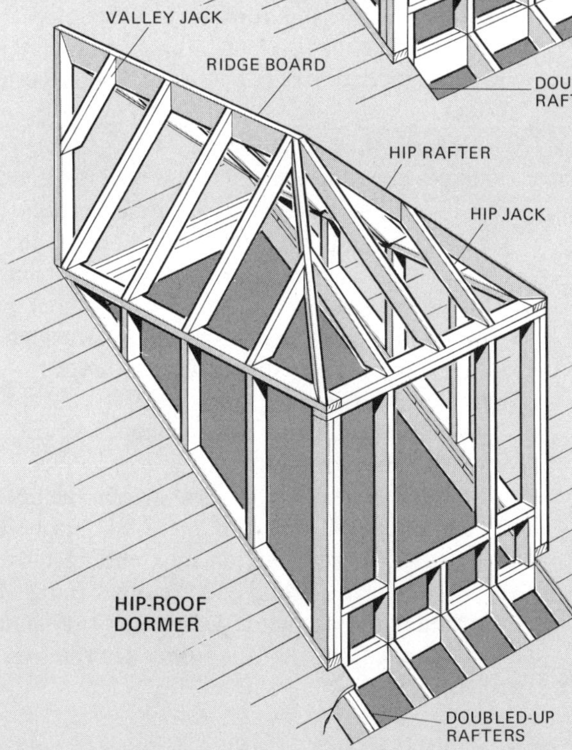

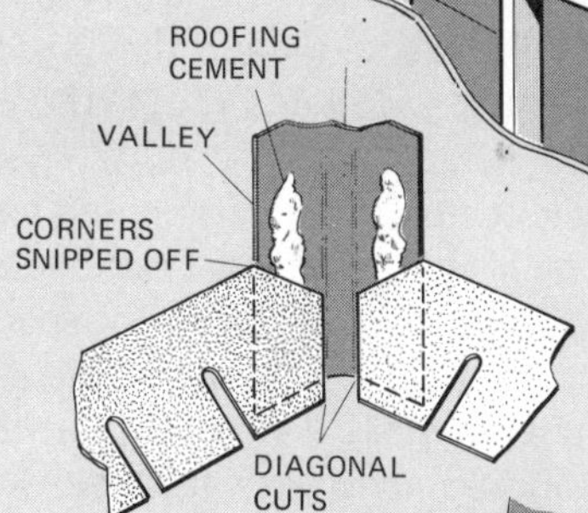

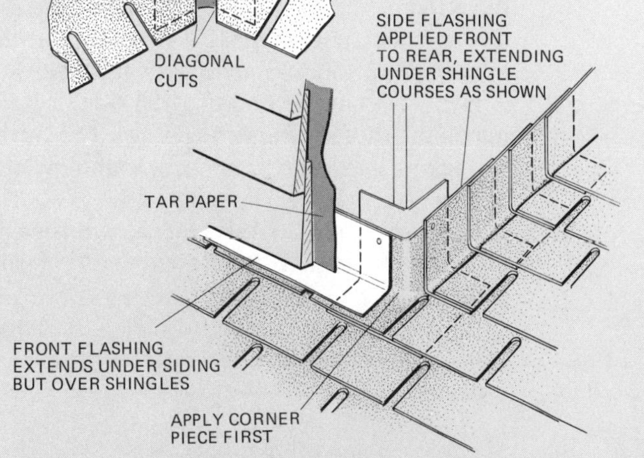

are with hammer and saw and in knowing your limitations. With the exception of a large Dutch colonial dormer, the framing of a single-window dormer isn't as difficult as you may think. Weather is a primary concern. Since you must cut an opening in the roof, you'll need clear weather for at least a couple of days. But be prepared for rain with a tarp you can tuck underneath the shingles and weight it down with a sandbag or two.

There are four basic types of dormers, as shown on page 117. Select the one that best complements the style of your house. Most important is to have it conform to local building codes.

First lay out the dormer location carefully, then pry up the shingles within the area and about a foot beyond on all sides. Trim back the roofing paper to within a few inches of the shingle line. Before doing any cutting, double the rafters that will frame the opening, cutting the new rafters so they'll extend at least 3 or 4 feet beyond the top and bottom of the hole Then saw the roof boards along the inside of the doubled rafters, and across the top and bottom of the marked opening. The trimmed boards above and below will support the cut rafters until you can spike double headers. Note that the opening should extend one roof-board width past the marked-out area at top and bottom.

The lower edge of the upper double header should be located at ceiling height. The bottom header members have their top edges set flush, at a height that will put the sill 28 to 30 in. above the floor.

frame the front first

Whenever possible, the side walls of the dormer should be erected over the doubled rafter—on sole plates nailed through the roof boards and into rafters below, using 20-penny (20d) nails. Build the front frame first and nail it in place, bracing it plumb until the rafter plates are in position. Then add the side studs, spacing them 16 in. o.c., driving 16d nails down into them through the rafter plates, and toenailing their lower end to the sole plate with 10d nails.

Next, cut out one end of a 1x6 ridge board to match the roof slope, leaving it overlong; level it by tacking it to a temporary prop standing on the header above the sash opening. Now, lay out and cut a master rafter and use this as a cutting pattern for all dormer rafters except the valley jacks.

Since spans are short in dormer construction, light framing stock is often selected. It isn't unusual for dormers to be framed with 2x4s (or even 2x3s).

Nail the rafters in place with 10d nails, starting from the outer end; then trim the ridge board flush with the outer rafters. A shed-type dormer, such as the gambrel shown, avoids all ridge-board fitting.

The rough window opening is centered in the front frame and should be 4¼ in. wider than the sash unit you select. Whether the trimmer studs are single or double depends on their proximity to the corner posts. When they're close, as in three of the framing details on page 117, double trimmers aren't needed. The fourth detail shows a flush-with-wall dormer where the corner posts are merely nailed to existing studs to extend a section of the wall upward; in this case, the rough framing of the window calls for double trimmers.

how a cornice turns corners

The front cornice construction depends on which type of side cornice you choose. In any case, the roof boards run only to the inside face of the front rafter, where they are nailed to a 2x2 cleat fastened along the upper inside edge of the rafter itself, to create the front overhang. In plain cornice construction, this overhang is braced by trim, but for the box type you extend the plancier (or soffit board) its own width beyond the front rafter so you can "turn the corner" with it, nailing the front plancier to a second cleat fastened along the lower front edge of the rafter. Though sketches show the roof boards beveled flush with the side fascia or sheathing, they may project an inch or so if you prefer an overhang effect.

Before shingling, lay a 14-in. sheet-metal valley where dormer and house roof meet, bending it until it lies flat against both roofs (see sketches, page 116.) Snap chalk lines up the valley to indicate where shingles must be trimmed. The top corners are also snipped off to shed water toward the valley. To avoid nailing through the valley, anchor the diagonally cut edges of the shingles with cement.

Where the dormer walls meet the roof, use step flashing, starting with a corner piece and working back each side, as shown in the bottom sketch, page 117. The side pieces should be 6 in. long, with the vertical flange extending at least 3 in. up under the siding and the other flange 4 in. out under the shingles. Don't nail the shingles through the flashing. The front strip rides on top of the shingles.

SALT AND PEPPER SHAKERS for picnics and camping may be made from 35-mm film cans. Cover the ends with foil, hold the foil with rubber bands and poke tiny holes in the top. The metal cap makes the shakers watertight.

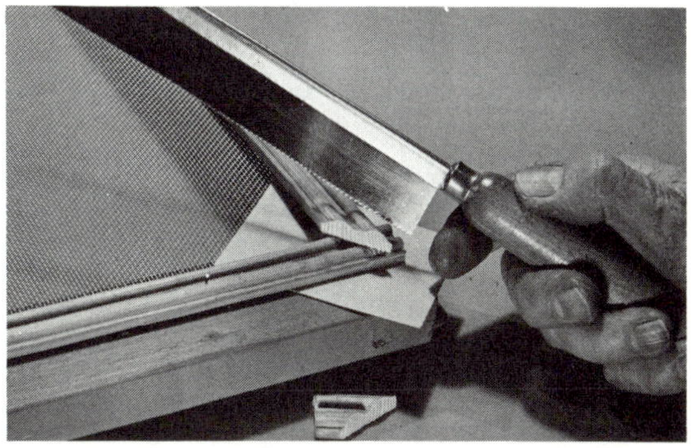

WHEN MITERING THE MOLDING at the corners of window screens, you'll want to get a close-fitting joint. The secret is to let the strips lap, slip cardboard underneath and saw both at the same time.

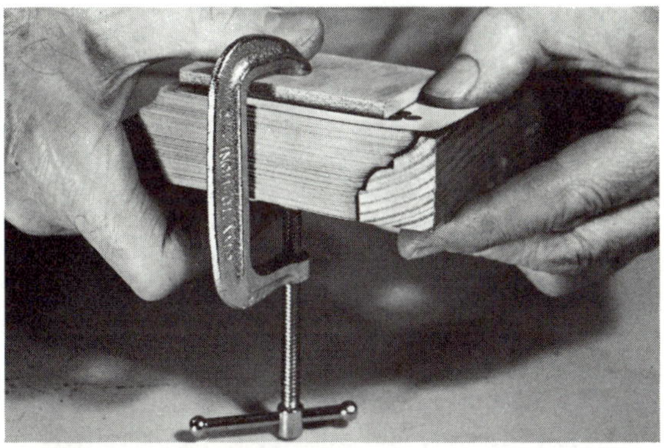

A DECK OF PLAYING CARDS and a C-clamp will pinch-hit for a contour gauge when you copy the profile of the molding. Crowd the deck firmly against the work and hold with a clamp.

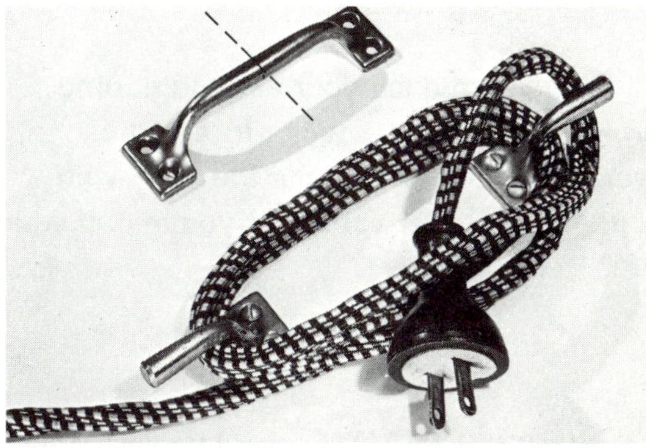

CLEATS FOR STORING appliance cords and anchoring clothesline can be quickly made from a window-sash lift. Cut the lift in half with a hacksaw and file the ends until they are smooth.

ANGLE-IRON PADS allow you to clamp a larger surface with fewer clamps. Placed under the jaws of a clamp, the pads distribute pressure evenly over the area which they cover.

BUTT JOINTS fastened with corner irons can be drawn tighter with the aid of a cardboard shim. Place the shim under one leg while you fasten the other leg.

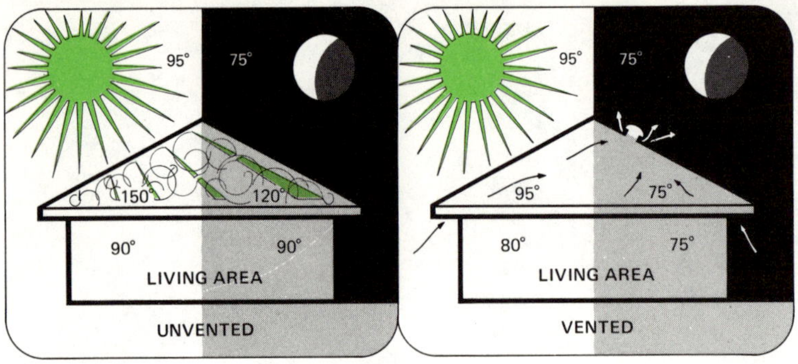

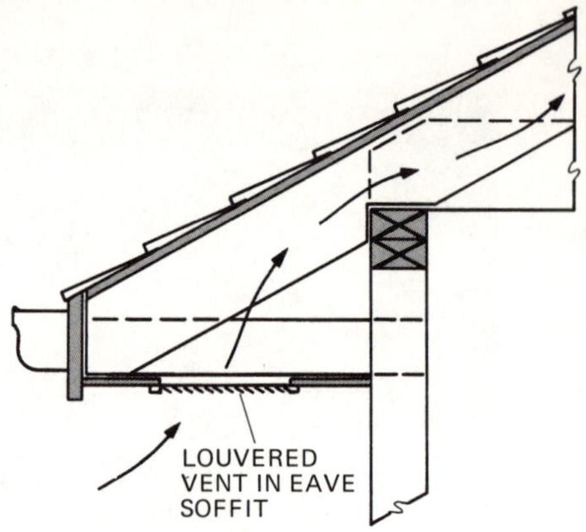

Cool your attic to cool your house

You can reduce your airconditioning bills and keep your house cooler in summer by lowering the temperature in the attic with a wind-driven or power ventilator you install yourself

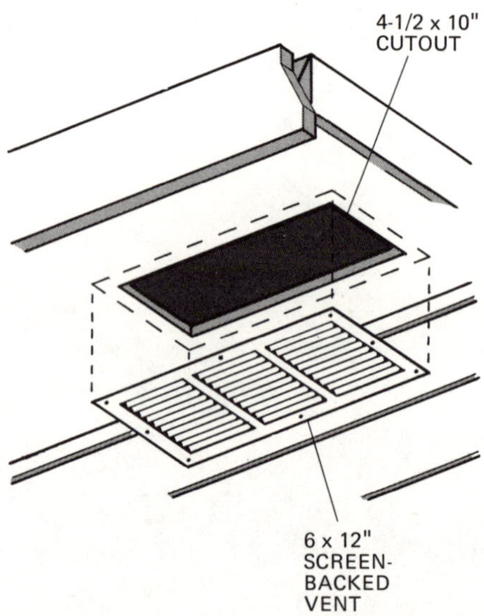

■ YOU'VE HEARD of a speed trap; what about a heat trap? Chances are, you have one under your roof.

Step into your attic on a sweltering day. You won't stay long: It's like entering an oven. When super-heated air is trapped in the attic of your home, the temperature is often as much as 60° F. higher than outside. When daytime temperatures reach 95°, it can be as much as 150° in the attic. When the sun goes down, the outside temperature may drop 10° or more. Inside, however, the house continues to stay miserably hot because your attic "oven" is still at work. It takes about eight hours for the attic air to cool down to match the night air. And then, before you know it, the sun is up again and the house begins heating.

The solution, of course, is not to let the heat build up but to replace it throughout the day with fresh cooler air from the outside. When attic temperature is kept low, heat can't radiate to rooms below. Consequently, it takes less cooling to keep your home comfortable on hot days and nights and, in turn, costs less to cool it since your airconditioning system runs less. Even without airconditioning, you'll feel the difference.

To lower attic temperature significantly it takes more than the small gravity-type vents normally found in roof or gable. On hot days, such stationary ventilators cannot by gravity alone remove heat fast enough to prevent temperature buildup. It takes an automatic exhaust fan—power or wind-driven.

Fans that are automatic and have built-in thermostats start by themselves at a preset temperature. When attic temperature reaches 90°, for example, the fan is set to turn on and run throughout the heat of the day, pulling cooler air in and forcing hot air out. The fan runs until the temperature is below 90°, then shuts off automatically.

Flushing excess heat from your attic is accomplished best when there is an adequate number of air intakes along the eaves. With the fan located at the highest point in the attic and the intake vents at the lowest, uniform air flow is assured.

SEE ALSO
Airconditioners . . . Winterizing, homes

AUTOMATIC 16-in. Hunter fan is designed to mount in gable opening. It gives a complete air change every five minutes in an 8500-cu.-ft. attic.

Screenbacked vents (8 x 16 in.) are easy to install in the roof's soffit, but where the roof has no overhang, gable louvers must provide air intake. Ideally, through-the-wall intakes would also be installed in the gables at the attic floor line.

Your home will have a lot to do with the type of exhaust fan you install. So you should take a good look at your house before you make a purchase. If it has a conventional-pitch roof, you have a choice of installing a fan that mounts flush in a gable or one that mounts on the roof. If it has a hip roof, and no gables, the fan will have to be one that's designed to mount in the roof.

Fans for moving air out of the attic are of two types—wind-driven and power fans. The one you choose will depend on how much air you need to move and the cost of energy in your area.

An efficient attic-cooling device, the wind-driven ventilator is gaining acceptance in many energy-short areas of the country. Since it is powered by the wind, it uses no electricity. By cooling the attic continually, it eliminates oven-like heat which, in turn, saves on airconditioning.

Since a wind-driven ventilator is turned by the slightest breeze, it keeps attic air moving, preventing a heat buildup that often reaches temperatures up to 140-150° F. In a well-ventilated attic, less heat is absorbed by the insulation and there's less to radiate down through the ceilings.

Even when there's no wind, a turbine ventilator continues to draw out the heat. Air drawn in through attic vents and escaping through the ventilator causes the unit to turn.

As a rule of thumb, one 12-in. ventilator is recommended for each 1000 sq. ft. of attic space; two units are best for 1200 sq. ft.

The photos on these pages show how easy it is to install wind-powered ventilators. The ventilators shown are a product of Triangle Engineering Co., Box 7464, Houston, TX 77008.

INSTALLING A power vent fan in the gable end of a house requires cutting a suitable opening for it, framing with short 2 x 4 studs and headers and lining with a frame of ¾-in. stock and 1⅛-in. casing. Exterior cover is carefully cut to fit snugly against the casing of frame, then caulked. Dimensions here are for a 16-in. Hunter fan (Model 22082) which has louvers that seal opening when the fan is off. Bead of caulking is also applied to flange of ventilator when fastening to casing with screws. Fan pulls air through louvers in opposite gable to flush the heat from one end to the other.

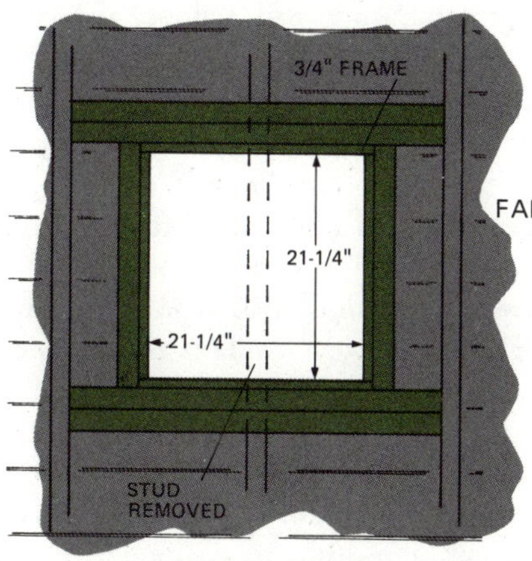

OPENING (REAR VIEW)

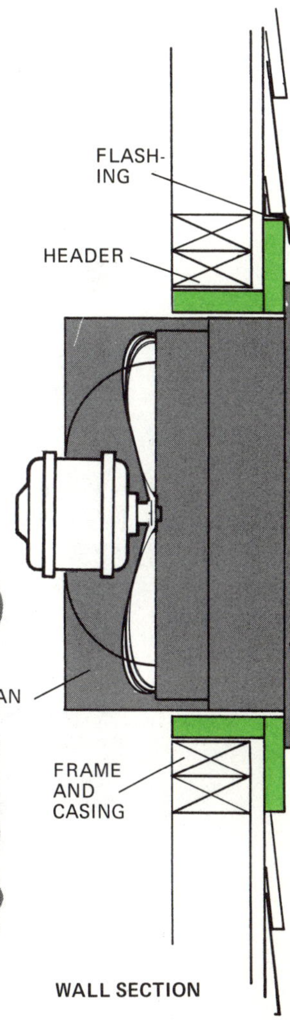

WALL SECTION

power ventilators

Power ventilators do a more efficient job of cooling than the wind-driven models because

INSTALLING A WIND-DRIVEN OR POWER VENTILATOR

Wind-driven turbine (left) by Triangle turns with slightest breeze, and escaping attic heat turns it when there is no breeze. The Vent-A-Matic power vent (below, left) is a low-profile ventilator designed for mounting on a roof. It has a 14-in. fan, turns on and shuts off automatically, and works best when intakes are around eaves.

1. LOCATE VENTILATOR from inside attic and at least 24 in. below ridge on rear side of roof.

2. CENTER BASE over pilot hole in roof and use inside of the base to scribe a hole in roof shingles.

they use electricity to move the hot air out and the cooler air in. Power ventilators are thermostatically controlled. Set to turn on automatically when the attic temperature reaches 110° F., the fan will run until the temperature is reduced to approximately 96° F. A cool attic means a cooler house day and night, and it is claimed that the lower room temperature will reduce airconditioning load as much as 30 percent.

Not only will a power ventilator keep your house cooler but it will reduce the possibility of spontaneous combustion in the attic. It will also prevent excessive heat and moisture from deteriorating attic insulation and the shingles.

As for power ventilators, two types are available. The larger, more powerful fans are designed to be mounted in a gable end of the house. Whether you can use this type will depend on the shape and construction of your home. The other type is the Vent-A-Matic power ventilator. It is a smaller, circular fan and is designed to be mounted directly in the roof.

The gable-mounted fans give a complete air change every five minutes when installed in an 8500-cu.-ft. attic. To install this model, you will have to cut an opening in the gable end of the house. This involves removing one of the existing studs, then building in a frame of 2 x 4 studs and headers. This frame should be lined and a casing built per the manufacturer's supplied dimensions. It is important to caulk carefully around the entire opening to prevent air leaks. Sufficient air intakes should be provided, especially around the eaves, so that the fan is not laboring to keep the air moving.

If a roof-mounted Vent-A-Matic fan is better suited to your house, you can count on one ventilator adequately cooling a home with up to 2000 sq. ft. of living space. Its 14-in. fan does the best job when the attic has at least 300 sq. in. of air intake located along the eaves.

The fan is enclosed in a housing of Cycolac ABS plastic, a durable space-age material that will outlast sheet metal and never needs painting. The ventilator is made by the Butler Engineering Co., Box 728, Mineral Wells, TX 76067. It measures 27½ in. sq., has a dome 8½ in. high and is operated by a 1/10-hp, 115-v. motor.

The unit should be mounted close to the center of the roof and near the roof ridgeline. Keep in mind that for a neat-looking installation, the unit should be visible only from one side of the roof. This will require the unit to be moved down from the ridge line until it can't be seen from the street.

Installation of a roof-mounted power-ventilator is almost identical to installation of a wind-powered ventilator. The first step is to locate the fan. This should be done from the inside of the attic. By working from the inside you will be able to locate the unit between the roof rafters. When you have determined the best spot, drill a hole up through the roof with an electric drill.

Then go outside and locate the hole. If you have trouble locating the spot, have someone

3. **USING CIRCLE** as a guide, cut away shingles with a sharp knife. Cut ½ in. outside the circle.

4. **CUT HOLE** through roof boards with a sabre saw or by hand with a keyhole saw, following the circle.

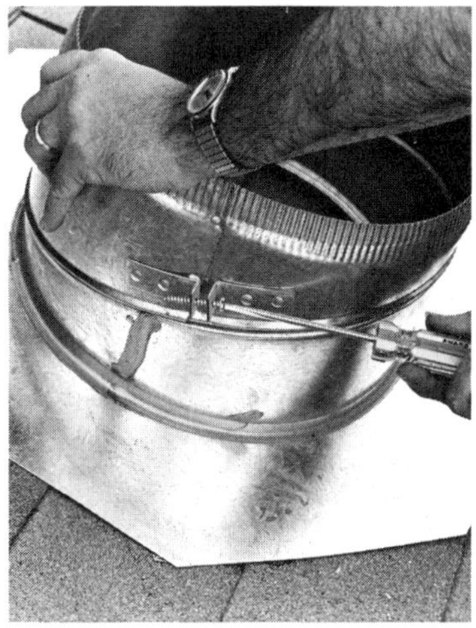

5. **WITH SCREWDRIVER,** loosen the locking screw on adjustable-pitch base so you can turn it.

6. **WHEN LOOSE,** grip top section and turn sufficiently to make the top of the base level.

7. **RETIGHTEN SCREW,** then slide the top half of flashing up under shingles, removing nails in the way.

8. **SECURE BASE** to roof with eight roofing nails driven through the flange, then caulk the heads.

9. **PLACE VENTILATOR** over crimped base; check installation by placing level across the top.

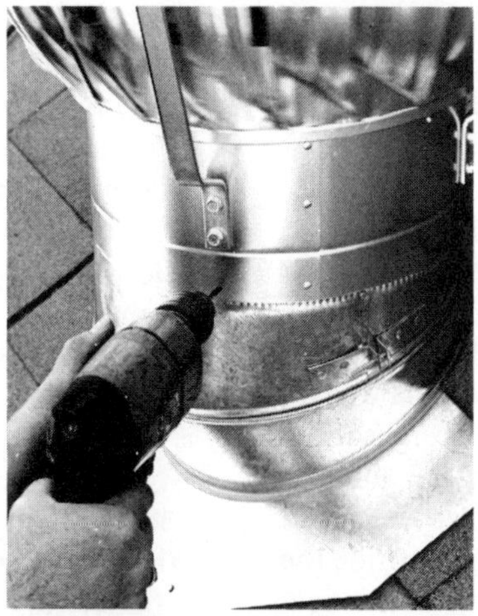

10. **USE BASE-RING** holes as guide in drilling matching holes around and through the base flange.

11. **LOCK RING** to flange with No. 8, ½-in. sheet-metal screws. Drive screws home for tight fit.

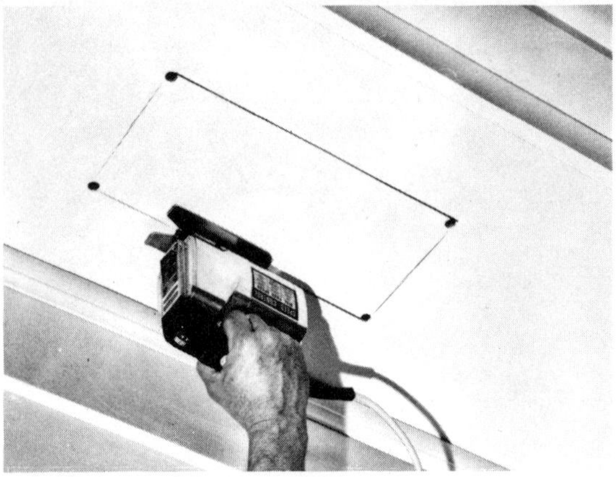

UNLESS you have adequate air intake through which cooler air can be pulled as hot air is exhausted, you can't expect maximum efficiency from your ventilator. Holes are cut in soffit and then capped with louvered cornice vents.

AFTER WIRING, check the proper operation of a powered ventilator with a 60-w. bulb. On a cool day the fan should come on when heated by the bulb and cycle off when the bulb is removed.

shine a flashlight through the hole from inside the attic.

Using the hole as a reference point, draw a 27-⅜-in. square outline on the shingles with a crayon or piece of chalk. This will be used to locate the metal base of the Vent-A-Matic unit.

You are now ready to cut the hole. Begin by fashioning a wood compass from a lumber scrap. Drive a nail through one end and drill a hole 17-⅜ inches away to take a crayon for marking. Place the nail in the hole in the roof and carefully scribe a circle on the shingles.

Next, cut through the shingles along the scribe line. This can be done using tin shears or a sharp knife. Clear out the shingles from inside the circle and remove any roofing nails.

Adjust the compass to draw a 15 in. diameter hole and draw a second hole inside the cleared area. The 15-in. hole is cut through the roofing boards using a sabre saw or keyhole saw. Start in the center where the hole was drilled and work your way to the outside.

You are now ready to install the ventilator. With the unit parallel to the ridgeline of the roof, slide the plastic flange up under the shingles, starting at the center of the hole. Position the unit squarely with the 27-⅜-in. outline you marked on the roof. Align the unit with the shingle lines. Continue to slide the flange under the shingles until the round housing can be centered and placed in the hole. You may have to go inside the attic to verify that the unit is properly positioned.

Nail the exposed portion of the flange to the roof. Galvanized roofing nails should be used to prevent rust. Check the unit for leakage using a garden hose. Because of the way the fan is positioned under the shingles, it should not leak. If it does, use butyl rubber caulking along the edges of the flange.

electrical installation

The control box for the unit should be screwed to an attic rafter. When connecting to the 110-v. line, follow the wiring diagram furnished by the manufacturer. All wiring should meet local building codes. If you have questions about proper installation, consult an electrician.

You are now ready to verify proper operation of the unit. The checkout procedure can be used for both roof and gable-mounted models. Put a 60-w. bulb in a drop cord. Turn on the current to the fan on a day when the attic is cool. The fan should not start. By bringing the bulb near the thermostat in the control box, you should be able to get the fan to start operating. If not, check all electrical connections carefully. Likewise, the fan should shut off when the bulb is removed from the vicinity of the control box.

when to install

The best time to install any attic ventilation device is in the spring. There is nothing worse than prowling around in an overheated attic to connect a fan and verify its operation. And by installing it before you need it, you will reduce your airconditioning bills and keep your house comfortable all summer.

Housing on housing

I propose to build an insulated box over my combination electric furnace/airconditioner. It now sits outside, with insulated plenums and ducts under the house. As I believe the metal housing absorbs heat in the summer and radiates heat in the winter, I think a cover might add to the unit's efficiency. Does this seem like a worthwhile effort? I could provide a hole for the air intake and discharge.—Thomas L. Denton, Madison, Ala.

I strongly advice against covering it for the following reasons: Circulation of air is extremely important around your unit. You could create a condensation problem on your housing with resultant rusting. Besides, your unit should have been insulated on the inside by the manufacturer. Reputable manufacturers will have done all they can to increase their units' EERs (Energy Efficiency Ratio). This includes proper insulation.

Replacing laminate surface

The Formica laminate on my kitchen countertop needs replacing. Can the old surface be sanded sufficiently to glue on new Formica satisfactorily?—Marvin E. Davis, Tuscaloosa, Ala.

A laminated countertop can be covered *only* if you sand it sufficiently, removing all shiny surface. Use a medium-grit paper. Don't forget to sand any self-edges that may require re-covering. Dust, then wipe all surfaces clean with lacquer thinner. When resurfacing, apply two coats of contact adhesive on the sanded areas. Let the first coat dry thoroughly before applying the second coat. Make certain room is ventilated.

Cracked concrete foundation

The outside of the foundation wall of my older home is stuccoed. The inside is treated with what I think is a moisture-proofing material. The mortar between some of the blocks on all four walls has loosened, leaving small cracks inside and outside. Cracks occur all around some of the blocks, others zigzag. The mortar seems soft and crumbly. How can I correct this?—E.H. Dustman, Everett La.

Without seeing the problem, it's difficult to evaluate. The zigzag crack is most likely due to settlement in your footings, but if the crack hasn't grown or changed for some time, your settlement has probably reached its final position. The joints should be raked out (cleaned) a minimum of ½-in. deep, and pointed up with a mix of one part mortar cement to three parts of fine, clean mortar sand. Work the mortar in with a pointing tool (a 6-in. length of ⅜-in. dowel works equally well). If it is not practical to remove the stucco on the outside, fasten wire lath to the existing wall and add ¾-in. stucco over this. If you have any doubt as to the structural adequacy of the walls, you would be wise to consult a licensed structural engineer.

Rust stains on roof

I have rust stains beginning to appear on my white asphalt roof shingles. Can you tell me how to remove them, and if I can treat them so they won't reappear?—Dennis Evans, Saugerties, N.Y.

The Asphalt Roofing Manufacturers Assn. suggests one method. Spray a solution of one part chlorine bleach to three parts water on the area. Several applications may be required. Don't brush the roof, as you may dislodge the granules. Take care that the bleach runoff doesn't stain the wood trim. Make a dam to catch the bleach with a fabric dropcloth. Also cover base plantings. The only way to keep the rust from reappearing is to track down the source (antenna bracket or other metal) and treat it with a rust-inhibiting paint.

Bubble trouble

When our toilet is flushed, it bubbles from the bottom and empties poorly. Thinking our vent pipe was clogged, we hosed water through it from the roof outlet. The water seemed to go right through to the septic tank, indicating that the vent pipe was clear. The toilet still acts the same. Any suggestions?—Mary M. Hill, Chambersburg, Pa.

You've taken the one step most people forget—you've cleaned the vent. However, as that didn't cure your problem, you've got a few more possibilities. It could be an obstruction in the toilet itself, or in the branch line to the soil pipe. I know of a similar case in which the vent was clear, but the obstruction was a tree root in the line between the house and the tank. The line was eventually cleared with an electric auger (rooter) in the hands of a professional. These rooters can be rented by homeowners, but I feel that this is one case of "Penny wise. . . ."

Soldering aluminum gutters

Is it possible to solder aluminum gutters? If so, do I use a soldering iron or torch?—Joseph Cancilla Jr., North East, Pa.

Yes, it's possible, using the special solders available. I would prefer the torch as it gives faster, more uniform heating of the metal. (*Caution: The danger of fire in this area is particularly serious since the overhang materials have been drying in the sun.*)

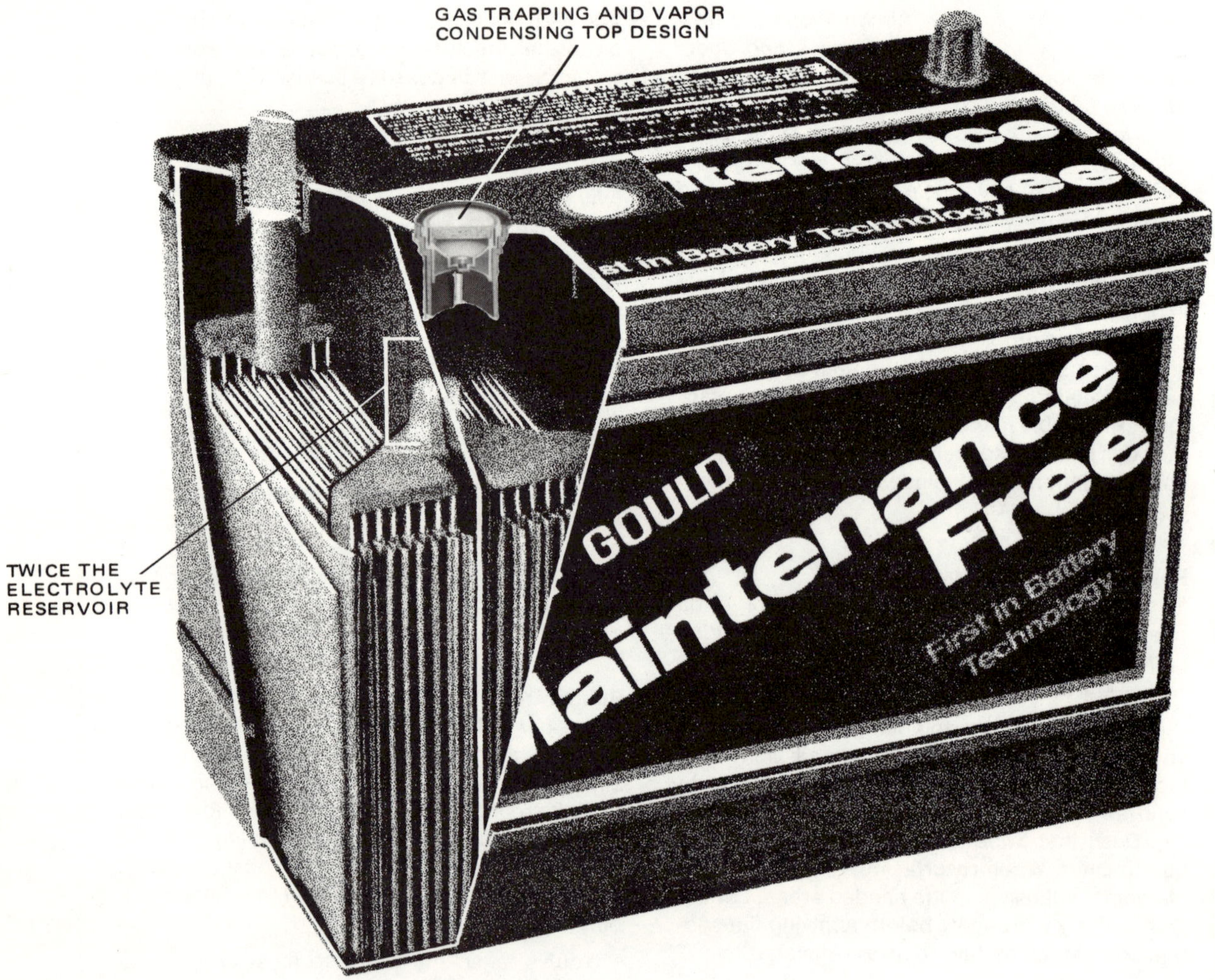

How to take care of a 'maintenance-free' battery

By MORT SCHULTZ

■ IN RECENT YEARS many of the major automakers have begun putting maintenance-free or low-maintenance batteries into their new cars. These also have become large sellers at retail stores, chain stores and oil companies. As such batteries become more popular, you should know how to maintain, test and recharge them.

SEE ALSO

Battery testers . . . Cables, auto . . .
Dieseling, auto . . . Distributors, auto . . .
Electronic ignition, auto . . .
Ignition systems, auto . . . Sparkplugs . . .
Tune-up, auto . . . Winterizing, autos

what is 'maintenance-free'?

Some batteries called "maintenance-free" by store personnel or instore advertising are really low-maintenance types. Major battery manufacturers spell out, by labeling on the battery or in literature accompanying it, if the unit is truly maintenance-free.

Maintenance-free batteries are more expensive than low-maintenance batteries. Both cost more than conventional batteries, but cost is not the only difference. Whether a battery is low-maintenance, maintenance-free or conventional depends on its grid construction.

Battery grids are lattice networks that hold pastes of active materials, which form the positive and negative plates. Grids also conduct electric current from the plates to the poles.

In a conventional battery, grids are an alloy containing 5 to 6 percent antimony and the rest lead. In a low-maintenance battery, grids are an alloy of 2 to 3½ percent antimony. In a maintenance-free battery, antimony has been eliminated and replaced by a calcium-lead alloy.

The degree of maintenance a battery requires depends on the amount of its antimony content. By "maintenance" we mean how often it is necessary to check cells for water loss and clean battery terminals, cable connectors and battery case.

Antimony causes a battery to accept current after the battery is fully charged. This overcharging leads to a loss of water (electrolyte) because excessive current reacts on water, turning it into hydrogen and oxygen.

Electrolyte loss presents you with three maintenance tasks. First, you have to replenish the water.

Second, gases given off through battery vents settle on connectors and terminals, causing corrosion that can impede the flow of current to the starter motor. If corrosion is not cleaned off, the engine could fail to start.

Third, gases escaping from vents can settle on the battery case and create a self-discharging path, draining battery strength. This will require you to have the battery charged frequently if you don't wash it to eliminate the electrolytic salts. Electrolyte is an electrical conductor. Calcium-lead batteries—that is, maintenance-free—do away with these tasks.

"Calcium-lead batteries just about turn themselves off when they become fully charged," states John J. Zalecki, national service manager of the Prestolite battery division. "They accept little more current." Therefore, in a calcium-lead battery, the gases emitted when overcharging takes place are reduced 90 to 97 percent. Water

THE TOPS of some maintenance-free batteries allow access to the cells. Lift off cover plates.

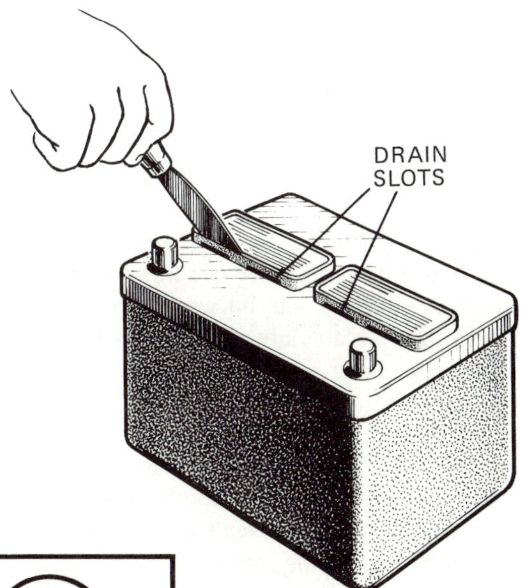

"EYE" IN SOME maintenance-free batteries indicates correct procedure to follow in no-start conditions.

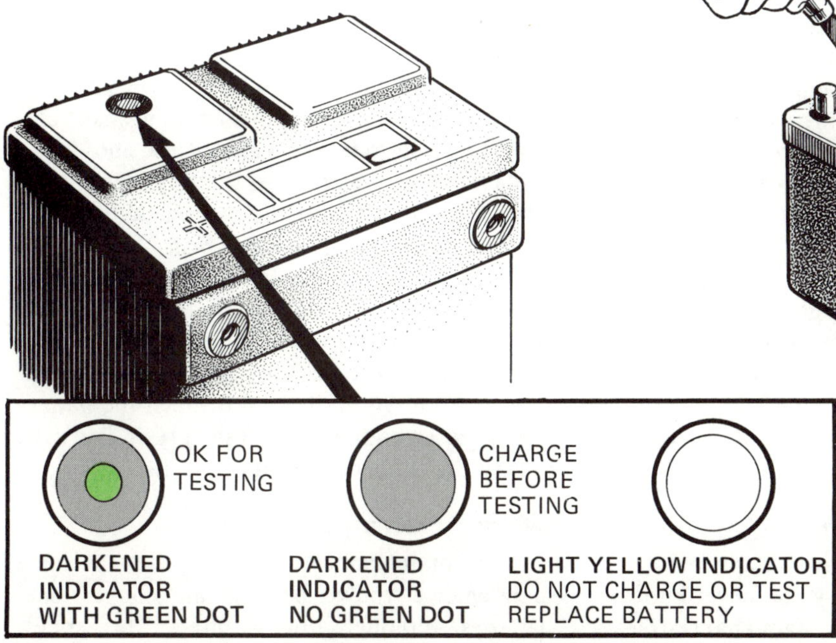

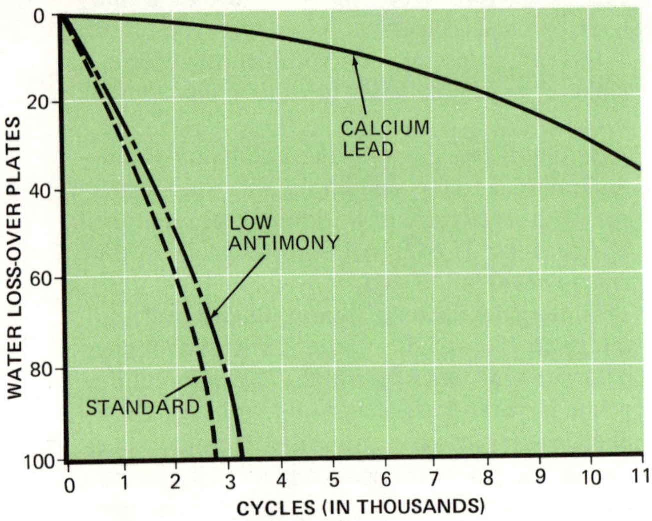

GRAPH SHOWS slight water loss of maintenance-free batteries using calcium-lead.

loss is kept to a minimum during a battery's lifetime.

"In a vehicle with the voltage regulator set to limit voltage to 14.2 volts, it's possible for a battery with 5 percent antimony to accept up to 6 amps. in overcharge current," Zalecki says. "A calcium-lead battery will accept an overcharge current of less than 0.1 amps."

two venting systems

Make no mistake about one thing: Every battery gives off gases. Calcium-lead and low-antimony batteries are no exceptions. Although many maintenance-free batteries look sealed (the familiar vent caps are not present), venting must be built into the battery in some way. A battery that isn't vented has no way to purge itself of gases that accumulate inside and can cause the battery to burst.

Two methods of venting a maintenance-free battery are used—through tiny holes in the sides or ends of the battery, or through a microporous disc. Either method permits flame-retardant venting; that is, it prevents flames created externally from traveling into the cell and igniting explosive gases.

installing a new battery

Installing a battery correctly is necessary to prevent damage, so let's run down the procedure.

When you buy a new battery you never know how long it's been in storage. Maintenance-free batteries have excellent shelf-life characteristics because of their low rate of self-discharge. They can remain in storage for at least 12 months without need for charging. However, you have no guarantee that a battery wasn't neglected. It may have been in stock long enough to lose charge. A booster charge of 20 amps. for two hours assures you that the battery will enter service fully charged. Charging is also advisable if the battery is being installed in cold weather or has been stored in a cold place.

Important: Do not charge a Delco Freedom battery if the visual indicator reveals a green dot.

removing an old battery

As the battery is charging, remove the old battery from the car, noticing the position of positive and negative terminals. To avoid accidental damage that the cross-switching of terminals and cable connectors may cause, mark pieces of masking tape (−) and (+) and place each on its respective cable: (−) on the ground cable (the one with one end connected to the engine block); (+) on the positive cable (the one that goes to the starter switch or starter relay).

Caution: Whenever you disconnect a battery, remove the ground (−) cable first. This minimizes the possibility of sparks shooting off that could ignite the hydrogen given off by a battery.

Inspect cables. If they are cracked, frayed or worn through, replace them. If cables are not worn, clean the connectors with a battery-cleaning tool or a wire brush. This may be the last time you will have to use a battery-cleaning tool. The small amount of gas given off by a maintenance-free battery is directed away from terminals and connectors, virtually eliminating corrosion.

Next, clean the battery hold-down and tray with a wire brush. Wash them with a weak solution of baking soda and water. Rinse and dry.

Place the new battery on the tray. See that its terminals line up with the correct battery connectors. *Connect positive cable first.*

Very important: Do not overtighten cable connectors. Doing so may distort the battery and cause early failure. Use a torque wrench. If the battery has side terminals, tighten bolts to between 60 and 90 in.-lb. or 6 ft.-lb. If the battery has posts extending from the top of the case, tighten the cable connectors to 15 ft.-lb.

servicing a battery

A *low*-maintenance battery requires the same maintenance you've been giving conventional batteries, although not as often. This entails checking the electrolyte level every 12 months or 10,000-15,000 miles, keeping the battery and connectors clean, and testing the state of charge when a starting problem appears to be caused by battery failure.

Maintenance-free batteries require service when a starting problem occurs. This is why Delco-Remy equips its Freedom battery with an "eye." Some think that the "eye" reveals whether the battery is good or bad, but this is *not* the case. The "eye," or visual indicator, indicates the level and specific gravity of the electrolyte in *one* cell.

You don't have access to the cells of the Freedom battery to check electrolyte level or test electrolyte specific gravity. This battery is sealed. "In normal vehicle operation, there is no need to view the 'eye' until a starting complaint is involved," states F.L. Bronnenberg of the Delco-Remy engineering staff. "Then the 'eye' reveals what procedure to follow."

If the "eye" has a green dot, it is safe to load-test the battery to determine if it is causing the starting problem. The amount of load placed on the battery depends on the model. The minimum voltage depends on temperature. The load-testing procedure for the Freedom battery is outlined in GM service manuals, and in Delco-Remy service bulletin 1B-116.

If minimum voltage is not attained during the load test (9.6 volts at 70° F. or above), replace the battery. The fact that the "eye" shows a green dot makes no difference. Remember: The "eye" doesn't tell if the battery is good or bad. If the "eye" is dark (no green dot), the battery should be charged before it is load-tested. Rate of charge varies with battery model and is outlined in service literature.

Caution: Charging should be halted when the green dot appears in the "eye" or when the maximum charge is reached, according to service instructions. If the "eye" is pale or light, do not charge or test the battery. The electrolyte has been depleted. Since water cannot be added, this is one situation that calls for replacing the battery.

cells are accessible

If your maintenance-free battery does not have an "eye," you have access to cells, although it may not seem that way.

Some companies make no attempt to hide cell openings. For example, the Red Camel maintenance-free battery, manufactured by ESB, has conventional battery caps. The caps can be removed, allowing water to be added if a voltage regulator goes bad and excess current is permitted to reach the battery. Excessive current increases gassing and will cause premature battery failure if water is not replenished.

The Roughneck and Liberator batteries, manufactured by Prestolite, are two types of maintenance-free batteries that have cells hidden, but accessible. With the Liberator, the center cover is removed by pulling straight up on the ends. After checking electrolyte level, the cover is placed in position and pressed down firmly until it seats.

With a Roughneck battery, a knife is used to cut through the top plaque center section. Removing the plaque reveals individual screw-type vent plugs.

Hold onto your battery hydrometer if you switch to a maintenance-free battery that allows access to the cells. You can check the battery's state of charge in the usual manner.

If you are hesitant about cutting through the battery to get at cells, there is another way to determine state of charge besides using a hydrometer. Ford suggests the following steps:

- Perform a battery capacity test.
- Wait one minute.
- Measure *no-load* battery voltage. If it is 12.4 volts or better, the battery is adequately charged. If no-load voltage is less than 12.4 volts, a booster charge should be applied.

avoid tipping

- Avoid tipping a battery, even a maintenance-free battery. It's possible that electrolyte could leak out of the vents.
- "The number one problem associated with discharged batteries is a loose generator drive belt," says J.R. Pace of ESB Inc.
- The charge voltage of maintenance-free batteries is more critical than with conventional batteries. A voltage regulator out of specification will result in a discharged battery if the setting is low, or premature water consumption if the setting is too high.

storage tips

- If you are going to store a maintenance-free battery, keep it upright in a cool, dry place. Avoid a place where the temperature will be above 80° F. High temperature increases the rate of self-discharge. To prevent freezing, do not store the battery where the temperature goes below 32° F.
- You can jump-start a maintenance-free battery in the usual manner. However, cover the battery's top and/or ends with a clean cloth to block vent holes. This will prevent gas that may escape from possibly being ignited by a spark.

Dents: how to get rid of them

By MORT SCHULTZ

Have you had a dent repaired by an auto-body professional lately? The price can be out of sight! You can do this work at a much lower cost with a few simple tools

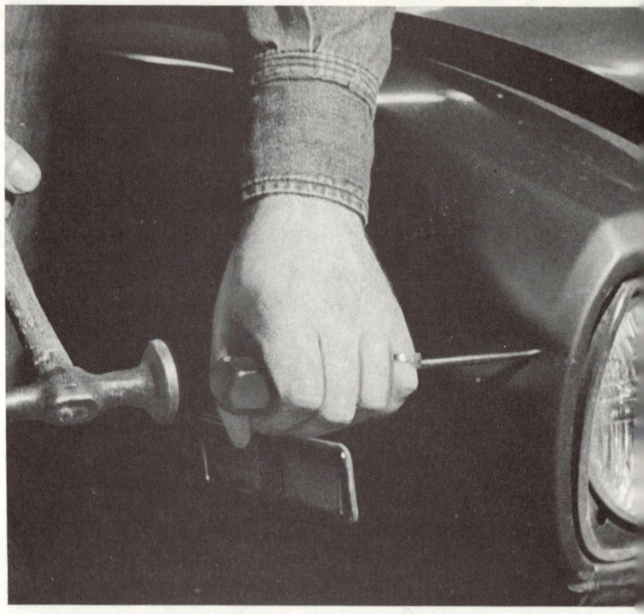

1 **PUNCH A HOLE** in the dent for a special tool called a slide hammer. This is the way to do it if there is no other way you can get behind it to push it out.

GEORGE GUDAT IS a professional who doesn't mind revealing trade secrets about his craft, which is auto-body repair.

"Car owners who have a mind to can repair dents and rotted areas themselves," he says.

When you consider what a professional can charge for repairing the minor kind of dent shown in the photo above, this is good news.

I recently spent several hours with George at the auto-body repair facility of Greenbrook American in Greenbrook, N.J., where he is body shop manager. The first thing that impressed me was that tools and materials you need to repair your car's body are readily available.

Consider the tool needed to straighten dents. It's called a slide hammer, and you can buy it at most auto parts or auto body supply stores.

Begin repairing a dent by punching holes in it an inch apart. Use an awl. Screw the slide hammer into a hole. It has a threaded tip. Slam the sliding arm back against the hammer's handle to straighten the dent. One blow should do. Go on to the next hole. (If the dent is shallow—say a maximum of three inches in diameter and one-quarter-inch deep—it isn't really necessary to pull it out if you don't have a slide hammer.)

Bare-metal the spot. This can be done easily enough with a grinding disc that's attached to an ordinary electric drill. Grind an area which is three to four inches *beyond* the dent.

You are now ready to mix the repair material, which is plastic body filler and hardener. You can purchase the filler in gallon and quart sizes.

The filler has an indefinite shelf life as long as the lid is kept on tight and it is not mixed with the hardener. The hardener comes in a toothpaste-type tube.

It is essential that the plastic filler and hardener be properly mixed together. Follow instructions on the container. Mixing is made easier by the fact that the filler is white or gray, and the cream hardener is in a color. You are able to see when the two are thoroughly blended.

Don't mix too much. For most dents, a glob of filler no larger than the size of a golf ball and strip of hardener about one-half inch long is sufficient. Mix them together on a clean, flat piece of cardboard or metal.

You have from 5 to 15 minutes working time after the filler and hardener are mixed, depending on the temperature. The hotter the day, the quicker the mix will set.

Avoid making repairs if the car's body is cool (under 60° F.) or damp. The filler will develop pinholes and will not set properly. The ideal working conditions are with the metal dry and temperature at 65°-75° F.

SEE ALSO
Autos, maintenance . . . Autos, ramps . . . Body care, auto . . . Brakes, auto . . . Ramps, auto repair . . . Tune-up, auto

Use a body-repair-compound plastic applicator to apply body filler. Applicators are available (three to a package, each a different size).

Apply the body filler in light coats until it is built up to a height of an eighth to a quarter inch above the surface. If you have ever spackled gypsum wallboard, use the same technique. Don't lay on globs—mold on one light coat after another.

Keep the filler off paint. It doesn't stick well and could eventually crumble.

Allow the filler to set up, but this doesn't mean that it should be permitted to get solid. You don't want it hard.

The filler is ready for the next repair step when you can put a scratch in it with your fingernail without having the material come up in a glob. At the ideal working temperature, this takes 15 to 20 minutes.

Using a Surform, "mold" the filler while removing excess. Surform, made by Stanley Tools, is available at hardware stores. It resembles a plane to which the Surform blade is attached. Blades are shaped flat for flat surfaces, half-round for contoured surfaces and rattail for tight curves.

Shave off 80 to 90 percent of the built-up filler, and then let the repair set until it gets very hard. This takes at least 30 minutes.

Now, using a sanding block fitted with a piece of 40-grit sandpaper, sand the area. Follow this with a sanding using 100-grit sandpaper attached

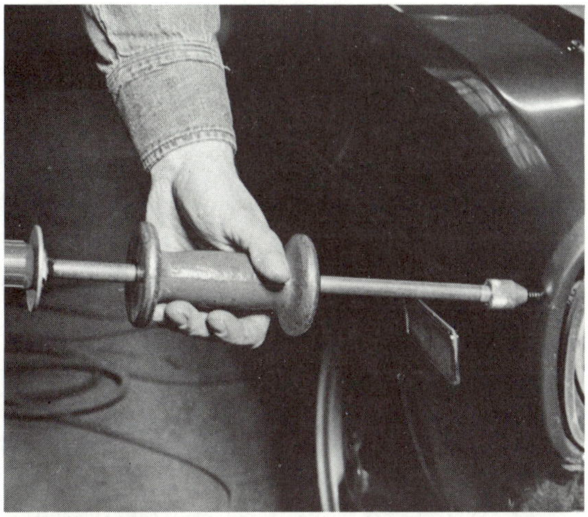

2 **THE SPECIAL** body-repair tool shown here is a slide hammer. The hammer enables you to pull out a dent after you have screwed it into a hole.

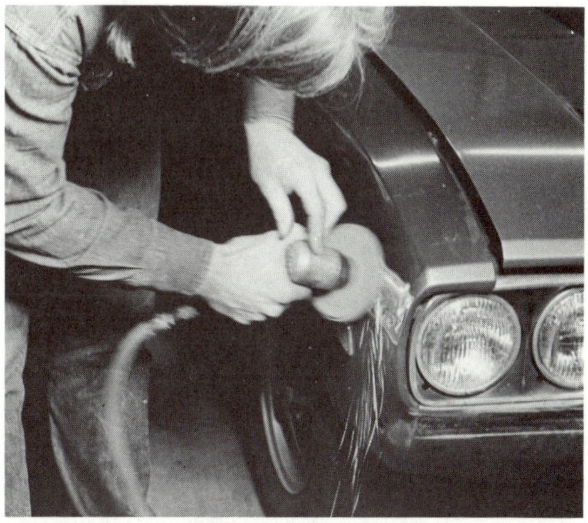

3 **GRIND THE AREA** around the dent right down to the bare metal with an electric drill. In this photo a pro is using a compressed air grinder.

4 **MAKE IT A HABIT** always to extend the repair area several inches around a dent so that the final filling and painting can be feathered.

5 **ADD THE CREAM** hardener to the plastic filler, following instructions, and mix them thoroughly. The applicator comes with the filler kit.

6 **PLASTIC FILLER** should be applied one layer at a time, and built up like spackling wallboard, until it is slightly higher than the body.

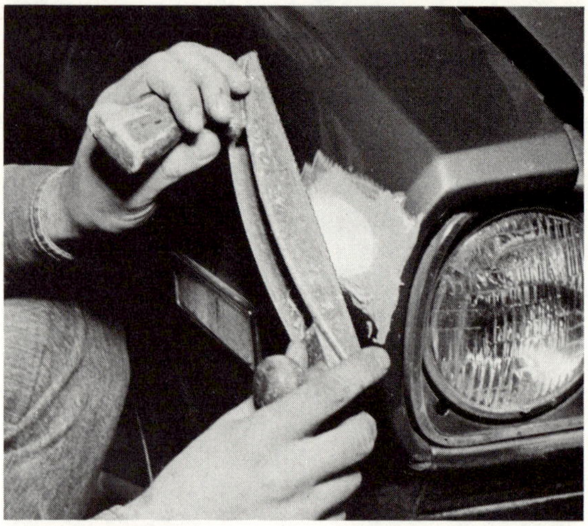

7 **SHAPING TOOL** such as a Surform is then used to remove any of the excess filler before you begin sandpapering the spot as flat as possible.

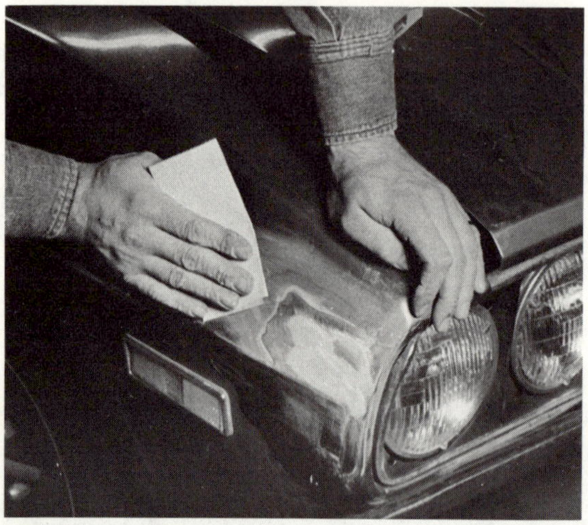

8 **TO FEATHER-EDGE** the repair, sand from the body paint area into the repair area. Be careful not to press down too hard!

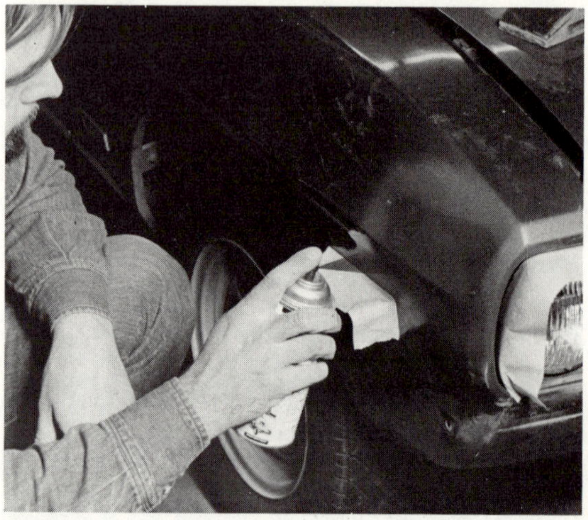

9 **APPLY PRIMER** to the repair area quickly and carefully. It's always a good idea to practice your spraying technique on a tin can first.

to the sanding block. Sand until the area is relatively smooth.

Avoid sanding the repair material while holding the sandpaper with your hand. You are likely to remove too much material and end up with a shallow spot.

You now need a piece of 220-grit, wet-or-dry sandpaper to feather-edge the paint around the repair area. Keep this paper wet, and sand from the paint edge into the repair area until you have a level surface. You should not feel any difference in the surface when running your hand over it.

If you are working near body trim or lights, mask them and apply a light coat of primer. Primer is available in spray cans. If primer oversprays on to paint, you can wipe it off. You really need not mask off paint around the area until you are ready to spray paint on the repair.

Let the primer dry—about 15 minutes—and apply a light coat of auto-body glazing putty. This material fills sandpaper scratches and other imperfections. Follow application instructions on the container.

Glazing putty comes in tubes, in quart cans and in gallons. It goes on very smoothly.

Allow the work to set and dry for at least an hour. Then, using No. 320 wet-or-dry sandpaper attached to the sanding block, lightly sand the entire repair. Follow with a coat of primer. Finally, mask off the area to keep overspray from getting on body paint, and paint the spot. To get the proper color, obtain the paint code from the identification plate attached to the car's firewall or door pillar.

There is usually no problem with ordinary colors, but it may be pretty tough getting an exact match if your car is painted with a metallic paint. Paint used on imported cars is also hard to match. The equipment used at the factory, such as electrostatic paint guns, can't be duplicated by most professional auto-body repairmen, let alone laymen.

If you find it hard to match your paint color with a spray-can product, you can buy a compressed-air supply and paint separately. You can buy paint made by automotive paint manufacturers in quart or gallon size from an auto-body supply house.

The compressed-air kit is an aerosol supply to which is attached a glass or plastic container into which paint is poured. One such kit is called Preval.

handling body rot

There are three ways to tackle a body rot problem. Two methods won't cost you much, but they are temporary. The third is more costly, but it is permanent. The least expensive and easiest way to do the job is with aluminum tape, which comes in four-inch-wide rolls. Break off pieces of rot and grind the area down to bare metal.

Place the tape over the rot, making sure that it extends at least one inch beyond the damage. Use 100-grit sandpaper to roughen up the tape. Then continue the repair in the way I described above for repairing dents. This method will last about six months. Then, the repaired area will start bubbling out.

A longer-lasting (but temporary) repair can be made with a piece of sheet metal that's the same gauge as the metal of your car (in most cases, 20 or 22-gauge). Be sure the sheet metal extends one inch beyond the rotted area. Grind the damaged spot and attach sheet metal with a Pop-rivet tool that you can buy in hardware stores.

Roughen up the sheet metal with a grinding disc, and proceed with the repair as described above. Pay close attention to applying filler between the metal and car body. Feather the filler into the body so you can't see the contour made by the patch.

Here again you are attaching one piece of metal to another. Eventually condensation and dust will get behind the repair, and it will break down. Figure on getting no more than two years.

10 **SAND THE REPAIR** area until the plastic filler is brought down to the level of the surrounding area before you begin to feather-edge.

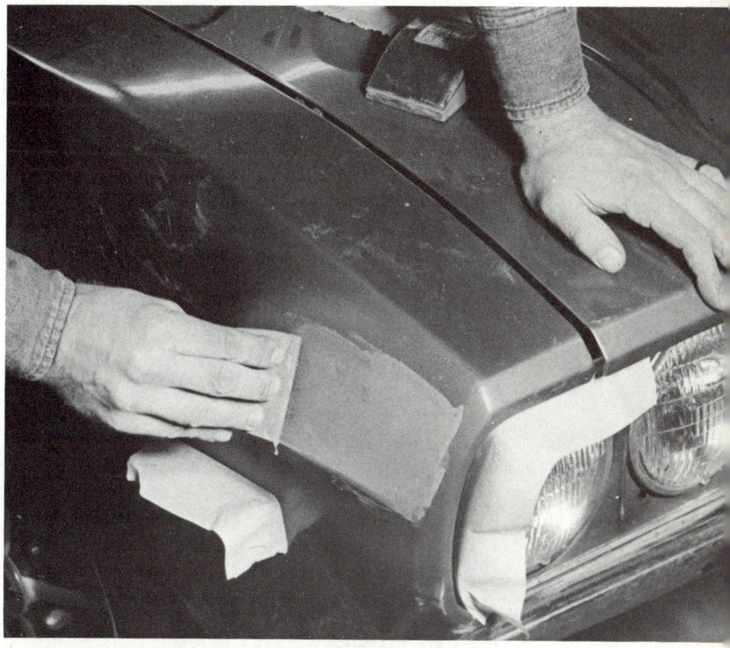

11 **AUTO-BODY** glazing compound is a final smoothing step. You are then ready to apply the paint to match the color of the car.

The permanent way of fixing body rot is by welding or brazing sheet metal right to the car's body. If you had a body shop do the job from start to finish, the cost might be considerable. But you can reduce it.

Have a professional do only the welding. Then, using the procedures outlined above, you finish the job.

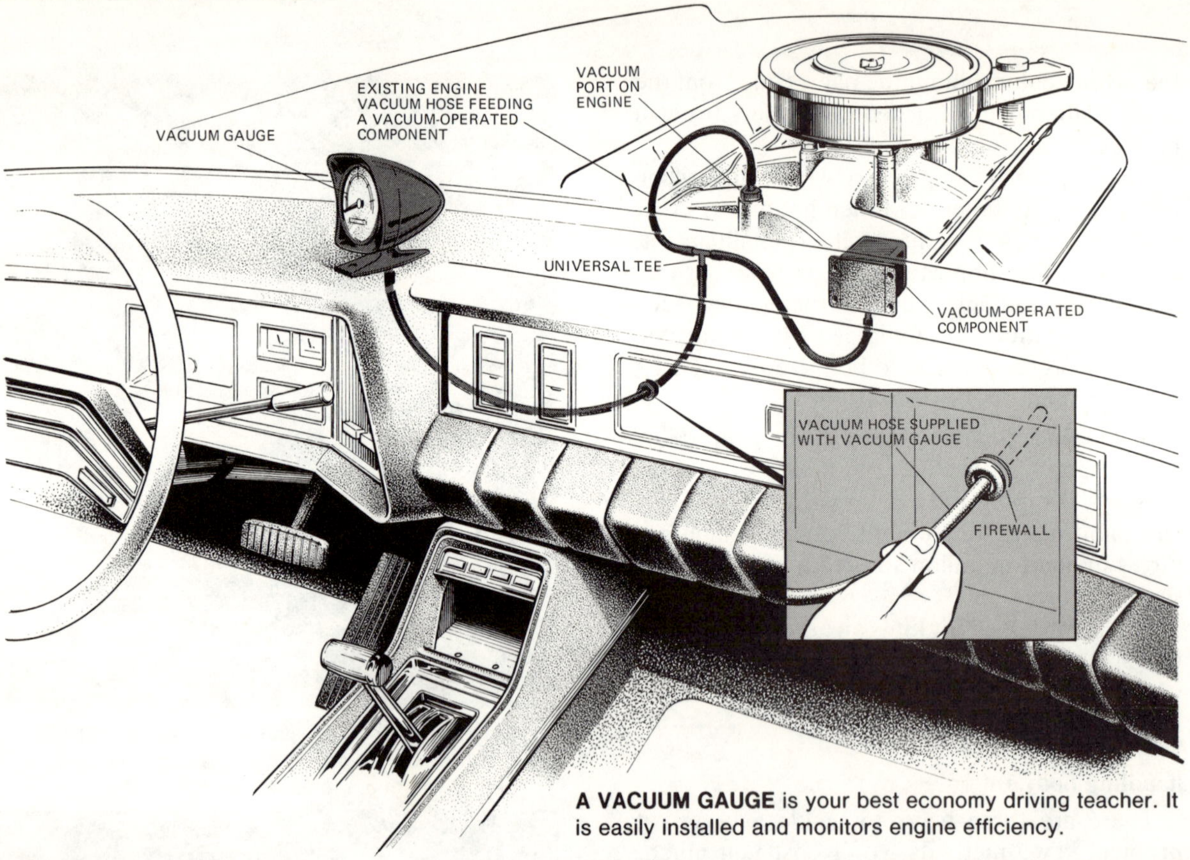

A VACUUM GAUGE is your best economy driving teacher. It is easily installed and monitors engine efficiency.

Improve your gas mileage by 30 percent!

SO YOU THINK you know all you need to know about getting the best gas mileage your car can give. Take this test and learn the truth:

1. **When does your car get its worst mileage?**
   a) After many hours on the highway.
   b) Climbing hills.
   c) In city traffic.
   d) The first few miles in the morning.
2. **When should you check your tire pressure?**
   a) When your tires are cold.
   b) At each fill-up.
   c) After you've driven 10 miles.
   d) After you've taken a long trip.
3. **How much energy loss is caused by one fouled sparkplug (V8)?**
   a) No appreciable loss.
   b) 3- to 5-percent loss.
   c) 7- to 10-percent loss.
   d) 25-percent loss.

SEE ALSO

Fuel systems, auto . . . Tune-up, auto

4. **To save gas when leaving a stop sign, you should:**
   a) Accelerate as fast as the car will go.
   b) Accelerate very slowly.
   c) Get to cruising speed smoothly, but as quickly as possible.
   d) Motion speedier motorists to pass.
5. **You'll increase fuel efficiency 20 percent by:**
   a) Slowing from 55 mph to 50.
   b) Slowing from 70 mph to 55.
   c) Driving normally at 20 mph.
   d) Coasting down inclines.
6. **How much gasoline does an average American driver use per year?**
   a) 200 gallons.
   b) 800 gallons.
   c) 1500 gallons.
   d) 2000 gallons.
7. **Which of the following costs you gas mileage?**
   a) Permanent roof racks.
   b) Underinflated tires.
   c) Accelerating slowly and gradually.
   d) All of the above.
8. **Which practice is likely to save the most gas?**
   a) Keeping engine filters clean.
   b) Using gasoline of the recommended octane.

c) Doing a regular tune-up.
d) Removing excess weight from car.

9. Which of these saves the most gas?
a) Installing radial tires.
b) Maintaining correct tire pressure.
c) Driving on underinflated tires.
d) Driving on overinflated tires.

10. Which of these conditions uses the most gasoline when driving at highway speed?
a) Driving with windows open and airconditioner off.
b) Driving with windows closed and airconditioner on.
c) Driving with vents open, windows closed and airconditioner off.
d) All conditions use the same amount of gas.

Answers: 1, d; 2, a; 3, c; 4, c; 5, b; 6, b; 7, d; 8, c; 9, a; 10, a.

Tens of thousands of Americans have been asked these questions by driving experts of the Department of Energy (DOE) and Atlantic Richfield Co. (Arco). DOE and Arco, acting independently, have conducted seminars to help drivers get the most mileage from a gallon of gasoline.

mileage up 30 percent

The purpose of the DOE and Arco quizzes and seminars was to demonstrate how little most of us know about driving economically. According to John W. Gendron, Arco senior vice-president, "A typical driver can improve his or her car's gasoline mileage by as much as 30 percent," using fuel-efficient driving and maintenance techniques taught by Arco and DOE, and using a vacuum gauge as a reinforcement tool to make your newly learned techniques become a habit.

The DOE program was designed primarily to retrain company and fleet vehicle drivers. The Arco seminar was aimed at private individuals. Frank Miller, who was a senior driver-training instructor with the DOE in Nevada, was the chief instructor for the Arco program.

save 160 gallons a year

Suppose the 30-percent estimate is ambitious—suppose the average saving is only 20 percent. Do you realize what this means? If each driver improves his gas mileage by "only" 20 percent, he will save 160 gallons a year.

You can understand why I got interested. That's why I had to find out if the Arco Drive for Conservation, as it's called, is effective. So I took the test.

The test at Arco's travelling exhibit was a driving test. The car sat on a Clayton dynamometer. It was equipped with a FloScan 660 miles-per-gallon gauge, a Halda Tripmaster that ticks off mileage traveled and a Stewart-Warner vacuum gauge.

wasteful vs. sensible driving

The results of my test were startling. Within 15 minutes, I had attained a 61-percent improvement in fuel economy. As impressive as this sounds, something else was proven that struck me just as hard.

This improvement in gasoline mileage was attained with a *decrease* by 12 seconds in the length of time it took me to get from point A to point B. In other words, driving hell-bent-for-leather to get somewhere wastes both fuel *and* time.

Yes, there was a catch. The test didn't allow the driver to handle a car the way he or she normally drives. Part A incorporated practically every bad driving sin in the book, except speeding, while Part B substituted sensible driving.

A volunteer driver from the audience was given instructions by a taped voice piped into the car through the loudspeakers. The program allowed for combination highway and city driving.

The first part of the program, taking six to seven minutes, engaged the driver in a series of erratic, gas-wasting maneuvers such as jack-rabbit starts and abrupt changes in speed.

It took me 6 minutes, 33 seconds to complete the first part of the program. The car averaged 10.34 miles per gallon of gasoline.

The same course of travel was then followed for the second part. This time, instructions called for smooth but rapid acceleration to reach the specified rate of speed; cruising up to a red traffic light hoping it will change and you won't have to stop the car; and, instead of lane jumping, maintaining a smooth driving rate in traffic.

This part of the test took me 6 minutes, 21 seconds to complete—12 seconds less than the time required in Part A. The car's mpg jumped to 16.66.

Although the 61-percent improvement in my case is not a realistic figure, because it doesn't take into account my usual way of driving, several of the gas-consuming habits experienced in Part A of the test are things I'm guilty of doing. Therefore, by changing these, I can realize a definite increase in fuel economy.

AUTHOR CHECKS the scores of his runs. First time he averaged 10.34 mpg in 6 minutes 33 seconds.

AT WHEEL, the author used a vacuum gauge on second run and averaged 16.66 mpg in 6 minutes, 21 seconds.

economy depends on driver

But how much of an increase can you actually expect? McDonnell Douglas Corp. used the same system as Arco to train people who drive for the company. It reported an overall 22-percent improvement in fuel economy.

Some drivers consistently achieve better automotive fuel economy than others, even when all other factors (vehicle size and type, driving cycle, weather) are equal. These differences can only be ascribed to the way in which the individual driver operates the vehicle. Such factors as acceleration rate, average speed, and braking and stopping techniques are known to produce significant effects on fuel economy. According to the DOE, "By practicing known fuel-efficient driving techniques, a driver can improve vehicle fuel economy by up to 20 percent."

How can you learn the driving techniques that will help you attain this significant improvement in fuel economy? One way is to practice the techniques described at the end of this article.

four ways to save gas

However, driving techniques alone won't allow you to attain maximum fuel economy. According to Arco, the optimum savings are realized by paying attention to four areas, as follows:

1. Driving: An improvement of 8 to 12 percent can be anticipated by following the practices outlined at the end of this article.

2. Speed reduction: DOE reports that driving at 50 to 55 mph instead of 65 to 70 mph uses 15 to 18 percent less fuel.

3. Maintenance: An improvement of 9 percent can be expected by keeping aware of some simple practices. They include inflating tires to correct pressure, keeping the air filter clean and keeping fan belts tightened to specification. The greatest improvement in gas mileage is attained by tuning the engine regularly, switching to radial tires, changing oil regularly and having the front end aligned.

4. Trip planning: DOE says that by planning trips you can improve mileage by 5 percent. This involves planning to do all the tasks you have to do at a particular location during one trip, so you don't have to drive back again.

manifold vacuum gauge helps

Another way to help your gasoline budget is to equip your car with a manifold vacuum gauge. The gauge, mounted on the dash, allows you to determine when the engine is operating at its greatest efficiency.

Manifold vacuum has a direct correlation to fuel consumption. When manifold vacuum is high, fuel consumption is lowest. Conversely, when manifold vacuum is low, as it is during rapid acceleration, fuel consumption is highest.

Basically, there are three types of in-car vacuum gauges: dial, indicator light and piston. The dial-type gauge indicates intake manifold by a pointer on a dial face. Many dial-type gauges show the amount of vacuum in relative terms, such as poor, fair and good. Others use numerals (zero to 30) marked in five-inches-of-vacuum increments.

The indicator-light gauge informs the driver of vacuum level through indicator lights (for example, green for okay, orange for fair, red for poor). This type of gauge is used in some cars, such as Cadillac, as original equipment.

With a piston-type gauge, the piston is pulled into its housing as vacuum increases. A different

COCKPIT of Arco test car comes with a vacuum gauge, FloScan mpg gauge and trip odometer.

VACUUM GAUGE is found as a stock Pontiac unit in the shift quadrant of the dashboard.

color is displayed on the piston dial at various vacuum levels.

DOE tested dial- and piston-type gauges at the Nevada test site in conjunction with its driver test program. It found that drivers using either type of gauge were able to attain similar increases in fuel economy during the highway segment of the test. Drivers indicated that, in traffic, the dial-type gauge was easier to follow than the piston type.

Vacuum gauges are relatively easy to install, requiring that you tap the gauge into a vacuum line subject to full manifold vacuum. Be sure installation instructions accompany the gauge you buy. Installation should take less than 30 minutes.

Gas-saving tips taught by ARCO and DOE follow. Some you've heard before. Others, I'll bet, will surprise you.

■ **Observe the speed limit** and maintain a steady speed.

■ **Don't tailgate** and don't cut in and out of traffic.

■ **Anticipate stops.** When approaching traffic lights, slow down by taking your foot off the accelerator and try to hit the green rather than racing up to the red and having to stop suddenly.

Also, back off on the gas pedal and let the car's rolling resistance help slow you down, instead of using heavy braking. Always brake with your right foot. People who use the left foot to brake often unconsciously keep light pressure on the gas pedal with their right foot.

■ **Keep windows closed at highway speeds.** Use vents or airconditioner to reduce the wind resistance your car meets with windows open. Avoid using airconditioning at lower speeds.

■ **In cold weather, try to keep the car warm** by turning up the temperature and letting vents force heated air through the car. If possible, avoid using the heater blower. If the blower is needed, keep it at the lowest possible setting.

■ **Drive slower when you're bucking a head wind.** Wind resistance is a key factor in reduced gas mileage at speeds over 40 mph.

■ **Shut off power-consuming accessories before you turn off the ignition,** so engine load is minimized the next time the engine is started.

■ **Don't rev the engine just before turning off the ignition.**

■ **Try to avoid idling the engine for more than a minute.** With the engine warm, it is more efficient to shut it off and restart it when you're ready to go. However, you have to judge whether the engine will restart in very cold or hot weather.

■ **Avoid unnecessary steering-wheel movement.** Each sideward movement of the tires causes drag, which increases fuel consumption. When making turns, back off on the gas pedal and let the car slow down on its own. Touch the brake pedal lightly, if you have to. Roll through the corner and accelerate back to cruising speed as rapidly, but as smoothly, as possible.

■ **Accelerate to speed as rapidly as possible, but smoothly.** Avoid jackrabbit starts.

■ **In cold weather, do not allow your car to warm up at idle for more than 30 seconds.**

■ **Accelerate slowly on sand, gravel, and snowy, icy or rain-slick roads,** so your wheels don't spin.

■ **Anticipate hills.** Gently press the gas pedal and maintain momentum to carry you over the top. Don't increase speed going uphill. Once over the crest, ease off on the gas pedal and let gravity help you down the other side.

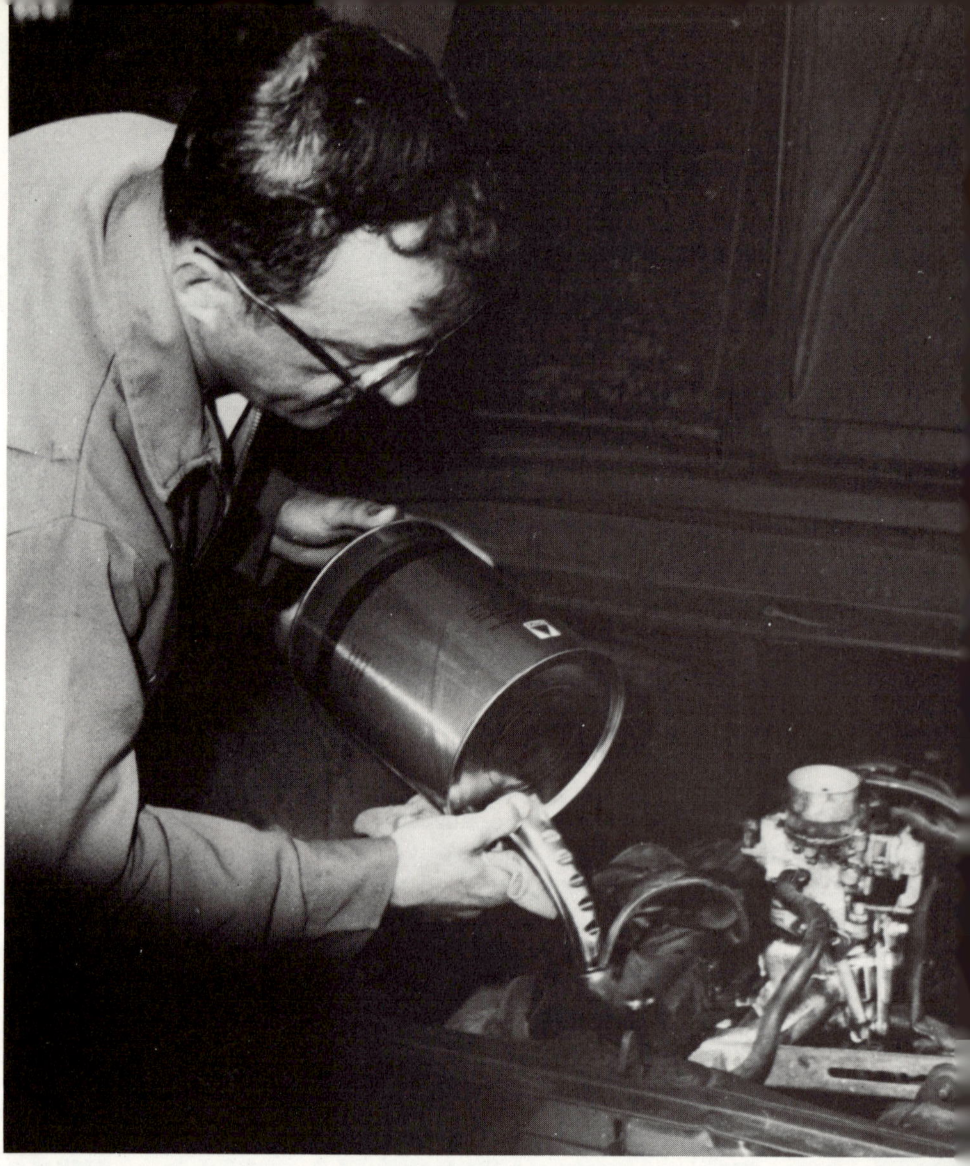

Do all of your own routine service

By MORT SCHULTZ

YOU CAN SAVE a lot of money by doing your own routine automobile service and maintenance. How much?

The answer: as much as 75 percent. No kidding.

So, if you now spend $200 a year to have a pro handle some of these services, you could save $150 by doing them yourself.

At least ten of the so-called ''routine but essential'' services outlined in the owners manuals of most cars are within the realm of automobile owner expertise. These services are listed in Table A along with the supplies you will need for each.

The major saving is in mechanic's labor. Say the labor cost of an oil change and chassis lube job is $10. Plainly, someone who does the work himself keeps that sawbuck.

Over a year, such savings become substantial. For example, the average car needs three oil changes and grease jobs a year. By our $10 hypothesis, the do-it-yourselfer saves $30 by taking on just that one easy job. And the more he does, the more he saves.

There is another saving that the car owner is going to realize when he begins doing work himself. Most professional mechanics charge abso-

SEE ALSO

Alternators, auto . . . Carburetors, auto . . .
Cooling systems, auto . . . Distributors, auto . . .
Engines, auto . . . Ramps, auto repair . . .
Steering and suspension, auto . . . Tune-up, auto

A LOW-COST hydrometer checks the specific gravity of battery electrolyte, revealing its state of charge.

RADIATOR COOLANT can be checked with ball-type hydrometer. Number of balls afloat gives the reading.

lute top retail price for every new part or other item of supply they put in a car, such as engine oil, sparkplugs, oil filter, air cleaner element and fuel filter. They profit on parts as well as on labor.

You can buy these same parts for as much as 50 percent less in stores with auto parts departments catering to individual car owners. These stores include such well-known ones as Sears Roebuck and J.C. Penney.

You can also purchase parts and tools through the mail at substantial savings by dealing with a large direct-mail company such as J.C. Whitney in Chicago.

Your one biggest expense when you set up a do-it-yourself auto facility is going to be tools . . . that is, tools other than the ordinary ones

PCV VALVE is easily removed from its seat for replacement. Replace any deteriorated hose as well.

SERVICES DO-IT-YOURSELFERS CAN DO

Service	Supplies Needed	Service	Supplies Needed
1. Change engine oil and oil filter	1. Fresh engine oil and a new oil filter	7. Service emissions control system	7. New positive crankcase ventilation (PCV) system valve
2. Lubricate chassis	2. Chassis lubricant	8. Check fluids (strength of battery electrolyte, level of power steering and brake fluids)	8. None
3. Replace carburetor air cleaner and fuel filter	3. New carburetor air cleaner and fuel filter	9. Rotate tires	9. None
4. Remove and service or replace sparkplugs	4. New sparkplugs if old parts are no longer serviceable	10. Service automatic transmission	10. Fresh automatic transmission fluid, new filter, and a new pan gasket
5. Set distributor points and time ignition	5. None		
6. Service cooling system	6. Fresh ethylene glycol antifreeze		

AIR CLEANER sits loosely in its housing on top of the carburetor. A new one is easy to install.

IF A SPARKPLUG socket didn't come with your car, you'll need one. Be sure to get the right size.

you can take from your home workshop, such as pliers, screwdrivers and wrenches.

These tools, while specialized, aren't complex and needn't be costly. A grease gun and a timing light will be the most expensive. Adequate versions of both are available for well under $10. As you extend your capacity, you'll need more tools—but you'll also be saving more so your budget need never be significantly wounded. If you truly need a tool, its first use will normally pay for its purchase. From then on, it's free.

Remember, too, that as with supplies, the price of tools varies significantly. It pays to shop around.

What about the work itself? Everyone of the tasks listed in the table on page 139 is easily handled by anyone not frightened by an engine and not shy about getting his or her hands dirty.

There isn't sufficient space here to go into detail concerning each of the services. However, here are some hints—many of them dollar-saving hints—that you may find helpful:

- Get a service manual. It will guide you in handling any special innovations relating to jobs on your car. Write the manufacturer's director of technical publications. Manuals cost less than $10.

You probably can get this information free-of-charge at your public library in an auto reference manual such as *Motor's Auto Repair Manual*.

The owner's manual that came with your car is another important publication. It will tell you how often the manufacturer recommends that each service be done. If you've lost yours, get another by writing the maufacturer.

- Before draining engine oil, warm up the engine. Empty half-gallon or gallon plastic bottles make handy receptacles. For ecology's sake don't pour oil down the drain. Recap the bottle tightly, mark it ''Used Oil'' in big letters and put it out for trash pickup.
- An oil filter in use will often become so tight you won't be able to free it by hand. Use a strap wrench if you have it. If not, you can save part of its cost by buying a 12-inch pipe hanger from a hardward store and wrapping it around the filter; placing a screwdriver through the hanger's holes will give leverage.

Before installing a new oil filter, coat its gasket with a film of oil. Tighten the filter by hand *only*.

- There are three main types of hand grease guns: one that you hand-fill with grease, one that accepts grease cartridges and operates like a caulking gun and a third for use either way. Most people prefer the cartridge type because it is less messy. However, grease bought in bulk costs about 30 percent less.

Get an extension for your grease gun; greasing out-of-the-way fittings, such as on upper ball joints, will be easier.

- The in-line-fuel filter of most cars is held by two small clamps. Slip them off the hose, remove the filter and replace it with a new one.
- Sparkplugs of engines in good condition and operated sensibly can be removed, cleaned and regapped until the recommended gap is no longer obtainable. Replace a plug that shows damage or can't be gapped to specifications.
- Distributor points need not be replaced until they show excessive wear or damage, such as pitting or dishing. When you put in new points,

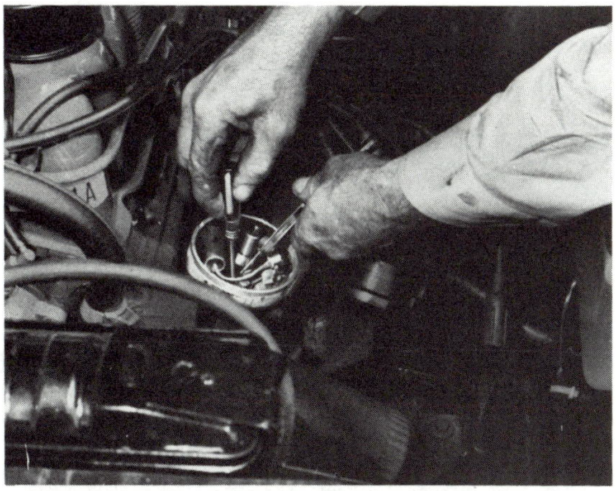

POINT-GAP feeler gauge is a small but sensible investment. Keep it oiled and free of grit.

DROP THE transmission pan to change filter and fluid. Remember to install a new gasket, too.

CHASSIS LUBE takes only a low-cost grease gun with a swivel arm. Cartridge-fill type is easiest.

also replace the condenser. To gap points, insert the specified feeler gauge between points and turn the adjustment screw until you feel some resistance on the gauge as you pull it from between the points.

As long as you have a timing light, use it more often than the carmaker recommends in his maintenance schedule. Performance of your car depends on maintenance of proper timing.

• Cooling-system service involves draining old coolant (be sure engine is warm), squeezing hoses to see that they aren't mushy (rotting), checking that clamps are tight, testing the radiator for leakage and testing the thermostat. A properly-cared-for system won't usually need a reverse flush.

Test coolant at least once a year with a hydrometer—the type shown on page 179 costs less than $2 and contains small balls which indicate the strength of the coolant by the number of balls that float.

• To service the emission-control system, disassemble all parts—including hoses, caps, canisters—and clean them. Most makers suggest that you replace the PCV valve every 24 months or 24,000 miles, whichever comes first.

• In addition to frequent checks of electrolyte with a battery hydrometer, wash the battery at least once a year with a baking soda solution and rinse with clean water. Tape tops of the caps to keep soda out of the battery.

• When rotating tires, include the spare.

• Warm up the engine before you drain the transmission, then drop the pan, replace filter, scrape off the old pan gasket, put on a new one, reinstall pan and fill transmission with new fluid.

ROTATING TIRES INCLUDING THE SPARE

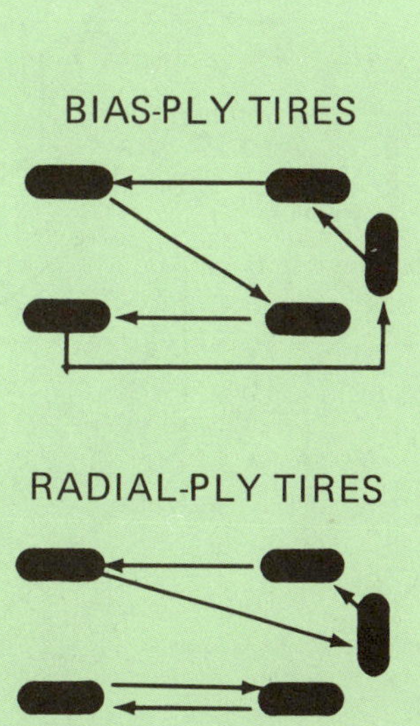

Build your own folding car ramps

WHEN YOU service any car, a pair of car ramps has the advantage of safety as well as convenience over the usual wedge-under-a-board setup. Those shown were made with stock 2 x 4s, fine for the job.

Mark and cut out the eight wood pieces needed for each ramp. Cut a notch to hold the end crosspiece in each 15-in. length. Then notch center boards to accept the smaller dowel when the ramp is folded. Bore the ⅞-in.-dia. holes for the larger dowel in these and the angled wood pieces. Locate and bore ½-in.-dia. holes for the smaller dowel.

Assemble the pieces as shown, using washers on the larger dowel. Fold to test for sufficient clearance in the "hinge" and respace the pieces on the dowel if necessary. Secure the dowel with screws. Fasten the end crosspiece in place. Then insert and secure the smaller dowel.

Have someone direct as your drive up the ramps. Apply the parking brake and place stops behind the rear wheels.

SEE ALSO

Autos, maintenance . . . Engines, auto . . . Ramps, auto repair . . . Tune-up, auto

TIME FOR an oil change? These ramps make it easy to slide under your car and do the work. They also fold for convenient, compact storage.

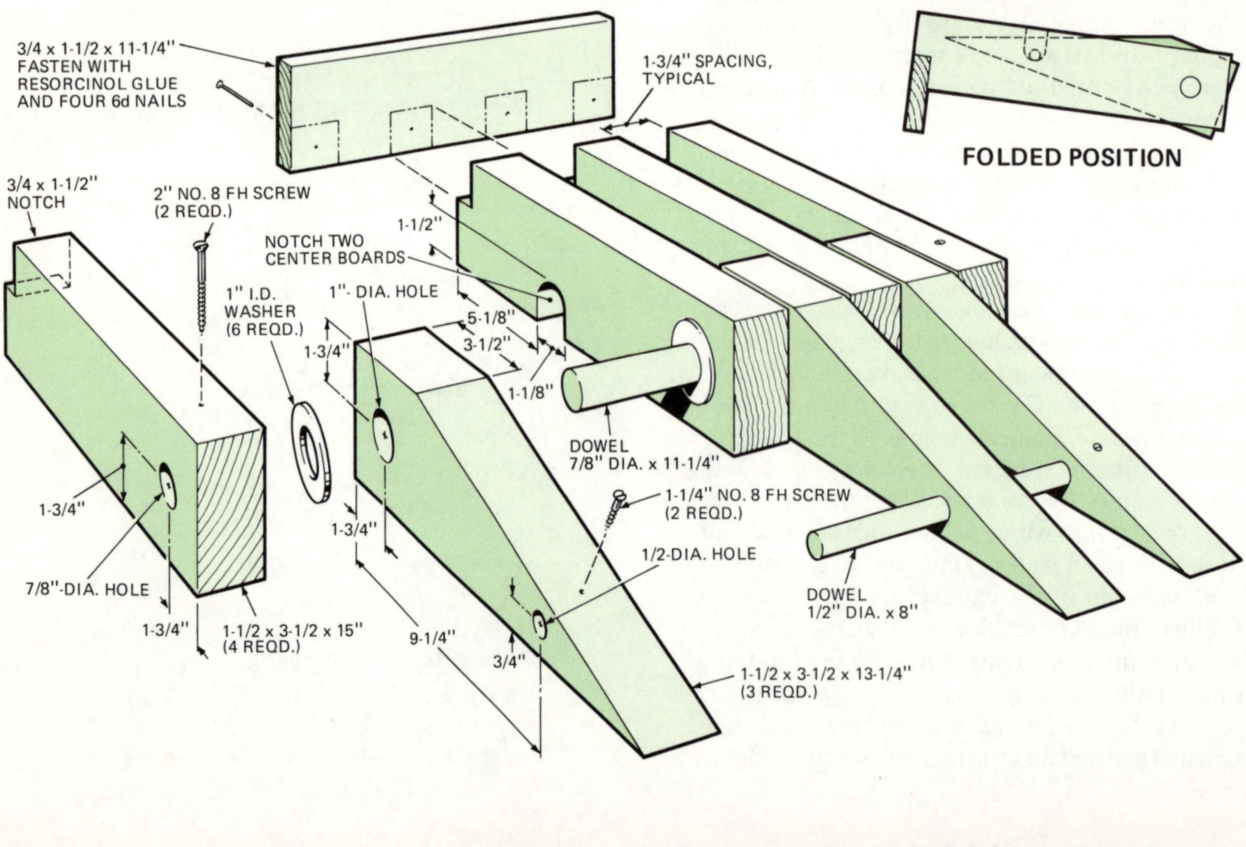

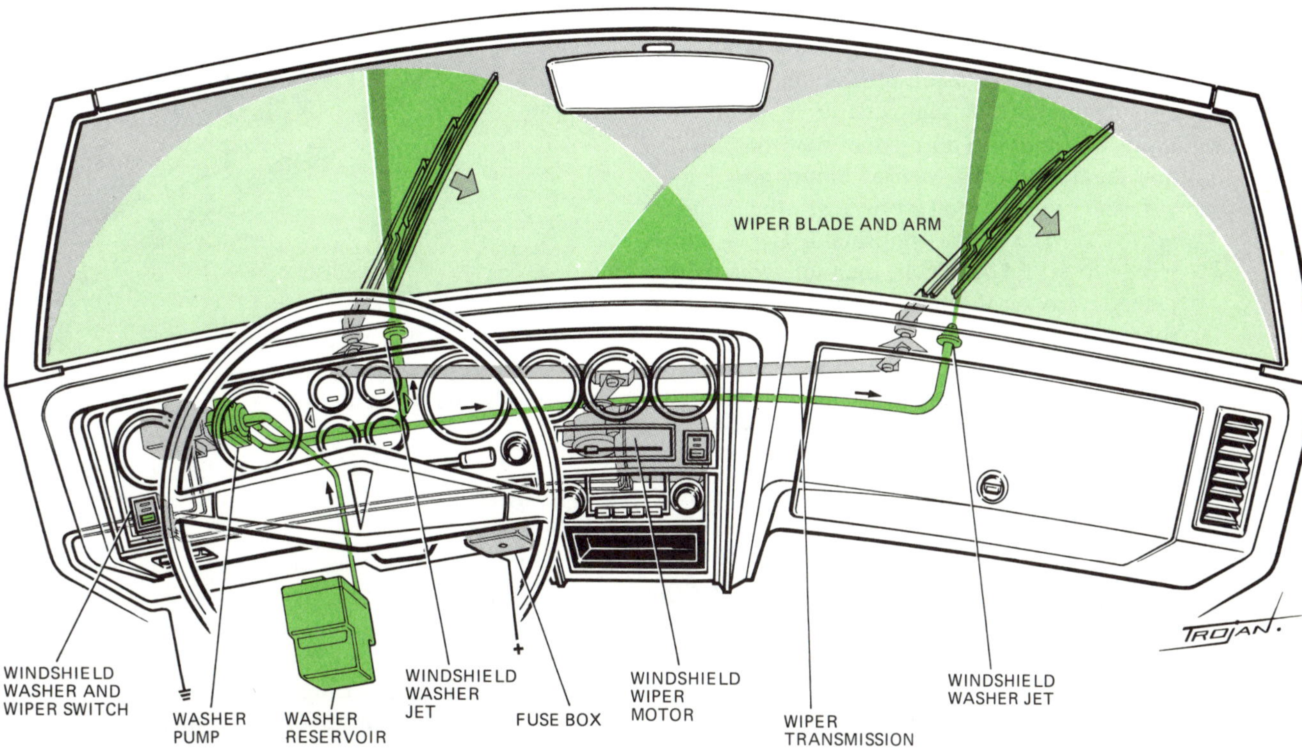

How to keep your windshield clean

By PACK BRYAN

IT'S A SAFE BET that, unless your car is new or you've replaced the wiper blades within the last few months, your wipers are streaking or skipping. Wipers usually don't go bad all of a sudden, so you're not likely to notice the progressive deterioration that's going on all the time.

The quickest, easiest, safest and cheapest way to keep your wipers working effectively in all kinds of weather is to install new refills every six to 12 months. You'll want to do it more often if you live in a heavily industrialized region, and may not need so many changes if you're located in a remote rural area. Air pollution, or lack of it, is the determining factor.

Most drivers go to the needless expense of buying new blades instead of refills. The blade is the whole assembly at the end of the wiper arm, and it rarely has to be replaced. The rubber that does the work is called the refill, costs only a fraction of the price of the blade and is usually all that has to be changed.

Between replacements, however, there's plenty that you can do to help the wipers do their jobs and assure clear vision in any weather. Begin by cleaning the glass inside and out at least once a week. Even if your glass looks clean as a result of frequent trips through an automatic carwash, the chances are you have a film of wax on the surface of the glass and on the blades.

SEE ALSO
Autos, maintenance . . . Carburetors, auto . . . Cooling systems, auto . . . Dieseling, auto . . . Engines, auto . . . Gaskets, auto . . . Leaks, auto . . . Ramps, auto repair . . . Rust, auto . . . Tune-up, auto

Glass manufacturers recommend that you treat the windshield as you would a fine mirror, so the old trick of using a dry paper towel or cloth to clean a dirty windshield on the theory that glass is "hard" just isn't valid. Use a mild detergent and water, or a solvent that has been made specifically for cleaning glass, to "float" the dirt away. Never use an abrasive or scouring powder, and don't try any car-polish compounds.

In the summer, road tar or bugs often build up on the surface of the windshield. Use a tar remover to get rid of the tar, then follow up with a detergent to cut the residue left by the tar-and-solvent mix.

To get rid of bugs, a plastic kitchen scouring pad (not metal) works well if one of the plastic net-covered sponges made for the purpose isn't available. Another method is to place a water-soaked towel over the windshield for half an hour or so. The moisture in the towel will soften the dead bugs.

WIPER-ARM TENSION can be checked with a professional gauge. Adjust or replace; don't bend wiper arm.

WIPER PROBLEMS—WHAT TO LOOK FOR

WIPER-BLADE and wiper-arm problems are sometimes apparent, as shown in the drawings. Often, though rubber appears good, it has lost its "life." To eliminate streaking, install refills on the blades.

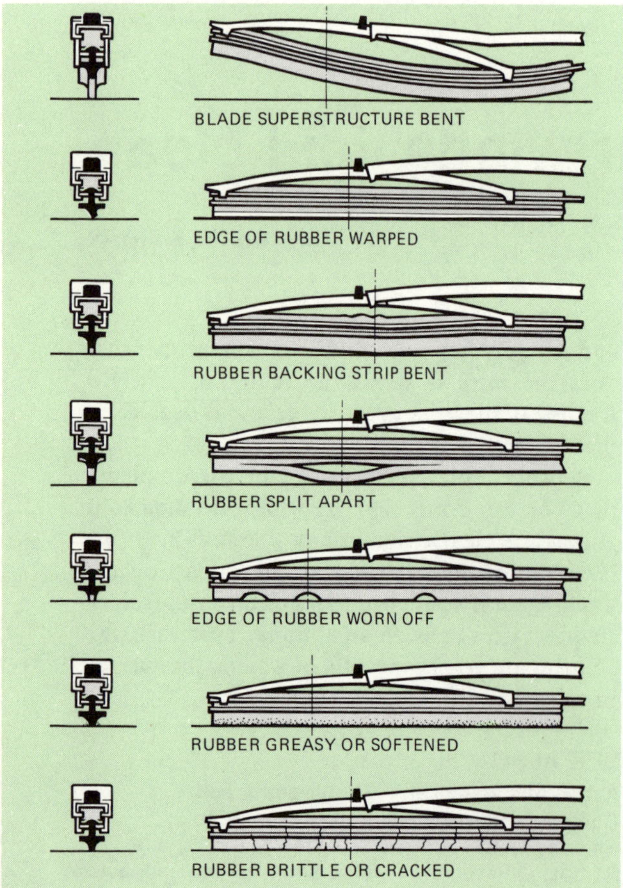

Don't let grime accumulate on the inside of your windshield until it rivals waxed paper for transparency. The build-up usually occurs more rapidly in cooler weather, when the windows are closed and the defrosters force a greater volume of air across the inside of the windshield.

Winter or summer, be sure to keep the windshield washer reservoir filled. Use washer solvent, rather than plain water. It cuts through road grime better.

Never pour boiling water on a windshield to melt ice or free the wipers. Cover the windshield at night with a blanket or a sheet of plastic to keep ice from forming. When ice *does* form, be sure to use a scraper that's made for the purpose. Glass manufacturers suggest frequent examination of these scrapers for nicks that appear in the edge of the blades. Replace any damaged scrapers before they get the chance to dig into the glass.

By federal law, every car manufactured must be equipped with a windshield washer, yet it is estimated that 30 percent of the washers installed in today's cars don't work.

If yours isn't functioning, it's a fairly simple task to locate the problem. First, check to see if there's fluid in the reservoir. Then listen closely: If you hear the pump running, it's likely there's an obstruction somewhere in the line.

Remove the hose at the pump outlet and blow through it. If the fluid squirts out of the nozzles, then the filter is clogged and must be cleaned. Use a solvent to cut any oily residue that may have accumulated on the screen.

If the filter is clean, examine the hose line for

breaks, kinks or obstructions; then check the nozzles. A straight pin or sewing needle will usually clean them out. If they've corroded closed, replacement may be necessary.

If the pump itself isn't running, check all electrical connections—the switch at the dash, the fuses, and the wiring running to the pump. If you still get no action, remove the pump or the pump-wiper combination and give it a bench test just to make sure that power has been getting to the pump. Refer to your dealer shop manual for the removal procedure to avoid damage to the wiper transmission assembly.

Adjusting the washers is simply a matter of bending the nozzles a little bit at a time until you have the stream hitting the correct spot on the windshield. That spot should be about two inches below the top of the wiper arc when the car is standing still. At expressway speeds, the stream will then hit the center of the wiped area.

Rubber refill edges must be sharp enough to cut through water, but remain soft and flexible enough to maintain contact with the glass. The edges must also be perfectly straight to assure uniform pressure throughout their length. When the edges go bad, or the rubber begins to harden, the blade skids across the glass like a bald tire.

Although a blade may tear when it's yanked away from a frozen windshield, it is chemical action that causes most blade deterioration. In fact, there are indications that "exercise" through frequent use can help to extend the life of a wiper blade. In dry, hot desert country, wet the windshield with a hose and run the wipers for five minutes every few weeks. It will help keep them soft.

arm tension

Until the early '60s, when electric wiper motors became standard, wiper-arm pressure was critical because of the low power of the vacuum motors then in use.

Today, heavy-duty electric motors permit the use of stronger springs in the arms. Average arm pressures have consequently more than doubled.

It isn't likely you'll need to test, but if you have to, here's how:

When the wiper arm is in a vertical position, remove the blade. Using a small pressure tester (most service stations will be able to find one in the back of the drawer), place the arm tip on the small platform and take your reading. If your car has a vacuum motor, the pressure should be about one ounce for each one-inch length of the blade. For an electrically powered system, pressure should be at least double that, and preferably be in the range of 32 to 36 ounces.

removing wiper arms

Arms are easy to remove, *if you use a puller tool.* You can borrow one at your local service station, or have the dealer do the job for you. Unless you have a fleet of cars requiring constant care, there's little need to buy a tool you'll probably never need again.

Lubricating the wiper system is a matter of applying just a few drops of oil to all possible points of wear. On the wiper arm, particularly if it's a double-arm parallelogram mechanism, keep the lubrication to a minimum to avoid dripping and smearing of the glass during wiper operation. Don't forget the under-hood linkage between the motor shaft and the two arm shafts.

TYPES OF WINDSHIELD GLASS DAMAGE

STONE NICKS or chips will not spread, but replace the windshield if they're large or directly in front of the driver. Outright breakage is glass that's shattered or cracked inside or out. Replace it. Strain cracks will spread; replace windshield. Star break has cracks radiating from point of impact; damage will spread, so replace windshield. Bull's-eye half moon is a chip that's not dislodged from glass; it won't spread. Sand pits, if there are enough of them, will impair vision. Windshield should be replaced.

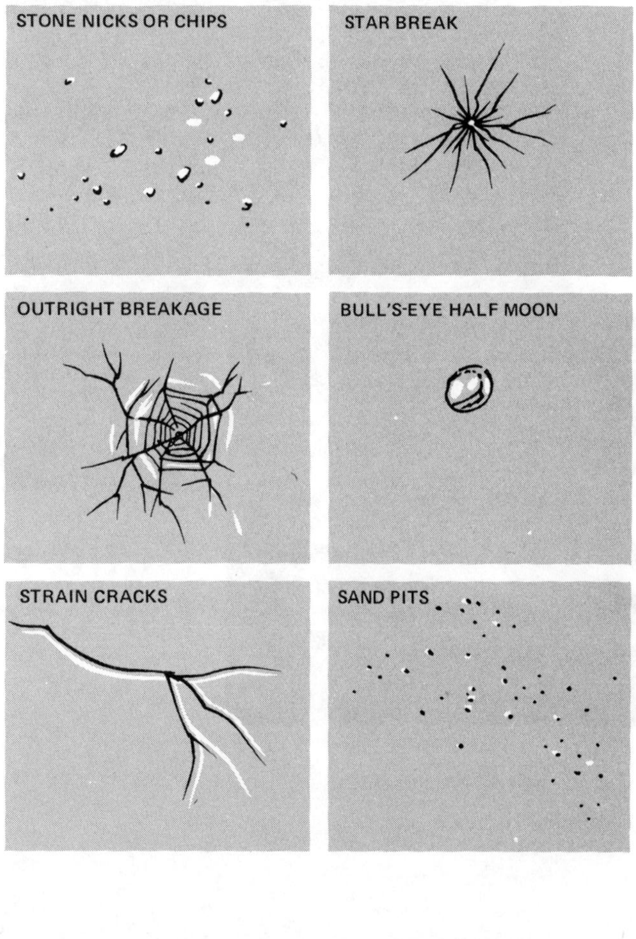

Build a flip-flop table for backgammon and chess

By HARRY HOBBS

SEE ALSO

Bridge tables . . . Chess sets . . . Cribbage boards . . . Game tables . . . Party tables . . . Pool tables . . . Shuffleboard tables . . . Veneering

■ THIS MULTIUSE, walnut game table will look great in your den or favorite game-playing nook. The table surface is a ready-made walnut and maple veneer face with a walnut border glued to walnut plywood. The apron is also of walnut plywood (good one side), while the legs are solid walnut. All parts (except the legs and veneer faces) are cut from a ½ x 30 x 30-in. piece of walnut plywood (good one side).

Start by cutting the plywood panel for the table top with a power saw fitted with a veneer blade. Make cuts in the order numbered on cutting diagrams. Some pieces will be exact size. Others, such as the gameboard, will be oversize, to be resized later. Next, cut the gameboard panel ⅛ in. smaller than the veneer face to allow for veneer overhang at the edges.

Use veneer glue for laying the veneer faces. The backgammon and chess faces are composed of many small pieces of veneer which are held together with gum tape on the "right" side, to be peeled off later. Apply contact glue to the tape-free side, quickly and fairly heavily. Also spread glue on one side of the panel.

Allow one hour and then apply a second coat to each surface. Wait another hour before laying the veneer face on the board with a slipsheet of brown paper between to prevent premature contact. Expose ¼ in. of glued board at one edge only. When you're sure of good alignment, finger-press veneer along the exposed edge. Withdraw slipsheet gradually, about 2 in. at a time. Apply pressure with a roller, but don't roll where slipsheet is underneath. When the slipsheet has been completely removed, roll hard over entire surface in the direction of veneer grain where possible. Turn the panel over on a hard, smooth, clean surface (such as particle board) and trim off veneer overhang before gluing the second face to the panel. Sand the edge gently. Do not sand outward across the veneer face.

To remove the gum tape backing from the veneer face, moisten a 3-sq.-in. area using water and a soap-free sponge. Wait a minute for it to

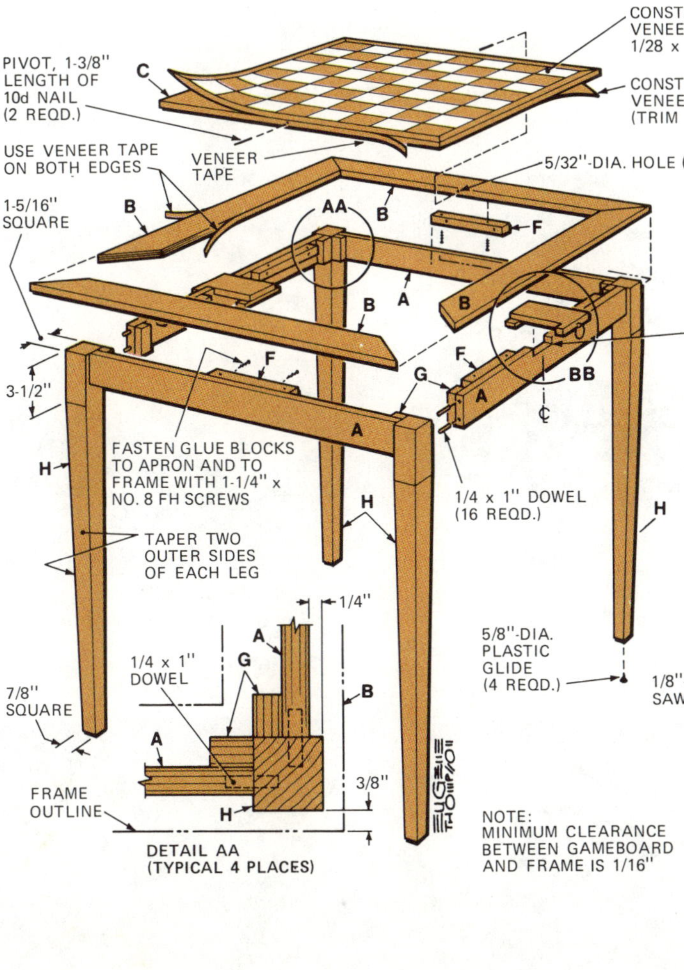

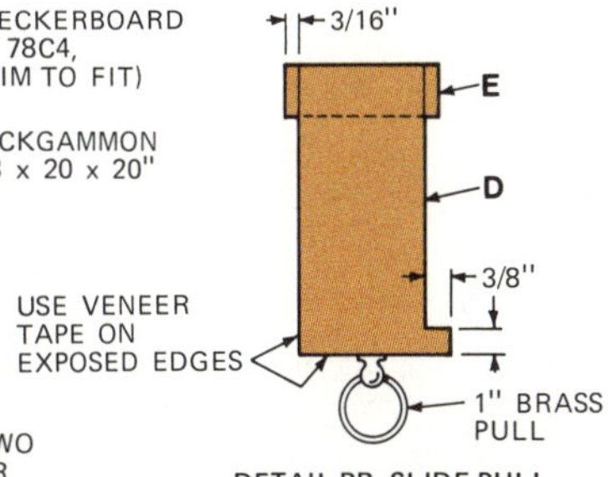

DETAIL BB, SLIDE PULL (2 REQD.)

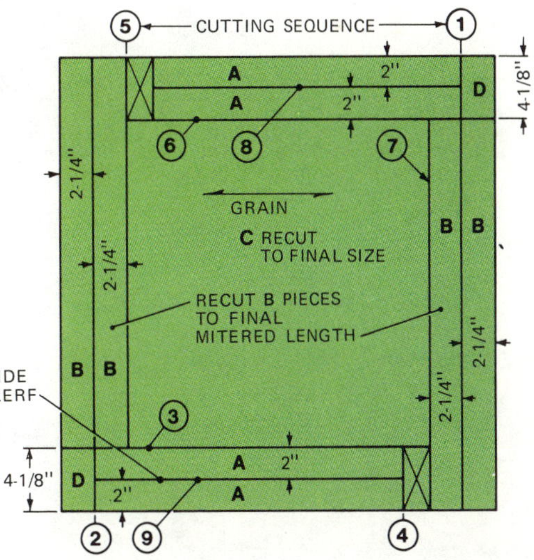

CUTTING DIAGRAM FOR 1/2 x 30 x 30" PLYWOOD

PHOTO SHOWS how to get all parts except legs from walnut plywood panel.

SPREAD GLUE on back of veneer and on plywood; recoat one hour later.

USE SLIPSHEET between coated game face and panel to assure alignment.

PRESS THE FACE with a roller for good bond and to prevent blistering.

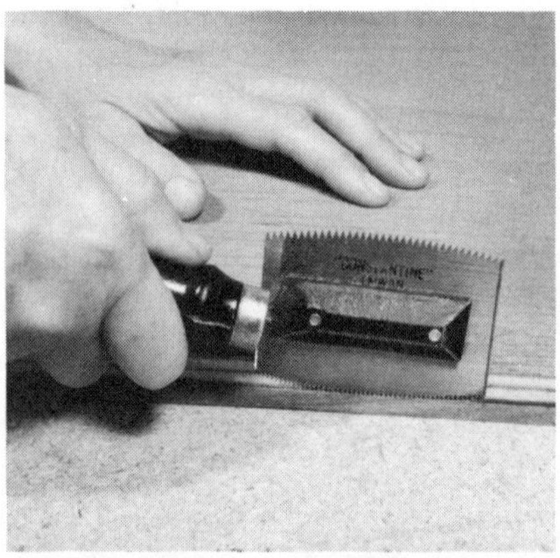

USE A VENEER saw or X-acto knife to trim the veneer overhang.

TO REMOVE gum paper on veneer, moisten small area and scrape with chisel.

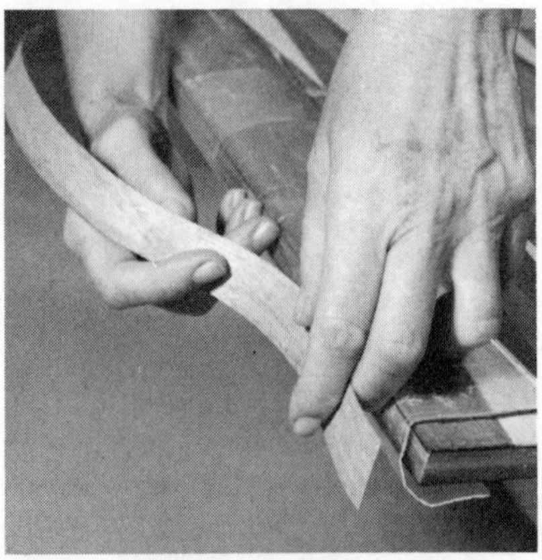

BOND VENEER trim to gameboard edges with veneer glue.

MITER FRAME members after measuring board and providing clearance.

POSITION FRAME members around board, lay out, mark for pivot points.

SIMPLE WOOD jig aids in boring off-center pivot holes in the frames.

INSERT NAIL pivots in gameboard (without glue) before assembling frame.

ASSURE SWING clearance with $\frac{1}{16}$-in. shims between board, frame.

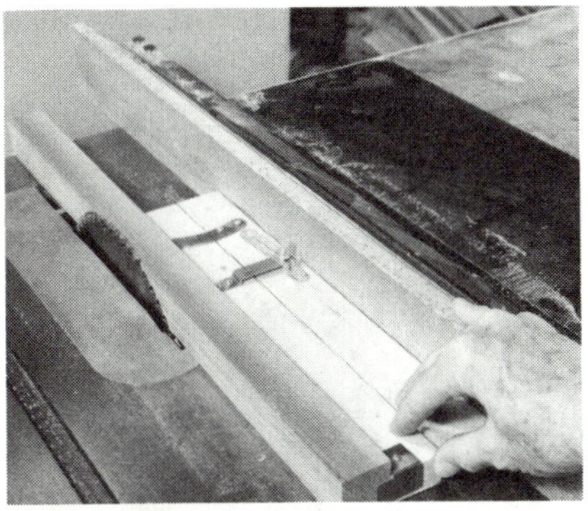

DRESS WALNUT stock for legs on jointer, taper with table saw.

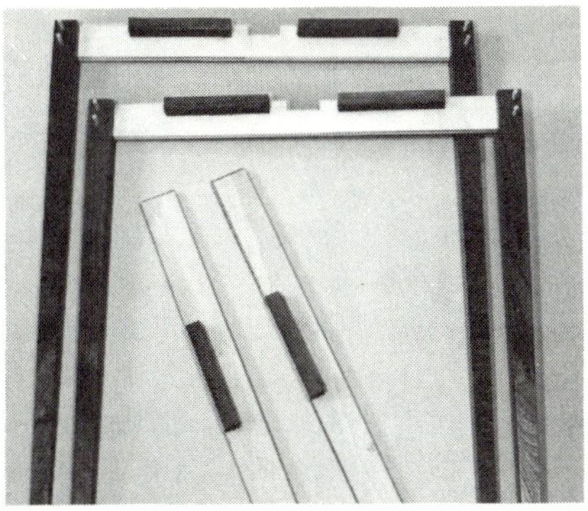

NOTCH TWO aprons for slides and fasten glue blocks flush to apron tops.

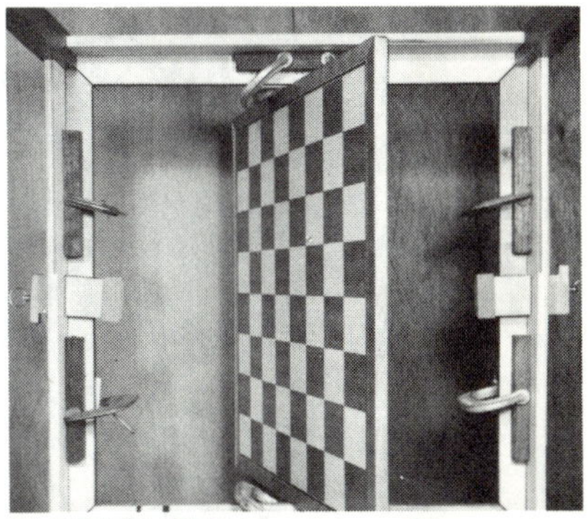

PLACE SLIDES in notches. Glue and clamp board frame to understructure.

soften, then scrape with a chisel. Peel off anything that shreds. Continue this way, *resisting the temptation to soak the surface, until the board is clean.* Don't try to sand off the tape and don't use solvents.

Cover the edges of the gameboard with 1-in.-wide veneer that comes in a roll. Again, use veneer glue and the slipsheet method. Trim off the overhang.

When mitering the four pieces that frame the gameboard, allow for the thickness of the veneer edging on both the gameboard edges and on the inside edges of the frame pieces—plus a minimum 1/16-in. clearance to permit the gameboard to pivot. Apply veneer edging to edges of frame *after* mitering.

To locate the pivot holes in two frame members and matching holes in the gameboard, lay the board on a flat surface and dry assemble four frame members around it. Measure the center point and mark it on the gameboard and frame. Drill 5/32-in.-dia. holes at center of edges at marked locations in two opposite edges of the gameboard.

Because the gameboard, veneered on both sides, is now thicker than the ½-in. frame, you have to lower the pivot hole in the frame so the gameboard top is flush with the top surface of the frame. Simply halve the thickness of the gameboard and use that dimension to locate the frame pivot hole by measuring offset from the good face. After drilling a hole in one frame member, use it as a guide for marking the second hole. A 16d nail, inserted in the hole, can be used to make a starter hole in the opposite frame member before drilling. Or use a jig to assure hole alignment (see photo, page 148).

Cut two segments of 10d nails for pivots. Working on a flat surface, insert pivots loose (no glue) in gameboard. Spread carpenter's glue on mitered ends of the frame. Lay members with walnut sides down so the frame and gameboard are flush on the side that becomes the table top. Apply a framing clamp around the frame and use one C clamp at each corner to hold wood scrap across miters, thereby keeping the joints flat. Before tightening the framing clamps, insert eight wood or plastic scraps 1/16 in. thick around the gameboard to obtain uniform clearance all around. After the glue is dry, remove clamps and add veneer edging around the outside edges of the frame.

For the legs, run walnut over a jointer or dress with a hand plane and then cut to length. Use a tapering jig on a table saw to taper two inside faces of each leg.

Make slides as shown. Apply veneer trim to edges and install brass ring pulls. Cut notches in two aprons for slides.

Cut glue-blocks from scrap wood and fasten to aprons with glue and screws. Then drill matching dowel holes in aprons and legs and assemble the understructure with glue.

Insert slides in their notches and glue understructure to frame/gameboard assembly. Add small glue blocks in corners to reinforce legs to aprons.

The choice of finish—varnish or oil—is yours. The gameboard should be finished before assembly. Drive furniture glides in leg bottoms.

MATERIALS LIST—GAME TABLE

Key	Pcs.	Size and description (use)
A	4	½ x 2 x 21¼" walnut plywood (apron)
B	4	½ x 2¼ x 24¾" walnut plywood (frame)
C	1	½ x 19⅞ x 19⅞" walnut plywood (gameboard)
D	2	½ x 2¼ x 4⅛" walnut plywood (slide)
E	2	¼ x ¾ x 2¼" walnut plywood (stop block)
F	6	¾ x ¾ x 6" pine (glue blocks)
G	8	½ x ¾ x 2" walnut plywood (glue blocks)
H	4	1-5/16 x 1-5/16 x 27" walnut (legs)

Misc.—30 x 30" checkerboard face (No. 78C4)*, 20 x 20" backgammon veneer face*, ¼" doweling, 2 1"-dia. brass ring pulls, 4⅝"-dia. furniture glides, 1¼" No. 8 fh screws, veneer glue, carpenter's glue.

*Game table veneer faces are available from Albert Constantine and Sons, Inc., 2050 Eastchester Rd., Bronx, N.Y. 10461. Complete game table kits are also available.

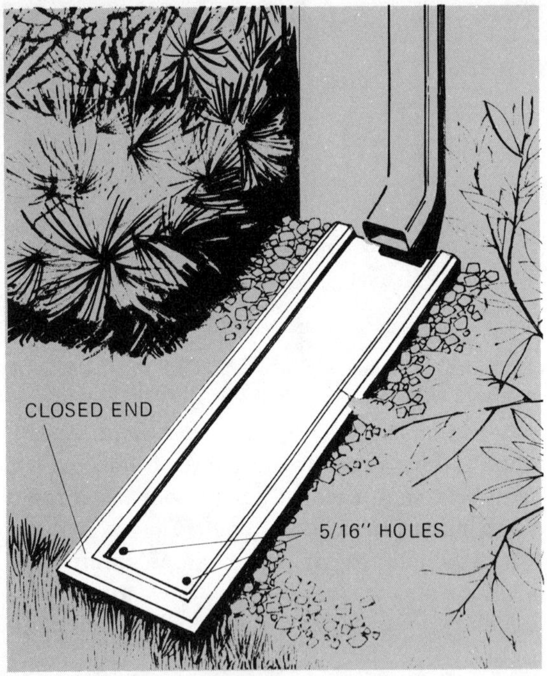

WATER FROM LEADERS is better diverted if the concrete splash block is reversed. Drill $^{5}/_{16}$-in. holes in each corner to allow the block to drain completely.—*Roland H. Bradley, Sarasota, FL.*

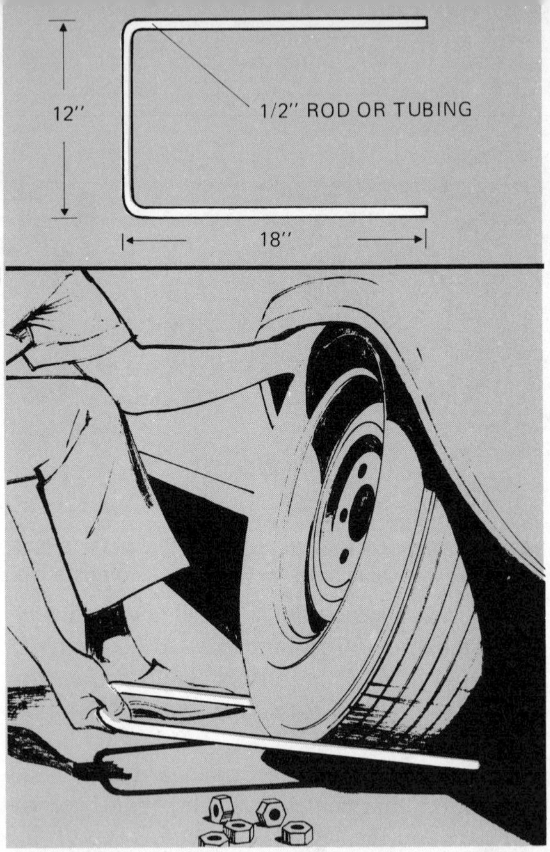

TIRE "FORK" that's formed from a ½-in. iron rod is a great aid for lifting a tire on or off its hub. The gadget will make your task easier, as well as minimize hand bumps.—*Charles H. Hardy, Whittier, CA.*

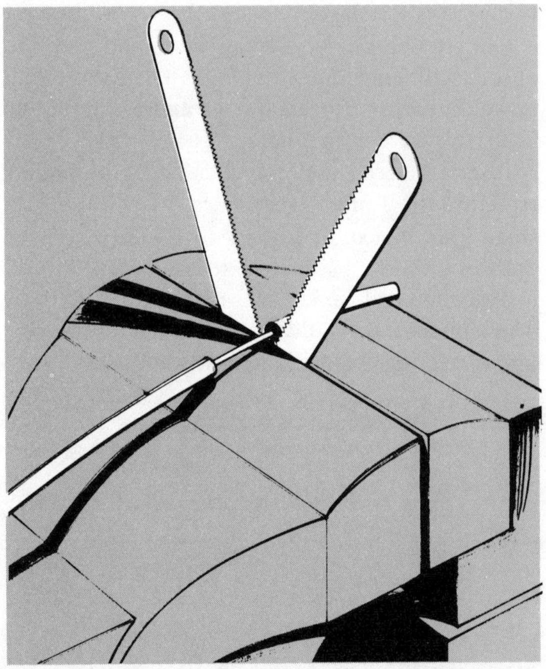

PEELING INSULATION from a wire is simple with this method. Clamp two sections of a hacksaw blade in a vise to form a V shape. Then pull the wire through with a twist.—*E. Dussault, Oak Park, IL.*

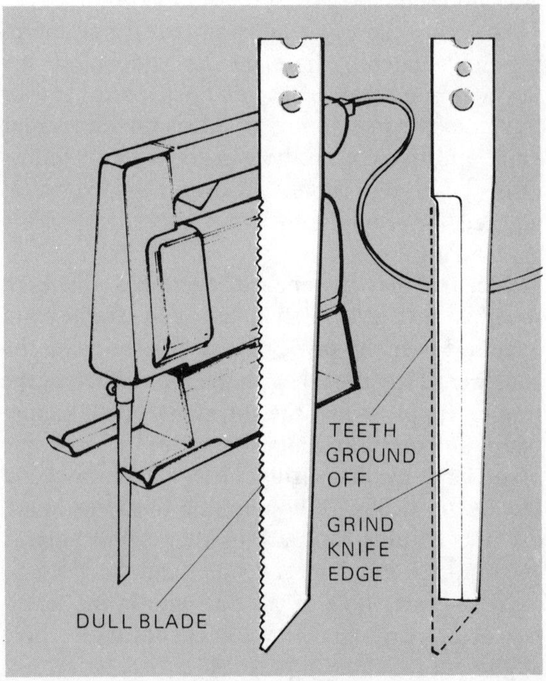

A DISCARDED SABRE-SAW BLADE can be put back to work cutting cardboard, cloth and paper after you grind off the teeth and sharpen the newly ground edge as pictured above.—*Andrew Vena, Philadelphia.*

LATEST GEAR includes ultralight packs and tents, and everything that goes inside.

New gear for backpackers

By WILLIAM T. McKEOWN

OUTER SPACE, believe it or not, is influencing what goes inside your backpack.

Lighter gear; stronger accessories; more waterproof and warmer clothing, sleeping bags and tents: these are just part of the bonus that has come back from the moon. Equipment that was designed for astronauts is now going far afield with hikers, and is making year-round camping possible.

Synthetics, with their assortment of trade names, are replacing many natural products. Expensive goose down, as a fill for cold-weather clothing, is still very warm for its weight, but once it gets wet, it loses its insulating efficiency. Then man-made products become superior. Down substitutes such as Thinsulate, Hollofil, PolarGuard, Sontique, Kodel and Quallofil are among the names that are becoming famous as insulating filling for quality cold-weather clothing and sleeping bags.

Frequently these materials are enclosed in coverings that have a remarkable trait called "breathability." Raindrops do not penetrate the fabric but microscopic pores allow water vapor from evaporating sweat to escape. Gore-tex, Klimate and, for larger and heavier tents, Evolution

SEE ALSO

Bicycles . . . Binoculars . . . Boat camping . . . Boating, white-water . . . Campers . . . Camping . . . Canoes . . . Emergencies . . . Exercising . . . Hunting . . . Map reading

FLEXIBLE FRAMES adjust to both the pack and wearer in a complete new backpack system.

CLASSIC COLEMAN stove still is ideal for cooking when there are several hungry campers to feed.

3 are materials that have this special ability. Now a backpacker can exercise without his jacket, gloves, cap and even boots becoming clammy from perspiration, and he doesn't have to worry about cold chills when he stops to rest. Tents made of these fabric laminates let breath vapor escape rather than coating the inner roof with a layer of frost.

Reflective metalicized materials, layered into astronauts' suits, minimize radiant heat loss into the frigid black void high above the earth. They're doing the same nearer home. Space Blankets and sleeping bags of Texolite are examples. Texolite alternates two layers of aluminized polyethylene, perforated to allow the escape of body moisture, with three layers of nylon mesh. Tests show a sleeping bag can be made 14 percent warmer with only a slight addition in weight.

Latest trends in backpack designs include more flexible frames that can be altered to fit the wearer better. Fabric material frequently is the tough, long wearing and abrasion-resistant Cordura nylon. Frames are sometimes enclosed, out of sight within the pack. Tents for hikers may weigh as little as two pounds, or even less, and are sometimes rigged "free-standing" so they may be picked up and moved while erected; guy lines and pegs no longer are required to hold these models upright.

Food, too, has become lighter to carry and easier to prepare—though no less expensive. The convenience of dehydrated and freeze-dried rations still has a high price tag, but improvements in preparation now have added to the variety and flavor of pack-foods available. Nearly all can be prepared quickly by cooking a short time in boiling water. Nutritious concentrated mixtures such as granola and breakfast bars can be found in most supermarkets. Recent special sterilizing methods make possible Kan Pak whole milk that is canned and has a shelf life of over a year without refrigeration. It, and other backpack and survival food assortments, are supplied by mail order from Stow-A-Way Industries, Cohasset, MA, and others. Hikers can save money by joining with friends to order pack-foods in bulk.

Pack stoves are lighter and more dependable. Mountain Safety Research in Seattle has a one-pound MSR Model GK stove that burns not only leaded, unleaded and aviation gasoline but also kerosene, stoddard solvent, #1 diesel and #1 stove oil. A quart of water can be brought to a boil in about 3½ minutes; a quart of gas can melt snow to make 48 quarts of water. Coleman's new Peak 1 backpacking division also has a compact high-performance stove that weighs less than two pounds and comes in an aluminum carrying case that opens to become two cooking pots. Matching it is a mini-version of the famous Coleman lantern.

Lithium dry-cell batteries were developed for the space program and are now available from a number of sources to power flashlights. They have double the voltage of standard cells, much longer life, and an even output that keeps light at maximum brightness for 90 per cent of the battery life. Unlike alkaline batteries, lithium cells also continue to operate at near peak output at below-zero temperatures. Because of their higher voltage, however, they require different flashlight bulbs. One popular use for the lights is in strap-on headlamps, a miner's style that leaves a packer's hands free for other chores. The new small penlight disposable flashlights are also favored by hikers because of their light weight.

Though each backpacker makes his own judgment, from experience, of which items weigh too much to be worth carrying, there are certain essentials that most campers would not do without. A canteen with water is basic, and modern hikers prefer the lighter models made of plastic. A Swiss Army knife is also favored. A belt cup for both drinking and cooking is another standard, as is a first-aid kit and sewing kit. A radio may be scoffed at by old-timers, but new very small models that can tune in the nonstop weather bands are particularly useful in areas where sudden storms may threaten.

Waterproof matches are hard to improve on, but some knowledgable packers search out magic novelty stores to locate trick birthday candles. These, mounted on a birthday cake, pop back into flame every time they're blown out. A stunt that is good for a laugh at a party can make all the difference when a camper is trying to start a fire or light a stove in a gusty rain. It's then that these no-blow-out candles become welcome camp companions.

BATTERIES power heating elements in heated socks, mittens. Mitts are made of nylon and leather.

CARRYING case for the Peak 1 backpack stove comes apart to become two cooking pots.

PEAK 1 PACKS have flexible frames that "customize" themselves to any user.

Bandsaw tips from the experts

By MANLY BANISTER

If you're among those do-it-yourselfers who are inclined to regard the bandsaw as a "wallflower," you'll be surprised at what this frequently underrated tool can do if given the chance. It far outperforms the sabre saw, for instance, in speed, tight turns, and smoothness of cut. Do you want proof? Go down to your shop and try the tricks described and illustrated on these three pages

SEE ALSO
Bench saws . . . Circular saw blades . . . Cutoff machines . . . Motors, shop . . . Power hacksaws . . . Power-tool stands . . . Radial-arm saws . . . Table saws . . . Workbenches . . . Workshops

■ STILL THE BEST and only tool for making curved cuts in thick stock, a bandsaw far outperforms the sabre saw in smoothness of cut, speed and tight turns. There's a trick to making tight turns even when using a narrow blade, and especially when the work calls for turns as small as ½-in. radius. A series of straight cuts is first made in from the edge of the work to the line of cut, dividing up the curve in segments as shown in the photo at the right. As you follow the curve with the saw, the waste falls free, giving the blade more room to make the turn. This stunt not only permits tight turns, but it keeps the blade from heating and burning the wood in negotiating turns of short radii.

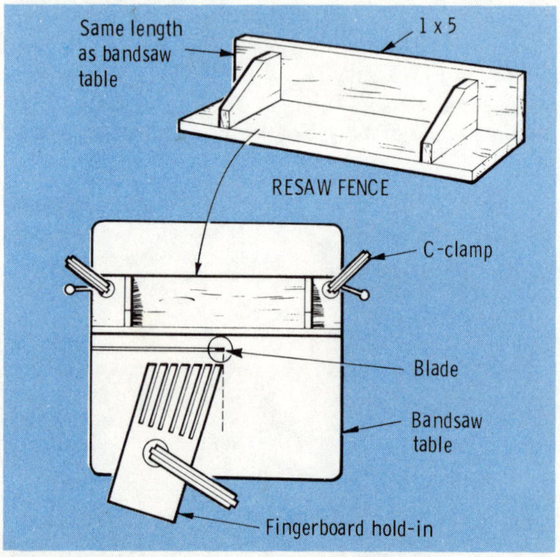

EDGE-RIPPING wide stock into thin boards is a job only a bandsaw can handle. It requires the use of a wooden fence to support and guide the work on edge, plus a slotted fingerboard to hold the work firmly against the fence. A ⅜ or ½-in.-wide skip-tooth blade is best, and a push stick is a must in feeding the work safely past the blade. Note the position of the hold-in board in relation to the blade. A series of parallel saw kerfs gives a spring action to the fingerboard when it presses against the work.

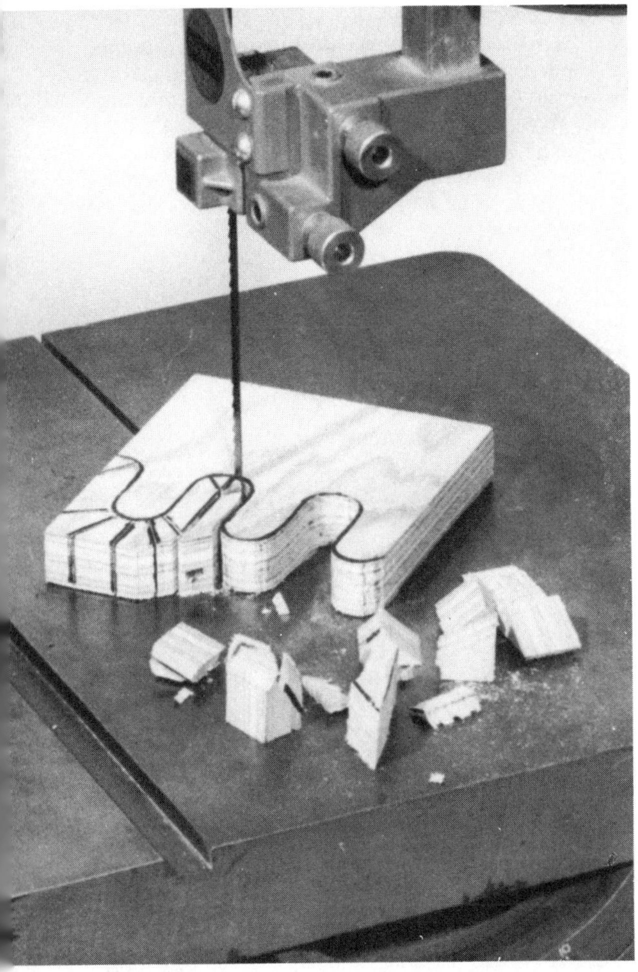

A WOODEN V-BLOCK cut on your circular saw to cradle the work makes your bandsaw extra handy for kerfing the end of turning squares, as well as for splitting dowels and doing other cylindrical work down the middle. In each case, the block is clamped in position to the bandsaw table so that the V-cut bisects the blade precisely.

WITH ITS TABLE tilted 45° and a wooden fence clamped to it, your bandsaw provides a quick way of roughing turning squares "in the round" prior to mounting between centers. The fence is positioned so that corners of the work are ripped off.

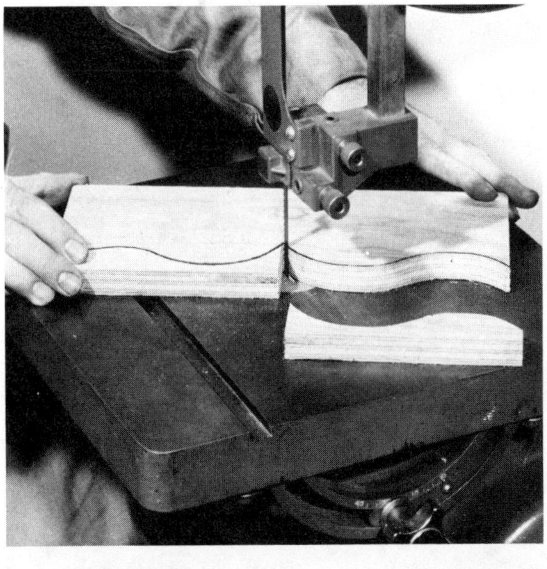

TO AVOID BECOMING "pocketed" when cutting a scroll in which two curves meet, always saw in first from the edge to the point of the pocket. The kerf frees waste when you reach the pocket, eliminating back-tracking. Complete the cut from the opposite end.

WHEN IT COMES to cutting perfect discs of any size, you can't beat a bandsaw and a circle-cutting jig. With the work impaled on an adjustable pivot point, you cut a perfect circle by merely rotating the work. The drawing below shows how the jig is made, designed to clamp to the edge of the bandsaw table. The size of the stock must be roughly the diameter of the disc to be cut so that the blade is on line when it enters the wood.

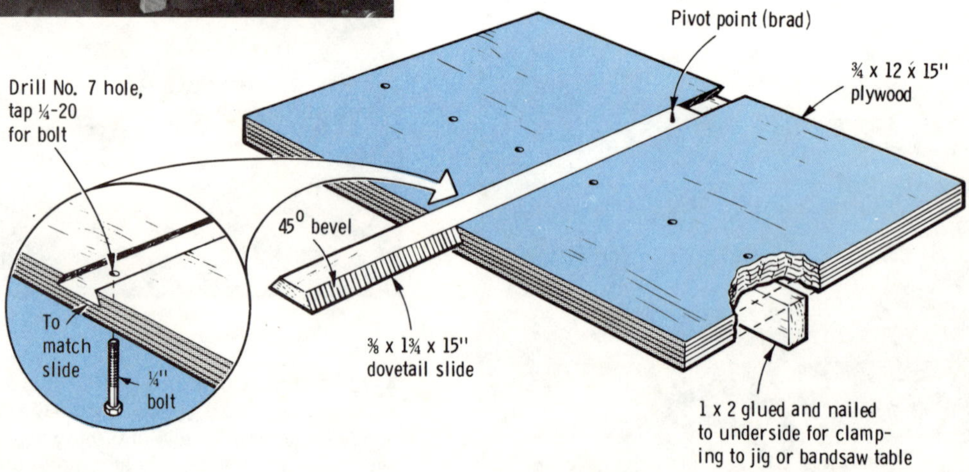

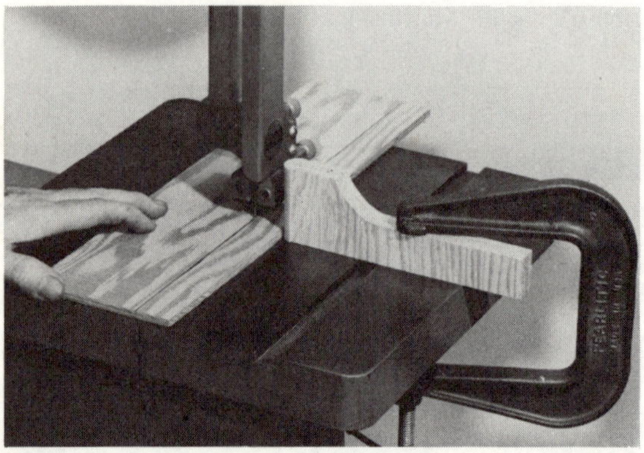

WHEN YOU FIND that the blade has a tendency to drift away from the cutting line while doing repeat ripping, a pivot fence clamped to the saw table will solve the problem. Having a rounded nose, the center of which is positioned to align with the front edge of the blade, the fence allows the work to be maneuvered to compensate for drift as the work is passed through the blade. The fence, of course, is located a distance from the blade equal to the width of the finished work. The work is held against the pivot fence at all times.

MASS RIPPING of identical widths on a bandsaw means less kerf waste than that created by a bench saw; this can add up to a considerable saving when cutting pieces in large quantities. If your saw is not already equipped with a fence, you can improvise one by clamping a wood strip to the table, using a try square to align it with the front of the table and parallel with the blade. A wide blade works best in straight ripping operations since it will not tend to drift as much as a narrow blade. It will always pay to switch to a wider blade.

How to fix bathroom plumbing problems

Left unrepaired, nagging plumbing problems can develop into costly repair jobs. Here's how to fix bathroom plumbing problems yourself

By RICHARD V. NUNN

when faucets develop the sniffles

■ Not only can a leaky, dripping faucet become hazardous to your nervous system, it can cost you money—especially if the problem is on the hot-water side. Both the water and the energy used to heat it can go down the pipes at the rate of 5–7 gallons per day at just one tiny drop at a time.

The source of trouble generally is a worn faucet washer which is fastened to the bottom of the faucet stem. The first repair step is to turn off the water at the supply valve below the sink or lavatory, or at the main valve where water is piped into your home from the utility or a well. After closing either valve, open the problem faucet to make sure the water supply is off.

With a screwdriver, remove the faucet handle. The screw holding the handle may be under a decorative escutcheon which can be pried up and out of its seat with the tip of a screwdriver.

Unscrew the faucet cap that holds the stem in the faucet housing. Use a pipe wrench padded with soft cloth or smooth-jawed channel pliers to turn the cap counterclockwise. Slip the faucet handle back on the top of the stem and turn out the stem counterclockwise. The stem is threaded. Once out of the housing, remove the handle from the stem.

The washer is at the bottom of the stem on compression type faucets. It is held with a brass screw. Remove the screw and pry out the washer. Fit the new washer into the seat and secure it with the screw. You may have to buff the edges of the washer with sandpaper so the washer fits tightly into or onto the metal seat. Some faucets have O-ring washers along the stem. Most have flat washers below the cap. Some have string packing. Replace these washers or packing along with the seat washer. The string packing is simply wrapped around the stem.

If worn washers are a constant problem, the faucet's valve seat may be pitted. To repair this, turn off the water and remove the faucet stem. Then insert and connect a faucet seat grinder—an inexpensive tool available at hardware stores—into the faucet housing. Screw the adjustable nut on the grinding tool down enough so the faucet's cap nut catches a couple of threads after it's placed over the adjustable nut on the threaded grinding tool shaft. Now turn the grinding tool clockwise by its cross handle. Tighten the cap nut as you turn. Make two complete revolutions with the grinder. Then remove the cap nut and grinder, replace the washers, and reassemble the faucet.

cartridge type faucets also drip

"Never drip" cartridge faucets do drip sometimes, and the repair is similar to repairing compression faucets except that the entire cartridge may have to be replaced if the washers in it can't be switched. You can buy special repair kits for these faucets; take the old parts to the store for a perfect match.

To repair a tipping valve cartridge faucet, turn off the water at the supply or main valve. Remove the handle with a screwdriver and the cap with a pipe wrench or channel pliers. Be careful not to damage the shiny finish.

A tipping valve faucet has a ball-shaped fitting under the metal cap. Under the plastic cap over the ball is a washer. Replace this washer. In the curved plastic socket in which the ball fits, you will see several more (usually three) O-ring washers inserted in the plastic. Pry out these washers with the tip of a screwdriver and replace them with new washers inserted with your fingers.

If the cartridge is a tube, remove the escutcheon and a stop tube behind the handle. These faucets usually have a retaining clip or two that hold the cartridge in its housing. Pull these clips

SEE ALSO

Bathrooms . . . Bathtubs . . . Drains . . .
Garbage disposers . . . Home improvement . . .
Plastic pipe . . . Plumbing . . . Sewage systems

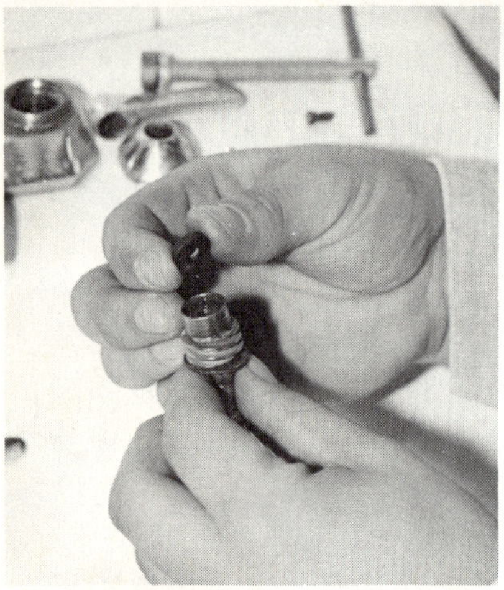

WASHER FITS into a metal "sleeve" at the end of the valve stem. Install the new washer with a brass screw usually provided in the washer package.

VALVE SEAT GRINDER fits into faucet housing. The cap goes over the threaded shank (slip out cross handle) and is screwed to the housing.

O-RING WASHER above ball is the one that usually leaks. Three more O-ring washers are located at the bottom of the socket in which the ball fits.

straight up and out with pliers. Then replace the entire cartridge with a new one.

The cartridge may be coded via a flat side. Make sure this side is facing the sink or lavatory as it is inserted into the housing. If the repair is to a tub or shower, the flat or coded side should always face up.

On some faucets, the spout has to be removed to get at the cartridge. First, remove the retaining nut holding the spout and metal sleeve in the faucet. Then turn off the spout which is threaded onto the faucet housing. Pad the wrench to prevent scratching the finish on the spout parts.

slow-flow bathtub drains

Hair and clay-like soap residue usually is the problem with slow (or no) flowing tub and lavatory drains. Cleaning the stopper mechanism is the solution. Sink drains are easier than tub drains.

For sinks, trace the lever that controls the stopper below the sink. It will be a wire rod that connects to another rod that slips into the drain. The rod is held to the pipe with a knurled cap. Unscrew the cap and pull out the rod. You can now remove the stopper. Clean the stopper and reassemble the rod assembly in reverse order.

Some sinks and lavatories have a stopper twisted onto the rod. Untwist the stopper counterclockwise, clean it, and replace it on the rod. The replacement can be tricky, since the unsupported rod will slide out of alignment in the drain pipe. Try jiggling the stopper lever to re-align it so the stopper can be reconnected to the rod.

For bathtub drains, remove the strainer and unscrew the stopper from the rocker arm linkage. Run water into the tub about ¼-inch deep. Then, with a plumber's suction cup, try to unblock the drain. Plug the overflow with a damp cloth, and use plenty of up/down action on the suction cup.

If this doesn't work, remove the escutcheon plate that holds the stopper trip lever. It is held by two screws. Then push aside the lever assembly. In this space, insert a flat drain auger or snake. The tip should go down through the opening until it is in the drainpipe under the top of the tub. Force the auger back-and-forth until you feel the debris block break.

HEIGHT ADJUSTMENT of a bathtub stopper is fixed by turning a nut. A spring at the other end of the linkage forces the stopper up or down. To remove the stopper, push it up with the trip lever and unscrew it.

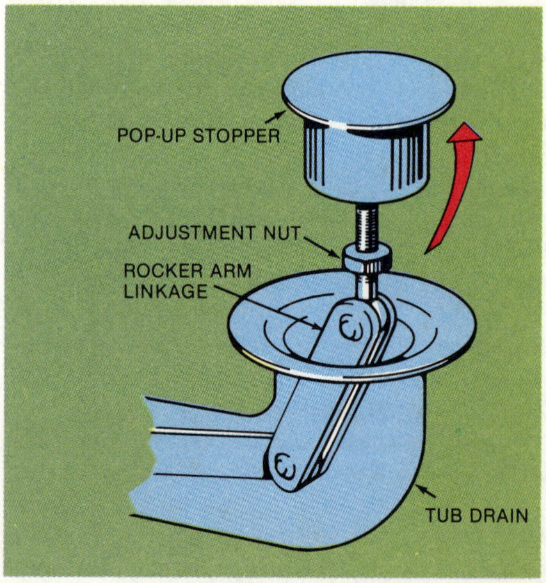

when a toilet runs constantly

The trouble usually is a worn tank ball, a pitted or worn tank-ball seat, or handle trip wires that don't properly release the tank ball so it drops solidly into the seat to shut off the water.

Take the lid off the flush tank. Then trip the handle and eyeball the wire linkage. If the wire is binding in the guides on the overfill pipe, turn the guide slightly on the pipe for alignment.

Tank balls often wear out, causing the ball to fill with water. Replace the ball. It is threaded to the lift wire which is connected to the linkage.

If the tank ball is worn where it fits into its metal seat at the bottom of the overfill tube, chances are that the seat is pitted or has a buildup of lime salts from water in the tank. Turn off the water at the supply or main valve; flush the toilet.

With medium steel wool, smooth the ball seat until it's shiny. If the seat is badly worn or pitted, you should replace the assembly.

incomplete toilet flushes

An inadequate water supply in the flush tank can result in incomplete flushes. The solution to this problem is extremely simple.

Remove the flush tank lid. If the toilet has a floatarm/float ball assembly, try bending the float arm gently upward. Flush the toilet. The tank refill should come to about ¾-inch from the top of the overfill tube.

Some flushing devices are adjusted by turning a screw at the top of the float arm lever on the ballcock assembly. Low-profile ballcock models (FillPro) are adjusted by turning a knurled plastic screw at one end of the assembly at the top. These screws adjust the water height in the tank, which should be about 3–4 inches below the top edge of the flush tank.

unclogging toilets the easy way

Any clogged toilet is messy to unclog. It is easier if you follow these procedures:

Do *not* flush the toilet. Remove any debris from the bowl by hand. Cover your hand and arm with several plastic garbage bags. You can get a grip through the plastic, although the material will restrict movement somewhat. With a dipper, remove as much water as possible from the bowl.

Seat a bulb-type plunger in the bowl, keeping the water line below the top of the plunger. Work the plunger up and down in the bowl. Use hard action on the plunger handle, but keep the rim of the plunger against the bowl surface. As you work you will feel the water moving in and out of the bowl. This vacuum breaks up the clog.

If the plunger doesn't work, try threading an auger with a hook on one end into the toilet trap. Crank the auger with its handle until the hook snags the clog. Then remove the clog on the end of the hook as you pull the auger out of the trap. To remove any remaining debris, flush the toilet several times.

BY REMOVING the overflow escutcheon, an auger or plumber's snake can be inserted into the drain pipe. Run the snake down the pipe until it makes the bend.

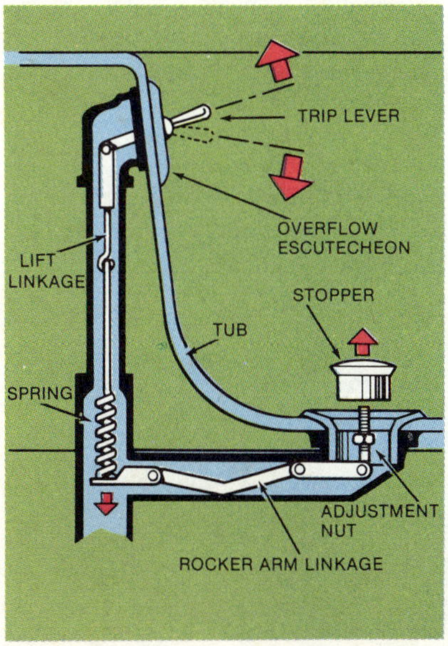

REMOVE the tank ball from its trip-handle linkage before you smooth the ball seat with steel wool. After cleaning you can see if the seat is pitted or worn, and needs replacing.

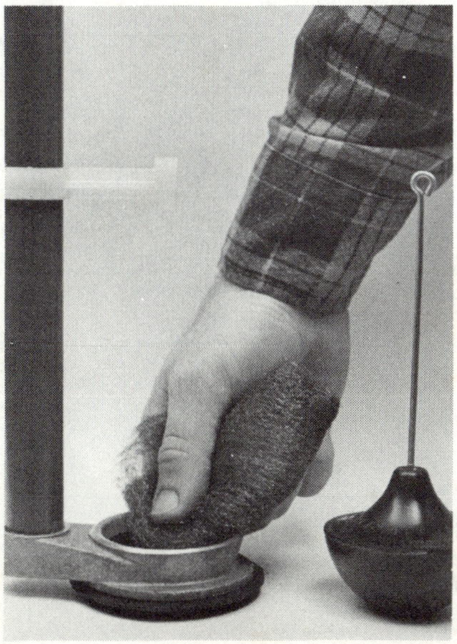

LOW WATER LEVEL is often the problem with incomplete toilet flushes. Try bending the float arm upward slightly. If there is water in the ball, the ball must be replaced.

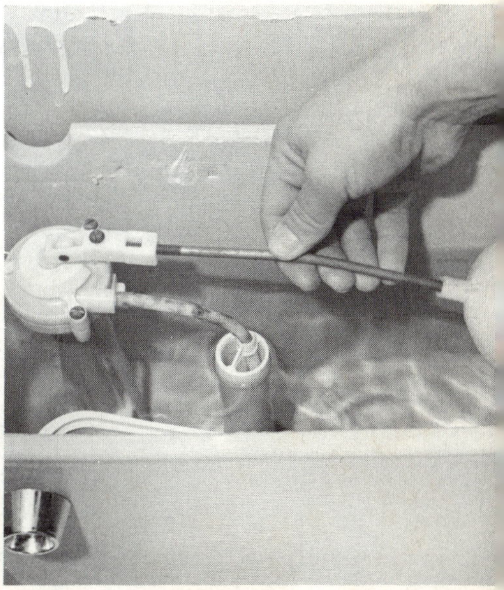

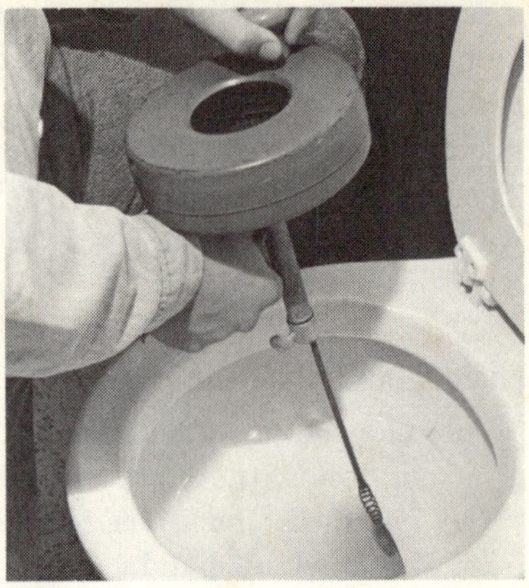

THE DEBRIS clogging a toilet seldom is in the water at the bottom of the bowl. It is in the toilet trap along the front of the bowl. Clean out all the debris you can see in the bowl, and dip out any excess water. Run a drum-type auger with a handle into the trap of the toilet. The hook on the end of the auger will snag any debris.

leaks under the toilet bowl

Water on the floor around the bowl of a toilet doesn't necessarily mean the toilet bowl is cracked. The leakage most often is caused by a faulty wax seal between the bowl and waste stack. To replace the ring, you will have to lift the toilet bowl. The job is not as difficult as it might seem, although it is time consuming.

First, turn off the water supply to the toilet and flush the toilet. Dip out the water in the tank and bowl. Remove as much as you can.

Remove the flush tank from the toilet by removing the bolts through the bottom of the tank and into the back of the bowl. Also disconnect the supply line from the shutoff valve at the ballcock assembly—not at the valve.

Two bolts usually hold the bowl to the floor. Remove these bolts (or nuts) with a wrench. If the fasteners are covered with ceramic caps, pry off the caps with a stiff-bladed putty knife or small prybar. The caps are usually set with plaster, or they are a snap-fit. You may have to clean the bolt threads before you can remove the bolts. If the bolts won't turn, saw them off with a hacksaw blade.

When the hold-down bolts are out, lift the bowl off the floor and tip it forward to trap the water inside the bowl. Then pour the excess water into the waste stack. Wipe the bowl clean.

At the top of the waste stack you will see what is left of a wax seal or ring. Under the seal will be a flange with two threaded bolts sticking out of it. If the bolts have been damaged, replace them and the flange. The cost is not prohibitive.

Since the toilet probably has been leaking for some time, the framing in the floor may be damaged. If so, cut short lengths of boards or dimension lumber to fit the width of the framing and spike these patches to the framing so they overlap the damage. What you're doing is reinforcing the old framing with new wood. If the old framing is badly damaged and you can't patch it, call in a pro for repairs. The damaged wood may not support the weight of the toilet properly, causing serious problems later.

Put the new wax ring over the mounting flange at the top of the waste stack. Then slip the mounting bolts into the holes in the flange. The flange is slotted so the bolts may be moved for alignment. With a putty knife, smear setting compound around the top of the waste stack. Then set the bowl over the flange and thread the bolts through the base of the bowl. The toilet must seat on the floor for support—not on the wax ring.

When the bowl is firmly seated, tighten the holding nuts. Be careful; don't overtighten.

A TOILET BOWL is fastened to a flange in the floor with two bolts. If the toilet has four bolts, the two front bolts usually are the flange bolts; the other two screw into the floor.

THE WAX SEAL—or ring—fits on the mounting flange. The flange is connected to the waste pipe. It's recommended that you replace the metal flange and bolts when you replace the wax ring. Have a helper seat the toilet over the flange as you align the bolts with the holes in the bottom of the toilet bowl. Keep the wax ring in the refrigerator until you install it. Heat will melt it.

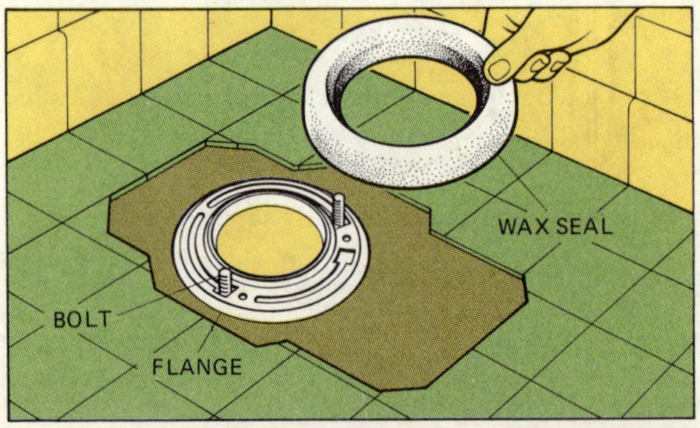

METRIC CONVERSION

Conversion factors can be carried so far they become impractical. In cases below where an entry is exact it is followed by an asterisk (*). Where considerable rounding off has taken place, the entry is followed by a + or a - sign.

CUSTOMARY TO METRIC

Linear Measure

inches	millimeters
1/16	1.5875*
1/8	3.2
3/16	4.8
1/4	6.35*
5/16	7.9
3/8	9.5
7/16	11.1
1/2	12.7*
9/16	14.3
5/8	15.9
11/16	17.5
3/4	19.05*
13/16	20.6
7/8	22.2
15/16	23.8
1	25.4*

inches	centimeters
1	2.54*
2	5.1
3	7.6
4	10.2
5	12.7*
6	15.2
7	17.8
8	20.3
9	22.9
10	25.4*
11	27.9
12	30.5

feet	centimeters	meters
1	30.48*	.3048*
2	61	.61
3	91	.91
4	122	1.22
5	152	1.52
6	183	1.83
7	213	2.13
8	244	2.44
9	274	2.74
10	305	3.05
50	1524*	15.24*
100	3048*	30.48*

1 yard =
.9144* meters
1 rod =
5.0292* meters
1 mile =
1.6 kilometers
1 nautical mile =
1.852* kilometers

Fluid Measure

(Milliliters [ml] and cubic centimeters [cc or cu cm] are equivalent, but it is customary to use milliliters for liquids.)

1 cu in = 16.39 ml
1 fl oz = 29.6 ml
1 cup = 237 ml
1 pint = 473 ml
1 quart = 946 ml
= .946 liters
1 gallon = 3785 ml
= 3.785 liters
Formula (exact):
fluid ounces × 29.573 529 562 5*
= milliliters

Weights

ounces	grams
1	28.3
2	56.7
3	85
4	113
5	142
6	170
7	198
8	227
9	255
10	283
11	312
12	340
13	369
14	397
15	425
16	454

Formula (exact):
ounces × 28.349 523 125* = grams

pounds	kilograms
1	.45
2	.9
3	1.4
4	1.8
5	2.3
6	2.7
7	3.2
8	3.6
9	4.1
10	4.5

1 short ton (2000 lbs) =
907 kilograms (kg)
Formula (exact):
pounds × .453 592 37* = kilograms

Volume

1 cu in = 16.39 cubic centimeters (cc)
1 cu ft = 28 316.7 cc
1 bushel = 35 239.1 cc
1 peck = 8 809.8 cc

Area

1 sq in = 6.45 sq cm
1 sq ft = 929 sq cm
= .093 sq meters
1 sq yd = .84 sq meters
1 acre = 4 046.9 sq meters
= .404 7 hectares
1 sq mile = 2 589 988 sq meters
= 259 hectares
= 2.589 9 sq kilometers

Kitchen Measure

1 teaspoon = 4.93 milliliters (ml)
1 Tablespoon = 14.79 milliliters (ml)

Miscellaneous

1 British thermal unit (Btu) (mean)
= 1 055.9 joules
1 calorie (mean) = 4.19 joules
1 horsepower = 745.7 watts
= .75 kilowatts
caliber (diameter of a firearm's bore in hundredths of an inch)
= .254 millimeters (mm)
1 atmosphere pressure = 101 325* pascals (newtons per sq meter)
1 pound per square inch (psi) = 6 895 pascals
1 pound per square foot = 47.9 pascals
1 knot = 1.85 kilometers per hour
25 miles per hour = 40.2 kilometers per hour
50 miles per hour = 80.5 kilometers per hour
75 miles per hour = 120.7 kilometers per hour